EDUCATION IN A COMPETITIVE AND GLOBALIZING WORLD SERIES

EXPANDING TEACHING AND LEARNING HORIZONS IN ECONOMIC EDUCATION

Enhancing Prospects of Longer-Term Sustainability of Cross-Cultural INSET Initiatives in China
Chunmei Yan
2009. ISBN: 978-1-60741-615-9

Multimedia in Education and Special Education
Onan Demir and Cari Celik
2009. ISBN 978-1-60741-073-7

PCK and Teaching Innovations
Syh-Jong Jang
2009. ISBN: 978-1-60741-147-5

Academic Administration: A Quest for Better Management and Leadership in Higher Education
Sheying Chen (Editor)
2009. ISBN: 978-1-60741-732-3

New Research in Education: Adult, Medical and Vocational
Edmondo Balistrieri and Giustino DeNino (Editors)
2009. ISBN: 978-1-60741-873-3

Approaches to Early Childhood and Elementary Education
Francis Wardle
2009. ISBN: 978-1-60741-643-2

Recent Trends in Education
Borislav Kuzmanović and Adelina Cuevas (Editors)
2009. ISBN: 978-1-60741-795-8

Expanding Teaching and Learning Horizons in Economic Education
Franklin G. Mixon, Jr. and Richard J. Cebula (Editors)
2009. ISBN: 978-1-60741-971-6

EDUCATION IN A COMPETITIVE AND GLOBALIZING WORLD SERIES

EXPANDING TEACHING AND LEARNING HORIZONS IN ECONOMIC EDUCATION

FRANKLIN G. MIXON, JR.
AND
RICHARD J. CEBULA
EDITORS

Nova Science Publishers, Inc.
New York

LIBRARY OF CONGRESS CATALOGING-IN-PUBLICATION DATA

Mixon, Franklin Graves, 1965-
Expanding teaching and learning horizons in economic education / Franklin G. Mixon, Jr., and Richard J. Cebula.
p. cm.
Includes index.
ISBN 978-1-60741-971-6 (hardcover)
1. Economics--Study and teaching (Higher) I. Cebula, Richard J. II. Title.
H62.M5345 2009
330.071'1--dc22

2009025492

Published by Nova Science Publishers, Inc. ✝ New York

CONTENTS

FOREWORD

Years ago, as an unimpressive undergraduate at Auburn University, I found myself searching for a discipline in which to major. I had tried Aerospace Engineering and had failed miserably (and literally). Emotionally bruised from my dismal performance in engineering, I decided to take an array of "principles" classes. Accordingly, I enrolled in classes from such disciplines as management, sociology, psychology, and economics. I discovered that I had a deep interest in the social sciences, and, in particular, economics.

My interest in economics was cultivated by an extremely talented instructor by the name of Michael Montgomery. At the time, Mike was an ABD from the University of Florida. Though in 1987 he was fairly inexperienced as a teacher, he was (and still is) a natural. His lectures were engaging and held students' interest even in an auditorium setting. I found myself wanting to know more about economics – even to the point of being willing to study and read the text. Though I did not know it at the time, I had found the discipline to which I would devote the remainder of my college years.

At the beginning of each new semester, as I gaze at the faces in my Principles of Microeconomics class, I wonder if any of my students are in a situation similar to the one I've narrated above. Is there some student who has a natural affinity for economics but is not yet aware of it? Can I make economics exciting enough to spark the interest of such a student? The essays and papers in this collection will help economics instructors present economics in a tangible fashion that students regard as relevant. By incorporating these ideas and applications economics educators are sure to be more effective.

Rand W. Ressler*
Edward Schlieder Professor of Economics
University of Louisiana at Lafayette

* Professor Ressler is also coauthor (along with Robert B. Ekelund, Jr. and Robert D. Tollison) of the popular principles text, *Economics: Private Markets and Public Choice*, 7th edition (© 2006 by Addison-Wesley). His research has been published in *Economic Inquiry*, *Journal of Economic Behavior & Organization*, *Southern Economic Journal*, *Public Choice*, and *Kyklos*, among other journals

About the Authors

Franklin G. Mixon, Jr. is a Visiting Professor of Economics in the Eugene W. Stetson School of Business and Economics at Mercer University in Georgia. Frank has published a number of articles on economics pedagogy that have appeared in the *Journal of Economic Education*, *International Review of Economics Education*, and the *Journal of Economics & Finance Education*. Frank also serves on the editorial board of the *Journal of Economics & Finance Education*. His research in areas outside of economic education has appeared in the *Journal of Money, Credit, & Banking*, *Journal of Economic Perspectives*, *Oxford Bulletin of Economics & Statistics*, *Journal of Applied Econometrics*, *Southern Economic Journal*, and *Public Choice*, among other outlets.

Richard J. Cebula is the *Shirley and Philip Solomons Eminent Scholar in Economics* at Armstrong Atlantic State University in Georgia. In 2007, Richard received the Southern Economic Association's prestigious Kenneth G. Elzinga Distinguished Teaching Award, and he currently serves as a Teaching Fellow in the Academy of Economics and Finance. Richard, the former editor of the *Journal of Economics and Finance*, is also included in the 3rd Edition of *Who's Who in Economics: A Biographical Dictionary of Major Economists, 1700–1996*. The author of a dozen scholarly books and 400 refereed journal articles, Richard currently serves as Co-Editor of the *Journal of Economics and Finance Education*.

Carlos J. Asarta is Assistant Professor of Practice at the University of Nebraska-Lincoln. Carlos is the recipient of the College of Business Administration Excellence in Teaching Award (2008) and the Bauermeister Faculty Award (2009) for outstanding teaching, research and outreach. His research focuses on the areas of economic education, assessment and economic literacy. Carlos is currently working on several projects involving the assessment of business and economics students at the college level. He is a member of the Council for Economic Education Research Committee and an active associate of the Nebraska Council on Economic Education and the UNL Center for Economic Education.

William B. Walstad is John T. and Mable M. Hay Professor of Economics at the University of Nebraska-Lincoln. Bill is an Executive Editor of the *Journal of Economic Education*, the leading academic journal in the field, and served a six-year term as chair of the Committee on Economic Education for the American Economic Association, the premier organization for economists. He is a national expert on testing and assessment in economic and business education, and has directed seven national test projects (e.g., *Test of Understanding of College Economics*). He is the author or co-author of several hundred scholarly studies on economic and business education, with his most recent books being

Entrepreneurship in Nebraska (Gallup Press) and *The Entrepreneur in Youth* (Edward Elgar). Bill is the Principal Investigator for the Teaching Innovations Program (TIP) in economics that is funded by the National Science Foundation. For his contributions to research and economic education worldwide he received both the Henry Villard Research Award and the International Award from the Council for Economic Education and the National Association of Economic Educators.

Christopher R. Bollinger is the *Gatton Endowed Associate Professor of Economics* at the University of Kentucky. Chris' research, primarily in the area of econometrics, has been published in numerous well-respected journals, such as the *Journal of Econometrics*, *Journal of Applied Econometrics*, *Journal of Labor Economics*, *Journal of Urban Economics*, *Journal of Business and Economic Statistics*, *Journal of the American Statistical Association*, *Review of Economics and Statistics*, and the *Southern Economic Journal*. He also serves as a Co-Editor of the *Southern Economic Journal*.

Gail Mitchell Hoyt is a Professor of Economics at the University of Kentucky. Gail has won numerous awards for teaching during her career, dating back to graduate school in 1991. She is the recent winner of the Panhellenic Council Outstanding Professor Award in 2005. In 2001 Gail won both the Alumni Association Great Teacher Award and Beta Gamma Sigma Teacher of the Year Award. Her research in economic education has appeared in the *Journal of Economic Education*, *Classroom Expernomics*, and *Teaching Business and Economics*. Gail currently serves on the Board of the American Economic Association's Committee on the Status of Women in the Economics Profession (CSWEP).

KimMarie McGoldrick is a Professor of Economics at the University of Richmond. KimMarie is an award-winning educator, who recently won the 2008 State Council of Higher Education Outstanding Faculty Award. She serves on the editorial boards of both the *Journal of Economic Education* and *American Economist*. KimMarie's economic education research has been published in the *Journal of Economic Education*, *International Review of Economics Education*, *American Economist*, *Feminist Economics*, *Journal of Excellence in College Teaching*, and *Effective Teaching*. Her work in labor economics and industrial organization has appeared in the *Journal of Sports Economics*, *Industrial Relations*, *Regional Science and Urban Economics*, and the *Southern Economic Journal*, among others.

Charles Kroncke is an Associate Professor of Economics and Dean of Business at the College of Mount Saint Joseph in Ohio. Before joining the faculty at CMSJ, Charles served on the Higher Education Quality Assessment Councils of Estonia (1996) and Latvia (1997-1998). Charles' research in economic education has been published in the *International Review of Economics Education*, the *Journal of Economics and Finance Education* and *Shaping the Learning Curve* (*i*Universe, 2005), a volume of essays devoted to the subject. Additionally, his work in the area of labor economics and other areas has appeared in *Economics of Transition*, the *Journal of Labor Research* and *The Independent Review*, among others.

Lynnette Smyth is an Associate Professor of Economics at Gordon College in Georgia. Lynnette's pedagogical successes extend back to her graduate school years, when she was named Outstanding Teaching Assistant in statistics. In recent years she has helped organize Gordon College's "Teaching Matters" conference series. Lynnette's research in the area of economic education has appeared in the *Journal of Economics and Finance Education*, as well as in a recent volume of essays titled *Shaping the Learning Curve* (*i*Universe, 2005).

Additionally, her research on academic dishonesty has been published by the *Journal of Business Ethics* and *Community College Review.*

James Davis is a Professor of Accounting at Anderson University in South Carolina. His pedagogical research has appeared in the *Journal of Accounting Education, Accounting Education* and the *International Journal of Accounting Education and Research.* From 1985 to 1988, James served on the editorial board of *Issues in Accounting Education*, while from 1984 to 1985 he served on the editorial board of the education research section of *Accounting Review*. Additionally, James has published numerous textbooks and textbook supplements, including six editions (from 1984-2002) of *Management Accounting* (with Wayne Morse and Al Hartgraves), which was published by Southwestern, and three editions of (from 1987-1989) *Accounting Information Systems: A Book of Readings with Cases* (with Barry Cushing), published by Addison-Wesley. In addition to his pedagogical research, James' other work has appeared in the *Journal of Business Ethics*, *Business Horizons*, and the *Journal of Information Systems*, among others.

Patrick Taylor is an Associate Professor of Economics at Millsaps College. Patrick has received a number of teaching accolades, including both the Millsaps College Distinguished Professor Award (1993) and the Howard Bavender Outstanding Professor Award (1999). To date he is the only current faculty member in the Else School of Management to have received either of these two awards. He also won the LEAD Award for Excellence in Student Advising in 2005. In 1992, Patrick participated in the Joint Council on Economic Education teaching workshop, held at Northwestern University. In addition to his pedagogical research, which has been published in the *Journal of Economics and Economic Education Research*, the *Journal of College Teaching and Learning*, and *Business and Economic Review*, he has published articles in the *Journal of Risk and Insurance* and the *Journal of Forensic Economics*, among others.

Kenneth Rebeck is an Associate Professor of Economics at St. Cloud State University and a Research Associate with the National Center for Research in Economic Education. He has published articles in the *Journal of Economic Education*, *Contemporary Economic Policy*, *Quarterly Review of Economics and Finance*, *American Economic Review-Papers and Proceedings*, and the *Journal of Economics and Economic Education Research.* He is also co-author of the *Basic Economics Test*, the *Test of Economic Knowledge*, and the *Test of Economic Literacy*, all national standardized test instruments for pre-college economics. In addition to these, Kenneth is co-author of the *Test of Understanding College Economics Examiner's Manual.* Kenneth is active in K-12 economic education, conducting teacher workshops for the Minnesota Council on Economic Education and working as an outside evaluator on economic education projects and materials.

Steven B. Caudill is the *Robert D. McCallum Professor of Economics and Business* at Rhodes College. Steven has published extensively in the field of economic education, including publications in the *Journal of Economic Education.* He current serves on the editorial board of another economic education journal, the *Journal of Economics and Finance Education.* In addition to his work in economic education, Steven's research in applied econometrics and statistics has been published in the *Journal of Econometrics*, *Review of Economics and Statistics*, *Journal of Applied Econometrics*, *Journal of Business and Economic Statistics*, and the *Journal of Applied Statistics*, among others.

James E. Long is a Professor of Economics at Auburn University. Jim's primary research interests are the economics of taxation and labor economics. His work has been published in some of the leading economics journals, such as the *Journal of Political Economy*, *Review of Economics and Statistics*, *Industrial and Labor Relations Review*, *Southern Economic Journal*, and the *Journal of Human Resources*, to name a few. Jim has also provided consulting and expert witness testimony to organizations in disputes involving fair employment practices.

Linda S. Ghent is an Associate Professor of Economics at Eastern Illinois University. The winner of numerous outstanding faculty awards since 1999, Linda is also the author of a number of pedagogical materials that accompany leading economics textbooks, such as Gregory Mankiw's *Principles of Economics* (Thomson Learning), and Walter Nicholson and Christopher Snyder's *Microeconomic Theory* (Thomson Learning). Professor Ghent's research in the areas of public and labor economics has been published in *Southern Economic Journal*, *Industrial and Labor Relations Review*, *Industrial Relations*, *Economic Development and Cultural Change*, and *Public Finance Review*.

Marie Truesdell is the Dean of the College of Business at Marian University. Marie was hired by MU as an assistant professor about a decade ago, and asked to establish an economics program, which she did in only a few semesters. She later secured a $750,000 grant from the Lilly Foundation to establish an entrepreneurship program at MU. Professor Truesdell's recent work on regulatory takings was published in *Review of Agricultural and Applied Economics*.

Jennie W. Wenger is Analyst and Project Manager for the Center for Naval Analyses (CNA). In this role, she conducts research and manages projects on military and civilian subjects, including high school completion rates and the impact of state education policies, cognitive and non-cognitive skills of high school dropouts, the National Guard Youth Challenge Project (a quasi-military program for high school dropouts), and performance of enlisted homeschoolers. Her work has been cited in the press, as well as forming the basis for a Congressional Report. Jennie has experience teaching in both high school and college classrooms; she has taught at the University of North Carolina Department of Public Policy as well as at the University of North Texas Department of Economics (where she received the Mortarboard Apple Polishing Award for outstanding teaching, as well as the Professing Women Award). Currently, she teaches microeconomics and policy in the Department of Public Administration and Policy at the University of Georgia.

Heather Smith is a Research Assistant in the Economics Department at Armstrong Atlantic State University in Georgia.

Dirk Mateer is a Senior Lecturer and the Co-Director of Undergraduate Studies in Economics at Pennsylvania State University. His recent research on economic education topics has appeared in the *Journal of Economic Education* and *Perspectives on Economic Education Research*. Dirk is also author of the popular economics text, *Economics in the Movies* (Thomson/Southwestern, 2005). In addition to these endeavors, he maintains a number of websites that provide teaching tools that are used throughout the academic world. These Internet-based tools include the banner site titled *From ABBA to Zepplin, Led: Using Music to Teach Economics*, which Dirk co-produces with Joshua Hall and Robert Lawson. Also included in Dirk's web-based pedagogical umbrella are *Flash Music for Economics* (with Andrew Rice), *Movie Scenes for Economics* (with Herman Li), and *Teaching Economics with You Tube*. Finally, his economic education research interests are not limited to higher education. In 1999, Dirk and colleagues Burton Folsom and George Leef entered the economic education policy arena when they published a book titled *How Reliable are Michigan High School Economics Textbooks?* (Mackinac Center for Public Policy, 1999).

Roger W. Garrison is a Professor of Economics at Auburn University. Roger was named Mortar Board Favorite Professor at his home university, where he has taught since 1978. Dating from the mid-1980s, he has been a regular lecturer on Austrian Economics for the Ludwig von Mises Institute and for the Foundation for Economic Education. His pedagogical research has been published in the *Journal of Economic Education*, while his work on Austrian Economics and other topics has appeared in the *American Economic Review*, the *Journal of Money, Credit, and Banking*, *Economic Inquiry*, the *Journal of Macroeconomics* and *History of Political Economy*, among others. In 2001 his book, *Time and Money: The Macroeconomics of Capital Structure*, was published by Routledge, and in 2003 Roger was named as the first Hayek Visiting Fellow at the London School of Economics. He currently serves on the editorial boards of the *Review of Austrian Economics* and the *Quarterly Journal of Austrian Economics*.

David R. Lange is a Professor of Finance at Auburn University – Montgomery. David's research on organizations and other issues has been published in the *Journal of Management* and the *Journal of Risk and Insurance*, while his pedagogical work has appeared in both the *Journal of Economics and Finance Education* and *Financial Practice and Education*.

Carel M. Ligeon is an Associate Professor of Economics at Auburn University – Montgomery. Carel's research in the areas of agricultural and aquacultural economics has been published in the *American Journal of Agricultural Economics*, *Journal of Food Distribution Research*, *North American Journal of Aquaculture*, and the *Journal of International Food and Agribusiness Marketing*.

Scott A. Kjar is a Visiting Assistant Professor of Economics at the University of Dallas. Scott teaches courses ranging from principles of economics to intermediate economics, and from American government to Austrian economics. The latter is aligned with his research interests, which include 19th Century history of economic thought and Carl Menger and the Austrian school of economics. Scott's research on the history of economics has appeared, or will appear, in the *American Journal of Economics and Sociology*, the *Quarterly Journal of Austrian Economics*, and *New Perspectives on Political Economy*, while his work in the area of American government has been published in *Public Choice*. Among other professional organizations, Scott is a member of the Association of Private Enterprise Educators.

David B. Skarbek is a PhD student in economics at George Mason University. The winner of San Jose State University's *James F. Willis Award for Excellence in Economics* in 2004, and the American Institute for Economic Research's *Roy A. Foulke Graduate Award* in 2008, David has held 10 different fellowships and scholarships since 2004. He has also been active in pedagogical research, having published in the *Economic Education Bulletin*. David's work on constitutions, market failures and regulation has been published in the *Journal of Law, Economics, and Organization*, *The Cato Journal*, *Dartmouth Law Journal* and the *Journal of Labor Research*.

Joshua C. Hall is an Assistant Professor of Economics at Beloit College in Wisconsin. Joshua has been awarded more than 10 academic fellowships since his career began just a few short years ago. Since then he has also won the award for the Best Educational Note in the *Journal of Private Enterprise* (2005), and he has published articles in both the *Journal of Economic Education* and *Perspectives on Economic Education*. His other, non-pedagogical research interests are in public finance and entrepreneurship. His work in these applied microeconomics areas has appeared in numerous academic journals, such as the *Journal of Labor Research*, *Economics Bulletin*, *The Cato Journal* and the *Atlantic Economic Journal*.

Scott A. Beaulier is an assistant professor of economics, the *BB&T Distinguished Professor of Capitalism*, and chair of economics at Mercer University in Georgia. Scott won the *Outstanding Graduating Senior Award in Economics and History* and the *Adam Smith Prize for Outstanding Undergraduate Work in Economics* at Northern Michigan University in 2000, and since then he has won more than five other academic awards and fellowships. His pedagogical work in economics has been published in the *Journal of Economic Education*, while his research in areas of Austrian economics, law, public finance and constitutional economics has appeared in the *Review of Austrian Economics*, *American Review of Political Economy*, *Kyklos* and *Constitutional Political Economy*.

Wm. Stewart Mounts, Jr. is a Professor of Economics and Associate Dean of the Stetson School of Business and Economics at Mercer University in Georgia. Dr. Mounts has won the Stetson School's top pedagogical award three times – in 1991, 1995 and 2001 – and he won Mercer University's SGA Teacher of the Year Award in both 1980 and 1981. His academic research has extended to economics pedagogy, where he has published in *Classroom Expernomics*. His more traditional research has been published in numerous journals, such as the *Journal of Money, Credit, and Banking*, the *Southern Economic Journal*, *Public Choice*, the *Journal of Applied Social Psychology* and the *Journal of Macroeconomics*.

Daniel Box is a graduate of Auburn University, with degrees in software engineering and applied mathematics. A National Merit Scholar Finalist coming out of high school, Box was the recipient of the *Parmer* Scholarship, the Engineering National Merit Scholarship, the University National Merit Scholarship and the *John and Rosemary Brown* Scholarship from the College of Science and Mathematics. During his undergraduate days at AU, Daniel was the only undergraduate student to work in AU's National Security Agency (NSA) Information Assurance Lab (IAL).

Steven B. Caudill is the *Robert D. McCallum Professor of Economics and Business* at Rhodes College. Steven has published extensively in the field of economic education, including publications in the *Journal of Economic Education*. He current serves on the editorial board of another economic education journal, the *Journal of Economics and Finance Education*. In addition to his work in economic education, Steven's research in applied econometrics and statistics has been published in the *Journal of Econometrics*, *Review of Economics and Statistics*, *Journal of Applied Econometrics*, *Journal of Business and Economic Statistics*, and the *Journal of Applied Statistics*, among others.

Stuart D. Allen is a Professor of Economics and Chair of the Department of Economics at the University of North Carolina at Greensboro. He is an award-winning educator, having won the University Alumni Teaching Excellence Award (1982), the Bryan School Outstanding Faculty Award (1985), and the MBA Association Faculty Excellence Award (1995). Additionally, Stuart has published articles in the *Journal of Monetary Economics*, the *Journal of Money, Credit, and Banking*, *Economic Inquiry*, *Public Choice*, and the *Journal of Macroeconomics*, among others. His writing on public finance pedagogy has appeared in the *Journal of Economics and Finance Education*, while his research on improving student learning in principles of economics has been published in *International Advances in Economic Research* and *Review of Black Political Economy*. From 1984 to 1993, Stuart served as the Director of UNCG's Center for Economic Education, and in 1994 the National

Council on Economic Education published his book (with Alan Stafford and John Clow), *Economics of Entrepreneurship*.

Kenneth A. Snowden, Jr. is an Associate Professor of Economics at the University of North Carolina at Greensboro. Kenneth teaches courses ranging from principles of economics to American and European economic history, and in 1996 he won the Bryan School's Outstanding Senior Faculty Teaching Award. Later, from 2003 to 2005, he served on the Teaching Committee of the Economic History Association. Additionally, Kenneth has published articles in the *Journal of Economic History* and *Explorations in Economic History*, among others. From 1994 to 1997, he served on the editorial board of the *Journal of Economic History*, while from 1996 to 1998 he served as a Trustee for the Cliometrics Society.

PART I. RESEARCH

In: Expanding Teaching and Learning Horizons
Editors: F. G. Mixon, Jr. and R. J. Cebula
ISBN 978-1-60741-971-6

Chapter 1

THE ACHIEVEMENT OF COLLEGE BUSINESS AND ECONOMICS MAJORS ON THE MAJOR FIELD TEST IN BUSINESS

Carlos J. Asarta and William B. Walstad

INTRODUCTION

The production of education can be characterized by choices derived from the scarcity of resources. In recent years, funding and enrollment concerns at colleges and universities have resulted in greater attention being devoted to improving the effectiveness and efficiency of higher education for students. As a result, universities and colleges are expected to assess and continuously improve the quality of their programs, and accrediting institutions have gained importance in the world of academia. Nichols and Nichols (2000) indicate that program assessment should focus on concrete, verifiable results, such as how much students have *learned* by graduation. The recent use in education of standardized testing instruments has opened the doors to new research that could further clarify and identify key inputs in the production and retention of knowledge.

The Major Field Test in Business (MFT-B) is a valid and reliable measure of learning outcomes from graduating college seniors enrolled in business and economics degree programs. It is designed to test understanding of core ideas and concepts in business and economics and the students' ability to analyze and solve problems, understand relationships and interpret material. Ideally, outcome assessment using the MFT-B should provide administrators with information that can be used to assess the performance of students relative to the goals and objectives of a college or department (Educational Testing Service, 1994). Standardized test scores also could be instrumental in comparing programs, identifying achievement trends or making resource allocation decisions (Black and Duhon, 2003). The performance of business students on the MFT-B, however, has been examined in only a limited number of studies, mainly because institutions use the test results for internal assessment purposes. Further research with this measure could identify key factors affecting the understanding of basic business and economics and serve administrators in formulating new policies aimed at improving programs and undergraduate retention of core business and economic knowledge.

This chapter, therefore, provides an extensive investigation of the results from an administration of the MFT-B to students completing their economics and business majors at a large Midwestern university. Detailed descriptive analysis of the achievement differences on the MFT-B is provided, based on a broad set of student characteristics such as gender, race, ethnicity, age and level of education, general academic ability, transfer status, being an international student, business or economic major, and coursework. Several regression models are specified and estimated to explain the effects of such student factors as major, coursework, and transfer status on the achievement of students taking this business and economics test. Model 1 specifically examines the effects of a student's major on MFT-B performance. Model 2 focuses on the performance of students on core business courses and their impact on MFT-B scores. Model 3 evaluates the effects of transferring a core business course on achievement on the MFT-B to its value in retaining core business and economic knowledge. The final model introduces interaction terms between the choice of major and student transfer of core courses to investigate the combined effects.

THE TEST

The Major Field Test in Business (MFT-B) is a two-hour multiple-choice test that contains 120 items. The testing instrument can be administered online or in a paper-based setting. Its main objective is to test student knowledge in areas considered by business schools and their accrediting agencies to be the "common body of knowledge." Such a "body" is assumed to include a common business core formed with knowledge in quantitative analysis, marketing, management, law, finance, economics, accounting and social and international considerations of modern business operations. Questions in accounting, economics, management, and quantitative business analysis and information systems each constitutes about 16 percent of the questions on the exam, while finance and marketing each constitutes 12 percent of the questions, and the legal and social environment represents 10 percent of the questions.

The economics section of the MFT-B is divided into three main categories that include topics in macroeconomics, microeconomics and international economics. The macroeconomic topics focus on national accounts and income determination, monetary and fiscal policy, the Federal Reserve System, and employment, inflation and growth. Microeconomic topics covered on the exam include market structures (i.e., monopoly), price theory, and supply and demand. Finally, the balance of trade and payments, international monetary systems, exchange rates, trade polices (including GATT, NAFTA and the European Union) and comparative advantage are the main topics covered in the international economics area of the MFT-B (ETS, Test Description, 2006).

There are two kinds of scores available for the MFT-B. Each test produces an individually reliable total scale score for each student (reported on a 120–200 scale) and the mean scale score for the group of students tested. Individual scores can be used to make decisions about the level of student achievement. The MFT-B test also allows institutions to collect scores that relate to a subfield within a major field of study (assessment indicator scores). Assessment indicators are reported for groups with at least five students and the scores are reported as a mean percent correct for the group in each of the assessment indicators. In other words, cohorts of students with a same major are created and the mean percent correct answers are reported for each of the subfields of the test (i.e., economics). Assessment indicators are not reported for individual students. Also, the MFT-B only scores correct answers and does not penalize individual students for omitting or guessing an answer to a question.

The reliability of the MFT-B is estimated using the Kuder-Richardson formula 20. Based on data from February 2003 to the present, the Kuder-Richardson coefficient is .89. A scale of reliability ranges from 0.0 to 1.0. The desired level of reliability for the reported total score is .90 or higher (ETS, Description of Test Results, 2006). A value of .89 indicates that the test can be used as a relatively accurate estimate of achievement for the purposes of assessing group performance.

Review of Potential Factors Affecting Achievement

Individual student characteristics are widely used as control or predictor variables in education production function models to explain the performance of economic and business students. The following section summarizes some previous research findings in economics and other business disciplines, and includes those studies which have used the MFT-B. The review primarily focuses on undergraduate education, but occasional references to studies of graduate students are cited.

Gender

Gender is an important control variable used in educational production function studies to explain student achievement in economics and business, but the direction of the gender effect is mixed. The performance and understanding of economics by males and females has been extensively studied in the research literature in economics and other disciplines.

Past studies in economic education show that males outperform females at the college or university level (e.g., Bolch and Fels, 1974; Siegfried, 1979; Williams, Waldauer and Duggal, 1992). Bolch and Fels (1974) examined the performance of students at Vanderbilt University on the College Level Examination Program (CLEP) of the Educational Testing Service. Their results imply that, even after controlling for verbal and math ability, men have a comparative advantage in elementary economics while women have a comparative disadvantage. Siegfried (1979) reviews the previous literature examining male-female differences and provides definitions for understanding and learning economics. Understanding is defined as the stock of knowledge at a point in time, while learning is defined as the increase of understanding over time. Siegfried finds that men tend to exhibit better levels of understanding than females while no difference was found in regard to learning between males and females. Siegfried also found that the performance difference between sexes increases as students enter high school and persist at the college level. Williams, Waldauer, and Duggal (1992) extended previous research on gender differences in economic knowledge by including student performance in courses at the intermediate economic theory level and in economic statistics. They found that the gender gap in economic understanding tends not to widen as students progress through college.

The gender results in economics, however, are mixed and more recent studies have found no gender difference in student performance on tests of economic knowledge (e.g., Hirschfeld, Moore, and Brown, 1995; Ziegert, 2000). Hirschfeld, Moore, and Brown examined the performance of males and females taking the Major Field Achievement Test in Economics and found virtually no differential performance by gender. Ziegert examined the relationship between personality type and understanding of economics as determined by standard measures of student performance (course grade or performance on the TUCE exam). Ziegert's results suggest that after adjusting for personality preferences, the differential performance by males and females disappears so that gender is not found as a statistically significant predictor of performance in economics.

The effect of gender on the performance in the MFT-B was studied by Bean and Bernardi (2002). The authors examined the association between gender and verbal and math SAT scores with performance on the MFT-B in a single institution, and found gender and verbal scores on the SAT to be the only significant variables in their model. Allgood and Walstad (2002) examined MFT-B test scores for 12,854 college seniors in schools of business and found that males outperform females. Finally, Black and Duhon (2003) examined the effect of gender on the overall performance in the MFT-B and found a test-score advantage for men over females after controlling for GPA, ACT scores, and age.

The effect of gender on performance has been studied in other business disciplines. In accounting, Mutchler, Turner, and Williams (1987) found that females outperformed males consistently over an 18-year period due perhaps to the quantitative nature of the subject. By contrast, Lipe (1989), Bouillon, Doran, and Smith (1990), and Park and Hayes (1994) found that student gender had no effect on academic performance in accounting courses. Lipe, however, found that male students performed better in courses taught by males and female students tended to performed better in courses instructed by females.

In finance, Borde, Byrd, and Modani (1996) found that the performance of males was superior to the performance of female students. Conversely, Borde (1998) found gender to be unrelated to performance in an introductory marketing course taught at a public university in Florida.

General Ability or Achievement

Academic ability is perhaps the most relevant variable in the production of knowledge and the only consistently significant explanatory proxy for undergraduate student learning in economics (Becker, 1997). Researchers have attempted to control for student ability with a wide range of measures, including high school rank, undergraduate grade point averages (GPA), the Scholastic Aptitude Test (SAT) scores and the American College Test (ACT) scores.

Early studies by Cohn (1972) and Bellico (1972) concluded that grade point averages and credits in mathematics were positively related to the performance of students in economics. The general finding in studies of economic education is that better SAT and ACT scores also tend to have a positive and significant effect in student achievement in economics (Barr and

Carr, 1980; Wetzel, O'Toole, and Millner, 1991; Laband and Piette, 1995; Ballard and Johnson, 2004).

In a recent study by Grove, Wasserman, and Grodner (2006), the authors investigate how the proxy choice of academic ability in previous research affected estimates of undergraduate student learning by testing over 150 specifications of a single model with different combinations of scholastic aptitude measures. The authors found the proxy choice creates large differences on the estimates of learning gains and suggested the use of college GPA and then either SAT scores or high school grades or rank to control for ability in single-institution studies. This finding is relevant given that their survey of 37 published articles cited in *Research on Teaching College Economics* by Siegfried and Walstad (1998) shows that, in 60 percent of cases, researchers used only a unique student academic ability set to control for student aptitude and randomly explained their choice for the proxy. Their results, however, should be taken as suggestive mainly because of the relative small sample size used in the study (n=117).

Most studies involving research with the MFT-B have focused on the relationship between intellect measures of business students and student performance. Allen and Bycio (1997) studied the relationship between GPA and other measures of intellect, and the performance on the MFT-B by examining two groups of business students at a single institution. Their first group consisted of accounting majors (n=65) while the other group consisted of all undergraduate business students who took the test (n=368), regardless of their major. Contrary to their hypotheses, the authors found a significant correlation between all of the GPA measures (i.e., core GPA) and intellectual aptitude measures (i.e., SAT), and test performance. The strongest association, however, was found between business core GPAs and the MFT-B scores.

Mirchandani, Lynch, and Hamilton (2001) also examined the MFT-B by including in their model several academic ability measures (GPA, SAT scores, and course grades) for a sample of 114 nontransfer students and 127 transfer students. The authors found that the best predictor for the performance of students on the MFT-B was the SAT score. The authors hypothesize that the stronger correlation between SAT and MFT-B scores may be due to comparable testing methods and the fact that both exams are developed by ETS. The effect of SAT scores on learning was studied even further by Bean and Bernardi (2002). The authors examined the association between verbal and math SAT scores and performance on the MFT-B in a single institution and found the verbal scores on the SAT to be the only aptitude proxy to be significant in their model. They conclude by noting that in their opinion, the data suggests that MFT-B score changes at an institution may be caused by SAT verbal score changes. The authors, however, were unable to control for important variables such as GPA.

Allgood and Walstad (2002) examined MFT-B test scores for all 12,854 college seniors in schools of business who took the MFT-B exam from January through June 1998. They found that students with higher GPAs outscored students with lower GPAs after controlling for many other student factors.

Finally, the effect of academic ability on performance has been studied in other business disciplines. Eckel and Johnson (1983) found that ACT math scores and performance in first year accounting courses were an accurate predictor of academic success in accounting, while Brown (1964; 1966) did not find a consistent relationship between college entrance test scores and the performance in undergraduate accounting courses as measured by course grades. Simpson and Sumrall (1979) and Schaffer and Calkins (1980) found that performances in economics and accounting courses, respectively, were the best predictors for success in finance. Finally, a student's GPA was found to be the most important predictor of performance in two introductory marketing courses taught by the same professor in a public university in Florida (Borde, 1998), and in an introductory finance course taught by four different instructors in a mid-size four-year liberal arts college (Dal and Baban, 1998), providing strong evidence that students who perform well in other courses tend to perform well in marketing and finance courses.

Race, Ethnicity, and International Status

Student race and ethnicity have often been used in models of student achievement in economics but the research findings have been mixed, with some studies finding white students tending to outperform non-white students, and others being unable to find any statistical difference between ethnic groups. At the college level, Borg, Mason, and Shapiro (1989) found race not to have a statistically significant effect in the performance of students in principles of macroeconomics even after controlling for student ability. Lopus and Maxwell (1993), however, examined ethnic differences in learning college economics and found that white students performed better than non-whites due to their preparation and learning styles. A study by Laband and Piette (1995) also revealed that white students perform better than non-white students in upper-level economic courses.

Personality types, however, may be an influential factor in the analysis of race and ethnicity. Borg and Shapiro (1996) used the Myers-Briggs Type Indicator (MBTI) to examine the relationship between student personality type and performance in principles of macroeconomics at the University of North Florida and found that the inclusion of the personality variable made the race variable (African American) insignificant on performance. The authors hypothesize that the lower performance in economics by minorities may be partially caused by personality differences. Ziegert (2000) replicated Borg and Shapiro's work by using a larger sample size and found similar results.

Moreover, Borg and Stranahan (2002) examined personality type and student performance in upper-level economic courses. The authors differentiated between Asian, Hispanic, African American and other students and found that African Americans when taken together as a group performed worse than members of other races. When African Americans, however, were grouped by personality type, they did not perform differently than nonblack students and nonblack students only performed better than African American students if they had specific temperament types (SJ and NT).

The effect of race, ethnicity and international status has been studied in other academic and business disciplines. Ward, Wilson and Thomas (1994) examined the relationship between classroom performance of African American students and their familiarity with basic business and accounting terminology by looking at a sample of African American students at a predominantly white university and a group of African American students at a predominantly black university. The authors find relatively low vocabulary scores for African American students and suggest that instructors should develop a "*sound terminology base for minority students*" so that they can "*understand the intricacies of business and accounting with less effort and increase their rate of success in completing the course.*"

Leppel (2001) explored the impact of race and Hispanic ethnicity on the business major and found that Asian and non-Hispanic blacks are less likely and Hispanics more likely to major in business than non-Hispanic whites. More generally, a summary of the literature on Hispanics and higher education achievement by Erlach (2000) found that Hispanics exhibit low levels of educational attainment that result in career disadvantages but "*those Hispanics who make it through the academic pipeline and start developing their careers seem to follow a track similar to those of the general population.*"

At the graduate level, Brahmasrene and Whitten (2001) surveyed certified public accountants to investigate factors determining the likelihood of success in the Uniform CPA Exam. The authors found no statistically significant difference between the five racial or ethnic groups examined (white, African American, Asian/Pacific, Hispanic and other). Clayton and Cate (2004) used discriminate analysis to examine MBA admission records to explore the factors that contribute to a successful graduate program completion at Northern Kentucky University. The results showed that the academic performance of whites and Hispanics was better than the performance of Asians in their MBA program.

A study by Tompson and Tompson (1996) surveyed faculty at two different business schools to identify behaviors that deter the academic performance and integration of international students. The most consistent response was the nonparticipation of international students in class discussion, followed by not asking for clarification, studying or working in groups made of international students only and sitting with other foreign students in class. Instructors, however, believed that the most negative impact on performance came from the violation of ethical guidelines regarding academic integrity. The study also speculated high attrition rates for international students due to the difficulty and stress created by the transition from a foreign high school to a university environment.

Age and Class Standing

The effects of age and class standing of students on performance have been studied in economics and other business disciplines. The overall assessment from the extensive research in this area finds age and years in school to either be insignificant or positively related to student achievement. Attiyeh, Bach and Lumsden (1970) and Laband and Piette (1995) found age not to be a significant factor explaining economic knowledge and performance. These findings are in accordance with the results reported in an early survey by Siegfried and Fels (1979). Conversely, Reid (1983) tested for factors that affect the economic knowledge of students upon completion of an introductory course in economics in a small, liberal arts university. The author included age in his model and found it to be a statistically significant variable, with older students performing better than those 21 years of age and younger. Reid's results corroborated previous findings by Barr and Carr (1980) and Manahan (1983).

School experience may matter based on education level. Cohn, Cohn, and Bradley (1995) found that upper-division students significantly outperformed lower-division students and recommended stricter requirements for attending principles of economics courses. Their class standing results supported previous findings by Bonello, Swartz, and Davisson (1984), Watts and Lynch (1989), and Watts and Bosshardt (1991) indicating that freshmen are at a disadvantage to sophomores and upper-division students.

Student age and class standing have been studied in other business disciplines. In management, Westerman, Nowicki, and Plante (2002) investigated the predictors of student performance and satisfaction, and found age to be a positive and statistically significant predictor of achievement. In finance, Simpson and Sumrall (1979), and in accounting, Brahmasrene and Whitten (2001), found that older students performed better than younger students. By contrast, in marketing courses, Borde (1998) found age to be unrelated to performance, as did Dockweiler and Willis (1984) in accounting.

Transfer Status

A 1992 survey of 11,000 college students conducted by the National Center for Education Statistics (NCES) at the U.S. Department of Education showed that the number of transfer students was on the rise, with over half of those being surveyed reporting that they had attended different institutions during their academic careers (NCES, 1996). A more recent study of community college students found that about 29 percent of students who began their postsecondary education in a two-year institution transferred to a four-year institution (NCES, 2003). These data indicate that an increasing proportion of students are being taught introductory economics in two-year college institutions. This trend raises questions about the quality of the education received by students who learn introductory economics or business in two-year colleges and then transfer to four-year colleges or universities.

The performance of transfer students on economic achievement was generally found to be either insignificant or worse than the performance of students entering four-year institutions directly. One of the first attempts in economic education to assess the effect of attending a community college on performance was undertaken by Bellico (1972) with 92 students at the University of Massachusetts. He found that students attending a community college had a negative but insignificant effect in undergraduate achievement in economics. Similarly, Arias and Walker (2004) included in their transfer student cohort any student who had transferred any credit hour regardless of whether the credit came from a two- or four-year institution and found transfer status not to affect student performance.

Borg, Mason, and Shapiro (1989) estimated the effect of attending a community college, and later transferring to the University of North Florida, on the achievement in principles of macroeconomics and found the effect for above-average students to be negative but not statistically significant. The effect, however, was negative and statistically significant at the one percent level for those students below average (where the below-average group was represented by students with SAT and ACT scores below 1004 and 22.98, respectively). The results for all students in the sample also were negative but only significant at the 10-percent level and the authors warned economic educators and policy makers about policy implications following their study by adding, "*Advisers should be concerned about placing freshmen or junior college transfers in the principles of macroeconomics course…however, we discover that the concerns are warranted for below average students but not for above average.*"

Borg and Shapiro (1996) examined personality type and student performance in principles of economics and found transferring from a community college to be negative and statistically significant in two of their three models. Although the authors did not divide the sample in two ability groups (i.e., above- and below-average), they suggested that the reasons for their findings were the selective admission processes undertaken by state universities in

Florida, where only about 15 percent, or what they called the "best and the brightest" of all graduating high school students are admitted.

In upper-level coursework in economics, Laband and Piette (1995) examined a sample of 2003 undergraduate students at Florida State University. The authors found that those students who had taken the macro/micro sequence of principles of economics at a community college tended to perform worse than nontransfer students in upper-level economics classes. The effect of verbal and math SATs was found to be insignificant and the authors concluded that their results could be explained by a lower quality of economics instruction at community colleges. Furthermore, using data from a 1992 U.S. Department of Education survey, Bosshardt and Watts (2005) reported that transfer students complete fewer economic courses on average than nontransfer students.

The effect of transfer status on performance in other business disciplines is similar to the ones discovered in economics. In introductory finance, Dal and Baban (1998) found transfer status to have a positive but insignificant effect on student performance. In accounting, Simpson and Sumrall (1979) and Borde, Byrd, and Modani (1996) found that transfer students from community colleges and other universities tended to be outperformed by students who did not transfer. In principles of accounting, Colley and Volkan (1996) evaluated the quality of course grades for transfer versus nontransfer students and found that principles' grades among transfer students were significantly worse than those of nontransfer students and these lower grades were significant predictors of lower performance in intermediate accounting courses.

An innovative study on transferring effects was undertaken by Borde (1998) with an introductory marketing class. The author divided transfer students into two groups, one group composed of students who transferred from community colleges and the other group consisting of students who transferred from different universities. Borde found that transfer students from community colleges tend to underperform when compared to nontransfer and transfer students from other universities (four-year programs).

Finally, Sauter (1984) investigated the effect of prerequisites and their transfer on the undergraduate performance of students in an operation management course at the University of Missouri. Using a sample of 700 students, Sauter found that those who take the prerequisite courses in other institutions do significantly worse than non-transfer students, and that taking the courses at community colleges versus other universities, magnified even further the difference in performance. Sauter concluded that the difference in performance was due to the lower math ability of transfer students. The author, however, was unable to control for the mathematical ability of the students and used the overall performance of students in the business school as a proxy for math ability.

One final point is worth noting about the above studies. The overall performance of transfer students to business degree programs at four-year institutions has typically been studied with course grades or some other local achievement measure. The measurement of achievement using a standardized test instrument such as the MFT-B has not received much attention in the literature and deserves further investigation.

Business Major

A limited number of research studies have examined the effect of a student's major on the overall business performance of graduating business students. The few findings seem to suggest that accountants are better prepared than students in other business disciplines after the completion of their business programs, while management and marketing students are at a disadvantage relative to other business majors. Further research is still needed, however. Studies with larger sample sizes, both at the group and major level should, and will, allow for better comparisons of achievement across majors. In addition, there are no available research studies that compare the overall business performance of economics majors with the overall performance of other business majors.

Karathanos (1991a) obtained "gain" and "value added" test scores by administering the Core Curriculum Assessment Program (CCAP) instrument to business students enrolling in their first business core course and students completing the core courses at a regional university in the Midwest. The author found the biggest score gain for students majoring in accounting (with a 77.6 percent gain in scores), while students majoring in management information systems experienced the smallest gain at a rate of 11.8 percent. Unfortunately, the sample size used to infer the results was small (26 students for the entering group and 21 students for the exiting group), so that it was not possible to conduct reliable analyses of subgroups by major.

Rosacker, Rosacker, and Lau (1995) examined business performance in specific business core courses to assess the academic quality of accounting majors versus that of business administration majors and found accountants to receive higher average course grades in 13 of the 14 business core courses examined. This finding could be explained by the higher overall GPAs and business core GPAs of accounting students in the sample when compared to business administration students. Of special relevance is the larger sample size used in this study (648 records) and the division of the sample group into two subgroups. An earlier study by Korte and Rosacker (1994) considered the difference in academic performance in seven business major areas and six business core courses, and also found accounting majors to be the best students in the school of business examined.

Allen and Bycio (1997) explored the relationship between a student's major and the performance on the MFT-B at a single and small institution in the Midwest. The authors studied a sample of accounting majors enrolled in various sections of the required capstone business course and a sample of 386 undergraduate business students who took the test, regardless of their major. The analysis was performed for majors that were represented by a minimum of thirty students, with accounting, finance, management and marketing being the only majors that satisfied the requirement. Accounting and finance students were found to score significantly higher than management and marketing students. No statistically significant difference, however, was found between accountants and finance students, although accountants tended to score higher. Marketing majors were the worst performers in the sample. The performance of marketing majors could be explained by the results of a recent study by Nonis, Philhours, and Hudson (2006) that found marketing students to spend less time attending lectures, preparing for class, preparing for exams, quizzes, projects and assignments, but spend more time at work than other business majors.

Black and Duhon (2003) also used the MFT-B to evaluate and improve student achievement in business programs. The authors examined a group of 456 students enrolled in a business core course at the University of Southern Mississippi. Unlike previous studies, they divided the sample into a group of management students and a group including all of the other business majors. After controlling for grade point averages, ACT scores, age and gender, they found that management students were at a statistically significant 3.57-point disadvantage when compared to other business majors. The authors suggest that other majors (i.e., economics) could be singled out for similar treatment, but such a study has not been conducted to date.

Overall Business Achievement and Course Effects

There is a limited amount of research examining the performance in specific business courses (i.e., the grade a student receives in principles of macroeconomics) and their overall effect on the achievement of business students before graduation. This issue is one that merits further research because it could allow administrators and educators to emphasize student learning in certain business areas to improve the overall business achievement of their students.

The two main standardized instruments used to measure the overall achievement of business students and the effects of specific course work are the Major Field Test in Business (MFT-B), which was previously described, and the Core Curriculum Assessment Program (CCAP). The CCAP was developed in 1987 in response to the need for outcome assessment in collegiate business programs, but only a handful of research papers have used this output measure (Karathanos, 1991a and 1991b; Jonas and Weiner, 1995), and none of these studies have examined the effect of specific business courses on the overall business performance of students. Karathanos (1991b) compared the MFT-B and the CCAP instruments to determine which assessment tool was a better outcome measure of collegiate business curricula. The author concluded that "*if an institution is comfortable using the 'national comparative data' approach, the Business Test has definite advantage over the CCAP instrument, particularly in terms of logistics and cost.*" Karathanos's conclusions probably contributed to the almost exclusive use of the MFT-B in assessment projects for business students and programs.

Mirchandani, Lynch, and Hamilton (2001) examined performance on the MFT-B for graduating seniors at Rowan University (Glassboro). None of the courses examined were highly correlated with performance on the MFT-B, with Principles of Statistics and Principles of Finance presenting the highest correlations at a value of about 0.3. Using factor analysis to reduce the number of independent grade variables, the authors were able to eliminate two of the 13 initially selected courses and found that quantitative courses, including Calculus, Accounting I and II, Finance, Operations Management, and Management Information Systems, have a positive and statistically significant effect on students' overall business performance. Qualitative and economics courses were not found to have a significant effect on the students' overall performance. Based on their findings, the authors suggest that business programs concentrate on the material in quantitative courses to improve the overall learning of business students.

Bagamery, Lasik, and Nixon (2005) extended the previous work by Mirchandani, Lynch, and Hamilton (2001) by examining the performance of 169 graduating students from Central Washington University on the MFT-B. The results showed that none of the grades in the 14 principles courses were highly correlated with the MFT-B score. The highest correlations were with Principles of Macroeconomics and Microeconomics (.53 and .43 respectively). The authors also performed factor analysis to reduce the number of course variables and created four factor groups (general, quantitative, accounting and management courses) that were regressed against the output measure. The authors found the grades for Principles of Accounting to explain 10 percent of the total variance in performance, and suggested one way to improve overall performance of business students was to improve student learning in this Principles of Accounting course.

DATA AND SAMPLE

The data set used in this study includes information on 689 graduating seniors who took the MFT-B during the 2005–2006 academic year in the College of Business Administration at the University of Nebraska-Lincoln (UNL). Graduating seniors from the College enroll in a Business Senior Assessment course during the last semester of their academic undergraduate program and are required to complete the MFT-B, as well as other assessment tests and instruments.

Data on a variety of variables were collected for this study. These variables included demographic characteristics, ability measures, transfer status, course grades and choice of major for the graduating sample of business students examined. A summary of the main dependent and independent variables used in the analysis and their definitions is presented in Table 1.

Table 1. List of Main Variables

DEPENDENT VARIABLES	
MFTB	Score on the Major Field Test in Business exam
DEMOGRAPHICS	
MALE	Student is male (YES = 1)
AGE	Student age at the time of examination
WHITE	Student classified as White (YES = 1)
ASIAN	Student classified as Asian (YES = 1)
OTHER	Ethnicity/race other than White or Asian (YES = 1)
ORIGIN	Student citizenship (U.S. = 1)
TRANSFER STATUS	
TRANSFCORE	Student transferring at least one business core course (YES = 1)
TRANSFOTHER	Student transferring other than business core courses (YES=1)
TRANSFCORECR	Student number of business core credit hours transferred
ABILITY	
SAT	Student score on the SAT or converted ACT
GPA	Student Grade Point Average at graduation
COREGPA	Student Grade Point Average in 11 business core courses

DEPENDENT VARIABLES	
OTHERGPA	Student Grade Point Average in non-business core courses
MAJORS/MINORS	
ACCGMJRS	Accounting or Agricultural Business (YES = 1)
BSADMJRS	Business Adm. or International Business (YES = 1)
ECONMJRS	Economics (YES = 1)
FINAMJRS	Finance or Actuarial Science (YES = 1)
MNGTMJRS	Management (YES = 1)
MRKTMJRS	Marketing (YES = 1)
ECONMNRS	Minoring in Economics (YES = 1)
COURSE GRADES	
MACECON	Principles of Macroeconomics
MICECON	Principles of Microeconomics
ACCG1	Principles of Accounting I
ACCG2	Principles of Accounting II
BLAW	Business Law
MRKT	Principles of Marketing
STATS	Business Statistics
FINA	Principles of Finance
ISYS	Management/Marketing Information Systems
OBMNGT	Managing Behavior in Organizations
ORMMNGT	Operations Resource Management
COURSE TRANSFERS	
TRANSFMACECON	Principles of Macroeconomic (YES = 1)
TRANSFMICECON	Principles of Microeconomics (YES = 1)
TRANSFACCG1	Principles of Accounting I (YES = 1)
TRANSFACCG2	Principles of Accounting II (YES = 1)
TRANSFBLAW	Business Law (YES = 1)
TRANSFMRKT	Principles of Marketing (YES = 1)
TRANSFSTATS	Business Statistics (YES = 1)
TRANSFFINA	Principles of Finance (YES = 1)
TRANSFISYS	Mngt/Mrkt Information Systems (YES = 1)
TRANSFOBMNGT	Managing Behavior in Organizations (YES = 1)
TRANSFORMMNGT	Operations Resource Management (YES = 1)
MAJOR AND TRANSFER STATUS	
ACCGMJRSTRANSFCORE	Accounting or Agricultural Business (YES = 1)
BSADMJRSTRANSFCORE	Business Adm. or International Business (YES = 1)
ECONMJRSTRANSFCORE	Economics (YES = 1)
FINAMJRSTRANSFCORE	Finance or Actuarial Science (YES = 1)
MNGTACCGMJRSTRANSFCORE	Management (YES = 1)
MRKTMJRSTRANSFCORE	Marketing (YES = 1)

Descriptive Results

Descriptive statistics for the entire student sample across all variables can be found in Table 2..

Table 2. Descriptive Statistics

	N	Min.	Max.	Mean	S.D.
TEST RESULTS					
MFTB	689	124	196	161.24	12.71
DEMOGRAPHICS					
MALE	432	0	1	0.63	0.48
AGE	689	20	42	23.09	2.55
WHITE	625	0	1	0.91	0.29
ASIAN	25	0	1	0.04	0.19
OTHER	39	0	1	0.06	0.23
ORIGIN	661	0	1	0.96	0.20
TRANSFER STATUS					
TRANSFCORE	366	0	1	0.53	0.50
TRANSFOTHER	128	0	1	0.19	0.39
TRANSFCORECR	366	0	21	4.91	6.15
ABILITY					
SAT	628	740	1520	1088.04	144.25
GPA	689	2.07	4	3.21	0.37
COREGPA	689	1.94	4	3.13	0.46
OTHERGPA	689	1.69	4	3.23	0.37
MAJOR					
ACCGMJRS	77	0	1	0.11	0.32
BSADMJRS	201	0	1	0.29	0.45
ECONMJRS	27	0	1	0.04	0.19
FINAMJRS	179	0	1	0.26	0.44
MNGTMJRS	112	0	1	0.16	0.37
MRKTMJRS	132	0	1	0.19	0.39
COURSE GRADES					
MACECON	680	0.67	4	2.87	0.78
MICECON	679	0.67	4	3.30	0.71
ACCG1	679	1.00	4	2.96	0.79
ACCG2	683	0.67	4	2.87	0.86
BLAW	689	1.33	4	3.35	0.65
MRKT	687	1.00	4	3.25	0.63
STATS	680	0.67	4	3.14	0.76
FINA	688	0.67	4	2.90	0.78
OBMNGT	687	1.00	4	3.14	0.71
OMMNGT	689	1.00	4	3.25	0.61
COURSE TRANSFER					
TRANSFMACECON	143	0	1	0.21	0.41
TRANSFMICECON	133	0	1	0.19	0.39
TRANSFACCG1	203	0	1	0.29	0.46
TRANSFACCG2	210	0	1	0.30	0.46
TRANSFBLAW	218	0	1	0.32	0.47
TRANSFMRKT	143	0	1	0.21	0.41
TRANSFSTATS	60	0	1	0.09	0.28
TRANSFFINA	7	0	1	0.01	0.10
TRANFSISYS	3	0	1	0.00	0.07
TRANSFOBMNGT	4	0	1	0.01	0.08
TRANSFORMNGT	4	0	1	0.01	0.08

The mean value of the dummy variables (0, 1) represents the percentage of students with a given characteristic. There were 296 students who completed the MFT-B test in the fall semester, 287 students who took the test in the spring semester and a total of 106 students who completed the instruments during the three available summer sessions.

The mean student age for the sample of graduating seniors was 23.09 years old, indicating that most students complete their degree in about five years. Of this group, 63 percent of students were males, 91 percent were white, and about 96 percent were U.S. citizens. Asian students accounted for about 4 percent of students in the sample and all other races and ethnicities combined accounted for the remaining 6 percent. The racial and ethnic composition of the senior group examined in this study is similar to that generally found at UNL.

A total of about 53 percent of the students in the sample had transferred at least one business core course from an outside institution. The mean number of business core credits transferred was 4.91 credit hours. The mean GPA was 3.21, which corresponds to a B- grade. The lowest GPA in the sample was 2.07 and the highest GPA was a perfect 4.0. The mean core GPA for the sample of students examined was slightly lower than the overall GPA at 3.13 points. The average SAT score was about 1088 points, with a sample minimum of 740 points and a maximum of 1520 points. Sixty-one students did not have an SAT or ACT score available. Examination of the proportion of graduating seniors by majors shows that about 29 percent chose business administration or international business as their area of concentration. Over one fourth (26%) were majoring in Finance or Actuarial Science. Economics majors were the least represented in the sample with about 4 percent of students specializing in that subject.

Information on the mean course grades for the 11 core business courses examined in this study shows that Principles of Macroeconomics and Principles of Accounting II exhibit the lowest mean quality point values with a 2.87 average. The highest mean grade belongs to the Marketing and Management Information Systems course, with a numerical value of 3.39. This quality point value is equivalent to a B+ letter grade. The maximum numerical value for each of the courses is 4 quality points while the minimum value varies, with several core courses exhibiting a mean of .67. The accounting class sequence is the only sequence that exhibits an average of less than 3 quality points in each of its courses. The economics sequence, which includes Principles of Macroeconomics and Microeconomics, is the only sequence where one of the courses is below 3 quality points and the other one is above. Students seem to perform considerably better in Principles of Microeconomics than in Principles of Macroeconomics. A limited number of course grades are missing from each of the courses examined, mostly due to difficulties translating transcripts and department credit validations.

The sequence of Principles of Accounting courses and Business Law were the courses most transferred by students in the sample, with a transfer rate of about 30 percent. About 20 percent of those who completed the sequence in Principles of Economics and Principles of Marketing transferred the courses, while only 9 percent of students transferred statistics. There were seven students allowed to transfer Principles of Finance, while management core courses were only transferred by four students and information systems by three individuals.

As shown in Table 3, the mean score on the MFT-B was 161 points, with a standard deviation of 12.71 points. The lowest achieving students during the 2005–2006 academic year received a score of 124 points on the exam, while the highest achieving students had a score of 196 points. Descriptive statistics on MFT-B scores by gender, age, race and ethnicity, origin, transfer status, ability measures, major and economics minor also are reported in Table 3. Male students scored on average about 2.5 points better than females. Males, however, registered the lowest MFT-B score in the sample at 124 points. Students 24 years of age or older scored slightly lower than students below the age of 24. White students, with an average MFT-B score of 161.95 points, outscored Asian students by almost 10 points and all other students by about 6 points. U.S. citizens performed about 3.5 points better on average than foreign students.

Examination of MFT-B scores and transfer core status reveals that students who started and fully completed their undergraduate business core training at UNL performed better on the MFT-B than those who transferred at least one business core course. The mean MFT-B score for those who transferred core courses was 157.80 points, while the mean MFT-B score for native students was 165.14. The sample of transfer students included the worst-performing individuals on the MFT-B with a score of 124 points, but also included the highest score at 196 points.

Ability, as it relates to the performance of students on the MFT-B, is examined through SAT and GPA subgroups. SAT scores are divided into two subgroups, one for students with entry SAT scores equal to or above 1070 points and another for students with entry SAT scores below 1070 points. The value of 1070 points is the median SAT entry score for the student sample examined in this study. There were 257 students who scored lower than 1070 points on the SAT and 371 students who scored at least 1070 points. Students with SAT scores equal to or higher than 1070 points outscored those with lower scores by about 13 points on the MFT-B, with an average score of 166.88 points.

Student GPAs were divided into four different groups, one for those students with cumulative GPAs below 2.5 and the other three in increments of one-half quality points. There were 314 students, or about 46 percent of the sample, who had accumulated an overall GPA between 3 and 3.49 quality points. There were 157 students with GPAs equal to or above 3.5 quality points, and only two students with GPAs below 2.5 quality points. Students in the highest GPA bracket also exhibited the highest MFT-B mean score at 169.22 points. Students with lower GPAs performed worse than those with higher GPAs. The lowest mean MFT-B score was found for students with GPAs between 2.5 and 2.99.

The performance of students on the MFT-B by major shows that economics majors performed better, on average, than any other major examined. The average MFT-B score for those majoring in economics was 168.96 points. Economics majors also exhibited the highest minimum score out of all the majors examined at 140 points. Accounting students exhibited the second highest mean MFT-B score at 167.09 points, while marketing students were the worst MFT-B performers, with a mean score of 156.59 points, or about 12.5 points lower than economics majors. The sample of Marketing students included students with the lowest score on the MFT-B, while accounting, business and finance majors had students with the highest MFT-B score recorded for the sample. Accounting, economics and finance majors performed on average above 160 points, while business, management and marketing majors performed on average below 160 points. Finally, those students with a major in one of the business disciplines previously described and a minor in economics performed relatively better than most majors, with an average MFT-B score of 165.10 points.

Table 3. Descriptive Statistics on MFT-B Scores

	N	Min.	Max.	Mean	S.D.
Gender					
Male	432	124	196	162.57	12.97
Female	257	132	196	159.01	11.96
Age					
<24	563	124	196	161.35	12.78
≥24	126	131	196	160.76	12.44
Race/Ethnicity					
White	625	126	196	161.95	12.43
Asian	25	132	173	152.16	11.01
Other	39	124	196	155.69	14.81
Origin					
US	661	126	196	161.39	12.66
Foreign	28	124	188	157.79	13.77
Transfer					
Yes	483	124	196	159.78	12.63
No	206	135	193	164.67	12.26
SAT					
<1070	257	131	181	153.64	9.90
≥1070	371	126	196	166.88	11.55
GPA					
3.5-4.00	157	132	196	169.22	11.52
3.00-3.49	314	126	196	161.77	11.97
2.5-2.99	216	124	189	154.72	11.03
<2.5	2	147	165	156.00	12.73
Major					
Accounting	77	126	196	167.09	13.36
Business	201	134	196	159.76	12.76
Economics	27	140	190	168.96	15.03
Finance	179	134	196	164.68	12.70
Management	112	131	189	159.46	11.38
Marketing	132	124	181	156.59	10.13
Minor					
Economics	79	134	196	165.10	13.55

The mean MFT-B score comparison by group shows several significant differences at the .01 level. Males performed better than females by 3.6 points. White students scored better than students from other ethnic groups or races by 7.6 points. Students who completed their core business training at UNL scored 7.3 points higher than students who transferred at least one business core course from another college or university. Students with SAT scores greater or equal to 1070 points or GPAs higher or equal to 3.5 scored on average significantly better than students with lower SAT scores or GPAs. In fact, the largest t-value found was exhibited by the difference in mean MFT-B scores between students with SAT scores greater or equal to 1070 and all other students.

Minor or insignificant differences were found with several variables. Students younger than 24 years old performed on average better than older students, but the difference was not statistically significant. MFT-B mean scores were significantly different at the .05 level between foreign and U.S. citizens, but the group size was small for this comparison. Further analysis of the difference in mean MFT-B scores by major is presented in Table 5.

The mean MFT-B score of marketing majors was significantly lower than the mean MFT-B score of all other majors in the sample. Management and business majors scored significantly lower on average than accounting, economics and finance majors. The difference in mean MFT-B scores between accounting, economics and finance students was not significant. Finally, the difference in scores between finance and economics, and management and business students, was negative but insignificant.

Table 4 presents further analysis of the difference in mean MFT-B scores by demographic characteristics and ability level. The mean MFT-B score of white students was compared to that of all other students in the sample, while the mean MFT-B score of students with GPAs equal or greater than 3.5 was compared to that of students with lower GPAs.

Table 4. Difference in Mean MFT-B Scores by Demographics and Ability

	Df-t	Mean Difference	*t*-value
Gender: Male~Female	572	3.56**	3.66
Age: <24~≥24	188	0.59	0.48
Race/Ethnicity: White~All Other	74	7.64**	4.36
Origin: Foreign~U.S.	28	3.60*	1.36
Transfcore: No~Yes	678	7.34**	7.90
SAT: ≥1070~<1070	598	13.24**	15.38
GPA: ≥3.5~Other	265	10.33**	9.76

** statistically significant at the .01 level, 2 tailed.
* statistically significant at the .05 level, 2 tailed.

Table 5. Difference in Mean MFT-B Scores by Major

Major	1	2	3	4	5	6
1. Accounting	0					
2. Business	–7.33**	0				
3. Economics	1.87	9.20**	0			
4. Finance	–2.41	4.92**	–4.28	0		
5. Management	–7.63**	–0.30	–9.50**	–5.22**	0	
6. Marketing	–10.50**	–3.17**	–12.37**	–8.09**	–2.87*	0

** statistically significant at the .01 level, 2 tailed.
* statistically significant at the .05 level, 2 tailed.

Further examination of the descriptive statistics by major as they relate to the transfer status, ability and course grades of those students who completed the MFT-B can be found in Table 6.

Table 6. Descriptive Statistics by Major

	Accounting (n=77)		Business (n=201)		Economics (n=27)	
TRANSFER STATUS	Mean	S.D.	Mean	S.D.	Mean	S.D.
TRANSFCORE	0.40	0.49	0.58	0.49	0.41	0.50
TRANSFCORECR	3.51	5.41	5.46	6.31	3.33	5.90
ABILITY						
SAT	1143.68	139.25	1068.77	152.30	1131.54	143.32
GPA	3.40	0.36	3.15	0.38	3.27	0.31
COREGPA	3.49	0.35	3.04	0.45	3.24	0.37
COURSE GRADES						
MACECON	3.27	0.70	2.81	0.80	3.18	0.56
MICECON	3.57	0.60	3.22	0.76	3.55	0.57
ACCG1	3.64	0.59	2.86	0.79	3.04	0.75
ACCG2	3.57	0.57	2.79	0.88	2.84	0.66
BLAW	3.56	0.48	3.28	0.69	3.47	0.55
MRKT	3.46	0.57	3.18	0.66	3.23	0.63
STATS	3.54	0.64	3.06	0.81	3.33	0.67
FINA	3.47	0.58	2.73	0.78	3.06	0.67
ISYS	3.43	0.51	3.31	0.61	3.33	0.55
OBMNGT	3.39	0.67	3.06	0.70	3.25	0.67
OMMNGT	3.52	0.57	3.12	0.57	3.36	0.52

	Finance (n=179)		Management (n=112)		Marketing (n=132)	
TRANSFER STATUS	Mean	S.D.	Mean	S.D.	Mean	S.D.
TRANSFCORE	0.49	0.50	0.53	0.50	0.59	0.49
TRANSFCORECR	4.63	6.34	4.93	6.11	5.11	5.97
ABILITY						
SAT	1107.99	126.79	1087.31	159.47	1064.80	122.11
GPA	3.27	0.38	3.16	0.36	3.16	0.33
COREGPA	3.26	0.45	3.03	0.46	2.99	0.40
COURSE GRADES						
MACECON	3.04	0.72	2.76	0.81	2.60	0.76
MICECON	3.39	0.68	3.15	0.68	3.28	0.70
ACCG1	3.08	0.79	2.80	0.76	2.72	0.71
ACCG2	2.90	0.82	2.79	0.79	2.63	0.89
BLAW	3.48	0.63	3.32	0.61	3.17	0.69
MRKT	3.34	0.62	3.16	0.64	3.20	0.59
STATS	3.28	0.67	3.03	0.80	3.00	0.75
FINA	3.20	0.66	2.69	0.77	2.65	0.74
ISYS	3.49	0.56	3.33	0.55	3.42	0.51
OBMNGT	3.28	0.71	3.03	0.74	3.05	0.68
OMMNGT	3.36	0.62	3.26	0.65	3.18	0.58

Business and marketing majors exhibited the largest proportion of core transfer students with about 60 percent of those majoring in these areas transferring at least one business core course from an outside institution. Accounting majors had the least proportion of business core transfer students, followed very closely by economics majors. There were 40 percent of accounting majors transferring at least one core course, while 41 percent of economics majors transferred at least one core course from an outside institution. Business students transferred on average more core credits than students in any other discipline. Business majors transferred on average 5.46 core credit hours, followed by management and finance majors with an average transfer of 4.93 and 4.63 core credit hours respectively. Economics majors exhibited the lowest transfer of core credits from outside institutions with an average transfer of 3.33 credit hours.

Examination of the mean SAT entry scores and GPAs of students by major reveals that accounting students exhibit, on average, the highest entry SAT scores and GPAs when compared to the other five majors. The mean entry SAT score for the group of accounting majors was 1143.68 points, while their mean GPA was 3.40 and mean core GPA was 3.49 quality points. Economics majors were ranked second both in terms of mean entry SAT scores and overall GPA. The average entry SAT score of economics students was 1131.54 points while their average graduating GPA was 3.27 quality points. The lowest mean entry SAT score and core GPA belonged to marketing majors with a mean value of 1064.38 points and 2.99 quality points respectively, while business students had the lowest mean GPA at 3.15 quality points.

Accounting students exhibited the highest mean core business course scores for 10 of the 11 courses examined in this study, and ranked second on the marketing and management information systems courses behind finance majors. Accounting students performed on average better in the economics sequence than economics majors, better in the Principles of Marketing course than marketing students, better in Principles of Finance than finance majors and finally, better than management students in operational and behavioral management. Finance and economics majors performed equally well in Principles of Macroeconomics, although economics students were on average better students in Principles of Microeconomics. Marketing and business students were the worst performers in Principles of Macroeconomics, while management students were outscored by all the other majors in Principles of Microeconomics. The lowest course averages were found for students majoring in marketing, business, and management, with marketing students exhibiting the lowest scores in six of the 11 courses examined, business students having two of the lowest scores and management students with the lowest scores in three of the courses. The average grade of economics majors was above 3 quality points for 10 of the 11 courses examined.

CROSS-SECTIONAL ANALYSIS

The education production function is the theoretical model used in this study. In education, the production function is some mathematical relationship describing how educational resources (inputs) can be transformed into educational outcomes (outputs). The production function then represents the maximum amount of output that can be produced for given levels of inputs and its general form can be expressed as $Q = f(X, S)$. For the purposes of this study, the inputs and outputs are related to undergraduate students and education in universities. Accordingly, Q is a vector of educational outputs (i.e., standardized test score), X is the vector of university-related inputs and S is the vector of non-university inputs. The internal process of transforming the educational inputs into output is known as the technology of education. This process is influenced by different variables related to the educational process such as pedagogical techniques or management. The general form of the *i*th educational production function using a linear approximation to the production of knowledge is given by:

$$q_i = a_i + \sum_{g=1}^{n} b_{ig} q_g + \sum_{h=1}^{k} c_{ih} x_h + \sum_{j=1}^{m} d_{ij} s_j + e_i$$

where a_i is the intercept, while $b_{ig}s, c_{ih}s$ and $d_{ij}s$ are the coefficients to be estimated, with $b_{ii} = 0$ and e_i being the stochastic term (Cohn and Geske, 1990).

The following regression models attempt to identify the factors that contribute to the retention and production of core business knowledge by graduating seniors and share similar independent variables, namely the demographic characteristics of students in the sample, their ability levels and transfer status as shown in Table 2. The first model specifically studies the influence of a student's major on MFT-B scores. The second model investigates the effects of student performance in core business courses and on MFT-B scores. The third model evaluates the impact of transferring core business courses on retention of business and economic knowledge as measured by the MFT-B. The final model introduces interaction terms between the choice of a major and student transfer of core courses to study the effects of both factors on student achievement on the MFT-B.

A one-tail test was used to assess the significance of model coefficients in cases where the direction of their expected effect was based on previous literature. A two-tail test was used to assess the significance of all other model coefficients.

Model 1: Effects of Majors

The estimated regression coefficients for Model 1, followed by the t-statistics in parentheses, are presented in Table 7. This model examines the effect of the choice of major on MFT-B performance after controlling for demographic characteristics, ability measures and transfer status. The regression equation was highly significant, with an F-statistic value of 51.77, and explained 49 percent of the variation in MFT-B scores.

The *B* coefficients show that gender, age, ethnic background, country of citizenship, SAT scores and the core GPA of graduating seniors and transfer of business core courses are highly significant in explaining the performance of students on the MFT-B. Consistent with previous findings by Black and Duhon (2003) and Bagamery, Lasik, and Nixon (2005), being a male was found to have a positive and significant impact, adding approximately 3.4 points to an MFT-B score. Older students performed significantly higher than younger students, with a 1-year positive age differential contributing to a higher MFT-B score of about .44 points.

Although no previous research was found related to the effect of ethnic background on MFT-B performance, previous findings in the economics and business literature (Lopus and Maxwell, 1993; Laband and Piette, 1995; Clayton and Cate, 2004) suggest that white students tend to outperform students belonging to other ethnic groups. Being a white student had a positive and significant effect on MFT-B performance, and added approximately 2.87 points to an MFT-B score.

Table 7. Choice of Major Effects on MFT-B Performance

Variables	*B*	(*t*-value)
(Constant)	93.13	(18.52)
MALE	3.42***	(4.61)
AGE	0.44***	(3.14)
WHITE	2.87**	(1.73)
ASIAN	–4.20 [c]	(–1.75)
ORIGIN	–10.80***	(4.74)
SAT	0.04***	(14.23)
COREGPA	6.76***	(7.55)
TRANSFCORE	–2.74***	(–3.73)
ACCGMJRS	1.28	(1.04)
ECONMJRS	4.24***	(2.34)
FINAMJRS	1.35*	(1.48)
MNGTMJRS	–1.30	(–1.26)
MRKTMJRS	–2.04**	(–2.08)
R Square	0.50	
Adj. R Square	0.49	
F	51.77***	

*** significant at .01 level, ** significant at .05 level, * significant at .10 level (1-tailed).
[a] significant at .01 level, [b] significant at .05 level, [c] significant at .10 level (2-tailed).

The estimated coefficient on Asian students was associated with a large and significant decrease in achievement relative to other races, suggesting the existence of family or community characteristics associated with a student's race that influence performance on the MFT-B.

The variable *ORIGIN* is highly significant and has the largest marginal effect on MFT-B scores among all other dummy variables in this model. U.S. citizens are found to be at an approximately 11-point disadvantage when compared to students from foreign countries. The examination of SAT scores for all foreign students admitted to UNL during the past eight years shows that their average SAT entry scores have increased considerably, providing for higher ability international students on campus [1]. In addition, foreign students are charged out-of-state tuition and tend to come from the top socioeconomic backgrounds in their countries. The negative coefficient was expected, but its size was certainly surprising.

Students who transferred at least one business core course from other institutions were at a 2.74-point disadvantage when compared to students who attended only UNL during their business core education [2]. Although different from previous findings by Mirchandani, Lynch, and Hamilton (2001) and Bagamery, Lasik, and Nixon (2005), the negative and significant *B* coefficient was expected for the group of graduating seniors. Conversations with business and economic faculty members revealed a widespread suspicion that the reason that some students take core business and economics courses at a local community college and then transfer the coursework into their degree program at UNL is that the community college courses are not as demanding. Although this conclusion is a tentative one and should not be extrapolated to institutions fundamentally different from UNL, a body of economics and business literature indicates that transfer students score lower than nontransfer students (Simpson and Sumrall, 1979; Borg, Mason, and Shapiro, 1989; Laband and Piette, 1995; Borg and Shapiro, 1996; Colley and Volkan, 1996).

Consistent with the previous findings is the highly significant and positive impact of SAT entry scores on MFT-B performance. This finding is not surprising; students who do well on one standardized test are more likely to do as well on other standardized testing instruments (Sacks, 1997). Equally consistent is the significant and large effect of a student's core GPA, with a 1-point positive core GPA differential contributing to a higher MFT-B score of approximately 6.8 points. Given this finding, it would be safe to say that students who do well on their core business courses will most likely perform well in a measure of core business knowledge.

Economics majors were the only students to exhibit a positive and highly statistically significant score advantage on the MFT-B, at about 4.26 points. The *B* coefficient for economics students, however, was expected to be positive and significant for two reasons. First, descriptive statistics showed that economics majors exhibited the highest mean MFT-B score in the sample. Second, informal interaction with several business students suggests that the materials covered in principles and intermediate economics are more difficult than the materials in other principles and intermediate business disciplines, excluding finance courses, which are similar to economics courses in their analytical rigor. For this reason, the expectation was that the brightest students would major in one of these two business programs and perform considerably better than all other business majors on the MFT-B. Finance students also exhibited a positive coefficient, but its significance was reduced to the 0.1 level. These students had a positive advantage of about 1.35 MFT-B points when compared to other business students in the sample.

The *B* coefficient for accounting students was found to be positive, but insignificant. The coefficient on accounting students was consistent with the findings by Bagamery, Lasik, and Nixon (2005), who found majoring in accounting to not have a significant effect on MFT-B scores. Students majoring in marketing were found to score significantly lower than all the other majors in the sample. In fact, students who majored in marketing were found to be at a 2-point disadvantage when compared to their business counterparts. The descriptive statistics previously presented showed that marketing students also exhibited the lowest mean MFT-B score in the sample at approximately 157 points. The performance of marketing majors could be explained by the results of a recent study by Nonis, Philhours, and Hudson (2006), who found that marketing students spend less time attending lectures, preparing for class, preparing for exams, quizzes, projects and assignments but spend more time at work than other business majors.

Model 2: Course Effects

The second model presented in this section examines the effect of business core course grades on MFT-B performance and controls for demographic characteristics, student ability and transfer status. The estimated regression coefficients for Model 2, followed by the t-statistics in parentheses, are presented in Table 8.

Table 8. Core Course Achievement Effects on MFT-B Performance

	B	(*t*-value)
(Constant)	94.25	(17.66)
MALE	3.55***	(4.75)
AGE	0.35***	(2.43)
WHITE	3.19**	(1.90)
ASIAN	–2.72	(–1.12)
ORIGIN	–11.17***	(–4.89)
SAT	0.04***	(13.96)
TRANSFCORE	–2.80***	(–3.74)
MACECON	1.49***	(2.66)
MICECON	0.57	(1.01)
ACCG1	0.68	(1.15)
ACCG2	–0.21	(–0.41)
BLAW	1.97 [a]	(3.10)
MRKT	0.78	(1.14)
STATS	–0.33	(–0.57)
FINA	2.23***	(3.77)
ISYS	–1.03*	(–1.41)
OBMNGT	0.14	(0.24)
ORMNGT	1.16*	(1.58)
R Square	0.50	
Adj. R Square	0.49	
F	37.65***	

*** significant at .01 level, ** significant at .05 level, * significant at .10 level (1-tailed).
[a] significant at .01 level, [b] significant at .05 level, [c] significant at .10 level (2-tailed).

The variable *COREGPA* was highly correlated with a variety of course variables and was excluded from this model [3]. The results exhibit similar coefficients, in terms of the size and signs, to those found in the previous cross-sectional analysis for the demographic, ability and transfer status variables. Asian students, however, were not at a significant disadvantage in this second model although the coefficient was still negative.

The performance on three of the 11 courses examined was found to be highly significant in explaining the overall MFT-B performance of graduating seniors. A 1-point grade differential in Principles of Macroeconomics, which requires students to understand the "Big Picture" as it relates to the nature and methods of economics, was found to contribute to a higher MFT-B score of 1.49 points. This finding differs from previous results by Mirchandani, Lynch, and Hamilton (2001) and Bagamery, Lasik, and Nixon (2005). These authors, however, performed factor analysis and were unable to identify the effect of single courses on MFT-B performance. Students who do well in this course will most likely do well in Principles of Microeconomics and Finance, which in total account for over 25 percent of the questions on the MFT-B test.

The Business Law course offered at UNL is a demanding class that focuses on law as it relates to business transactions. It emphasizes torts, contracts, sales, and related topics in the political and economic environment in which business functions and places an emphasis on the consideration of social and ethical issues creating pressure for change. It is not surprising to find the coefficient on this course to be positive and significant in explaining the performance of students. A 1-point grade differential in this core course was associated with a higher MFT-B score of 1.97 points. This finding diverges from previous literature results on the effect of qualitative courses on MFT-B performance (Mirchandani, Lynch, and Hamilton, 2001; Bagamery, Lasik, and Nixon, 2005). The performance on the business law course, however, is strongly related to the ability of students to read, analyze cases and come to conclusions. Students with excellent verbal and analytical skills would do well in this course, and would most likely have high SAT scores which have been linked to positive and significant effects on MFT-B performance. There is then a possibility that intellectually able students do well in the business law course and on the MFT-B, but that the performance in the law course has no sizable direct effect on the MFT-B performance. In fact, only 10 percent of the questions on the exam are devoted to the legal and social environment, making business law knowledge applicable to a relatively small percentage of questions on the test.

The highly significant and positive effect of the grade in Principles of Finance on the MFT-B performance of students was expected given previous findings by Mirchandani, Lynch, and Hamilton (2001). A 1-point grade differential in this course was associated with a higher MFT-B score of 2.23 points, which corresponds to the largest marginal effect of the course grades examined. Many economists would argue that Finance is applied microeconomics. It is very likely that students who do well in Principles of Finance are also competent in Principles of Macroeconomics and Microeconomics. In fact, the majority of double majors in our sample chose finance and economics as their areas of concentration. The *B* coefficient found for the Principles of Finance course grade came at no surprise given that about 26 percent of the questions on the MFT-B are based on principles of economics or finance and that the analytical skills needed to perform well in these courses are applicable to other subjects.

The *B* coefficients found on the *ISYS* and *ORMNGT* variables were significant at the .05 level. As expected, a 1-point grade differential in the Resource and Operations Management course contributed to a higher MFT-B score of 1.16 points. Surprisingly, and inconsistent with previous findings by Mirchandani, Lynch, and Hamilton (2001), the *B* coefficient on the Management/Marketing Information Systems courses was negative. Information systems courses focus on computerized data, information flows, uses, relationships and problems. Students who perform well on these courses tend to have strong computer knowledge and background and could potentially suffer from a lack of significant interest on business knowledge. For this reason, and although not expected, the negative and significant coefficient would make perfect sense.

The performance of students on the Principles of Accounting sequence was found to be insignificant in explaining MFT-B scores. Previous studies by Mirchandani, Lynch, and Hamilton (2001) and Bagamery, Lasik, and Nixon (2005) found the performance on these courses to have a positive and significant effect on the performance on the MFT-B. Descriptive statistics revealed that almost one third of students in the sample had transferred one or more of the accounting courses from other institutions. The grades in these courses were used in this model as reported by the outside institution. A plausible explanation for this finding is that an "A" grade from an outside institution may be representative of a lower letter grade at UNL. The grade, then, does not represent the quality of the knowledge acquired by those transferring students, but their attainment level at the outside institution relative to the other students in the course. In such a hypothetical case, a transfer student with an "A" in Principles of Accounting may know as much as a nontransfer student who received a "C" grade, making their performance on the transfer course not significant in explaining MFT-B scores.

Model 2 Extended: Course Effects by Major

Previous research on business education has shown that the effects of demographic characteristics and ability measures on student achievement vary by disciplines. Given these achievement differences by major, the expectation is that the effect of student achievement on core business courses will have a different impact on MFT-B scores depending on a student's area of specialization. An extension for model 2 was used to examine the effect of student achievement on core courses on MFT-B performance by major. The hypothesis tested is that majors who do well in their core areas of specialization score significantly higher on the MFT-B. This expectation is based on the idea that those who have a strong foundation are able to learn intermediate and advanced knowledge better, and that knowledge allows students to better solidify and comprehend the principles in other business areas.

Table 9 presents the estimated OLS coefficients for each of the majors in this study [4]. Each of the regressions presented in Table 9 was highly significant and explained between 41 and 56 percent of the MFT-B performance variability. To increase the sample size of those who received a strong academic background in economics, the group of economics majors was supplemented with those students who minored in the subject. The new sample size for the "Economists" group increased by 79 observations and totaled 106 students.

The *B* coefficients of the demographic characteristics and ability of students, as well as the transfer of core courses presented in Table 9, are generally consistent with the findings reported for the entire sample in Table 8. In general, the variables *MALE*, *AGE*, and *SAT* had a positive and significant effect on MFT-B scores, while the coefficients on the variable *ORIGIN* were negative and significant for all but economics, management, and marketing majors. The coefficient on *AGE* for the group of finance majors was, however, negative and significant, with a 1-year age differential contributing to a lower MFT-B score of about 0.6 points and suggesting that young finance students outperform their older peers in the amount of core knowledge they produce and retain.

Similarly, older marketing students were at a significant disadvantage when compared to their younger peers. The coefficients on the variable *TRANSFCORE* were negative and significant for all but management and marketing majors.

As it was expected, male economists performed better on the MFT-B than female economists by about 4.20 points, a coefficient that was significant at the .05 level. The significance and sign of this coefficient was consistent with previous literature findings. Economists with high entry SAT scores outperformed those with lower entry scores, and those who transferred at least one core course from an outside institution were at a significant 5.35-point disadvantage when compared to other economists who completed their business core education at UNL.

Table 9. Core Course Achievement Effects on MFT-B Performance by Major

	Accounting		*Business*		*Economists*	
	B	*(t-value)*	*B*	*(t-value)*	*B*	*(t-value)*
(Constant)	75.43	(3.82)	90.47	(8.40)	115.24	(6.26)
MALE	6.00**	(2.18)	3.58***	(2.56)	4.20**	(1.72)
AGE	0.62**	(1.74)	0.64**	(2.00)	0.01	(0.02)
WHITE	12.38**	(1.73)	2.40	(0.85)	−1.02	(−0.18)
ORIGIN	−15.43**	(−1.66)	−14.73***	(−3.46)	−7.11	(−1.10)
SAT	0.03***	(3.03)	0.05***	(8.54)	0.03***	(3.22)
TRANSFCORE	−5.91**	(−2.06)	−2.98**	(−2.07)	−5.35**	(−2.09)
MACECON	2.56	(1.17)	2.09**	(2.05)	1.57	(0.74)
MICECON	5.06**	(2.21)	0.39	(0.41)	0.56	(0.24)
ACCG1	−2.63	(−0.92)	0.79	(0.76)	−1.25	(−0.58)
ACCG2	1.50	(0.55)	−1.74**	(−1.99)	2.34	(1.25)
BLAW	3.21	(1.00)	0.99	(0.85)	4.46 [b]	(2.15)
MRKT	0.54	(0.20)	2.55 [b]	(2.13)	0.23	(0.10)
STATS	1.93	(0.78)	−0.29	(−0.28)	1.14	(0.55)
FINA	2.35	(0.76)	1.42*	(1.34)	4.48**	(1.81)
ISYS	−5.24**	(−1.80)	0.52	(0.43)	−5.06**	(−1.86)
OBMNGT	1.74	(0.85)	0.05	(0.05)	−1.39	(−0.68)
ORMNGT	1.24	(0.40)	−1.07	(−0.74)	−0.24	(−0.08)
R Square	0.56		0.54		0.55	
Adj. R Square	0.44		0.45		0.51	
F	4.44***		6.01***		12.99***	
	Finance		*Management*		*Marketing*	
(Constant)	119.81	(9.94)	77.72	(7.09)	120.73	(7.79)
MALE	4.84***	(2.67)	2.72*	(1.53)	2.62**	(1.73)
AGE	−0.59**	(−1.73)	0.81***	(3.12)	−0.72*	(−1.38)
WHITE	0.57	(0.14)	4.44*	(1.51)	3.03	(1.10)
ORIGIN	−8.45**	(−1.83)	−6.24	(−0.97)	−4.10	(−0.75)
SAT	0.04***	(5.08)	0.04***	(6.40)	0.04***	(7.10)
TRANSFCORE	−4.79***	(−3.02)	−1.29	(−0.79)	−1.56	(−1.04)
MACECON	2.34**	(1.77)	0.79	(0.65)	1.21	(1.17)
MICECON	−1.21	(−0.88)	1.26	(1.00)	−0.87	(−0.71)
ACCG1	−0.01	(−0.01)	−0.55	(−0.42)	0.73	(0.58)
ACCG2	1.59	(1.24)	−0.17	(−0.13)	−0.11	(−0.11)
BLAW	0.28	(0.20)	3.71 [a]	(2.60)	2.27 [c]	(1.85)
MRKT	0.84	(0.52)	0.13	(0.08)	−0.98	(−0.71)
STATS	0.35	(0.24)	−0.87	(−0.71)	−1.59*	(−1.37)
FINA	3.18**	(2.08)	2.81**	(2.33)	−0.62	(−0.57)
ISYS	−0.99	(−0.58)	−1.48	(−0.86)	−3.22**	(−2.01)
OBMNGT	−0.84	(−0.64)	1.31	(1.08)	3.20 [a]	(2.59)
ORMNGT	3.02**	(1.79)	0.98	(0.66)	2.19*	(1.52)
R Square	0.46		0.63		0.51	
Adj. R Square	0.41		0.56		0.43	
F	8.21***		9.34***		6.85***	

*** significant at .01 level, ** significant at .05 level, * significant at .10 level (1-tailed).
[a] significant at .01 level, [b] significant at .05 level, [c] significant at .10 level (2-tailed).

The results for the 11 core courses examined in this study vary widely by major. After controlling for demographic characteristics, ability and transfer status, the performance on the Principles of Macroeconomics course has a positive coefficient for all six majors, but it is only significant for business and finance students. A 1-letter grade increase in this principles course contributes to a higher MFT-B performance of 2.09 points for business students and 2.34 points for finance students. On the other hand, the performance on the Principles of Microeconomics course is only significant for accounting students, but at 5.06 points, its coefficient is the second largest exhibited by any of the core courses examined in this model. This finding suggests that accountants who do well in Principles of Microeconomics are better prepared for the MFT-B test and that the course work in this area supplements their accounting background and increases their core business knowledge.

Although the coefficients for the Principles of Accounting I course were not significant for any of the majors and exhibited mixed signs, the *B* coefficient on the second principles course in accounting was negative and significant for business and international business students. The coefficient in this particular class was also negative but insignificant for management and marketing majors. The negative coefficient for business majors implies that students who do well in Principles of Accounting II are at a disadvantage in terms of their future MFT-B performance. A final grade 1-point differential in accounting II contributed to a 1.74-point decrease on their MFT-B score. The coefficient on *ACCG2* was, however, insignificant in Model 2, but given that about one third of the students majoring in business, management and marketing transferred Principles of Accounting II from an outside institution, the possibility exists that their performance, as shown by the grades they received in this course from other institutions, may not be representative of the knowledge acquired. Students who transfer Principles of Accounting II with good grades may be lacking some of the basic foundations presented at UNL, therefore being at a disadvantage. This same rationale can be applied to the negative and significant coefficient found on the statistics course under the regression for marketing students.

The cross-sectional results found for the *BLAW* and *FINA* variables across majors were consistent with the coefficients found for the overall sample. In fact, the performance in the Business Law and Principles of Finance courses exhibited the only positive and significant coefficients in the "Economists" regression model. The coefficients on *BLAW* were also positive and significant for management and marketing majors, while the *FINA* coefficients were also significant for business, finance, and management students.

The *ISYS* variable was found negative and significant for three of the six majors examined. In fact, the coefficients found on this variable were negative for all but those students who majored in business or international business. A final 1-letter-grade differential in the information systems course contributed to a 5.24-point reduction on the MFT-B score of accounting majors, a result that was significant at the .05 level. The effect of a 1-point grade differential in this course was similar in size and significance for the group of economists and about two points lower for marketing students.

The sequence of core management courses presented mixed signs and significance levels. These two core courses were not significant in explaining the MFT-B performance of accounting, business, economics or management majors. A 1-point grade differential on the Resource and Operations Management course contributed to 3.02-point increase on the MFT-B performance of finance students, a result significant at the .05 level. This variable was also significant for marketing students, but its size was smaller and was only significant at the 0.1

level. The OB management course was only significant in explaining the performance of marketing students. A 1-point grade change in this management course was associated with a 3.20-point increase on the MFT-B score of marketing majors, a result that was highly significant at the .01 level.

Finance majors were the only students examined that exhibited a positive and significant coefficient on the principles course pertaining to their area of specialization. A final 1-letter-grade differential in the Principles of Finance course contributed to a 2.81-point increase on the MFT-B score of finance majors, a finding that was significant at the .05 level. On the other hand, the effect of student achievement in the core areas of a student's major did not have a significant and negative effect for any of the majors. This finding suggests that the amount of core business knowledge that students retain is not related to the students' performance in the principles courses for their majors, but it is related to the complementary nature of the other core business courses in the academic curriculum.

Model 3: Course Transfer Effects

Model 3 examines the effect of the transfer of specific business core courses on the MFT-B performance of business students after controlling for demographic characteristics and student ability measures. There were four core courses not included in the analysis because they were transferred by one, or less than one, percent of students in the sample. The variable *TRANSFCORE* was highly correlated with some of the transfer courses and was excluded from the regression equation.

The estimated regression coefficients for Model 3, followed by the t-statistics in parentheses, are presented in Table 10. As it was the case in Models 1 and 2, the regression equation was highly significant, with an F-statistic value of 46.18, and explained 48 percent of the variation in MFT-B scores. The OLS coefficients found on the demographic characteristics and ability measures were again similar to the coefficients found in Models 1 and 2. Male students outperformed females by roughly 3.8 points, a result significant at the .01 level. The coefficients on *AGE*, *ORIGIN*, *SAT* and *COREGPA* were also highly significant in explaining MFT-B performance. Older students significantly outperformed their younger peers. White students were at a significant 3.51-point advantage on the MFT-B, while Asian students were at a 4-point disadvantage, a significant result at the 0.1 level.

Several perplexing results were found for core economics courses. The estimated OLS coefficient on the transfer of Principles of Microeconomics course was associated with a positive and significant achievement gain of 2.45 points, suggesting that students who transfer Principles of Microeconomics from other institutions are at a significant advantage when compared to those who enroll and finish the course at UNL. This unexpected coefficient could be the result of specific instructor effects and grade inflation. In the presence of grade inflation, nontransfer students who received inflated grades on this principles course may not have the basic tools and building blocks necessary to fully comprehend basic microeconomics and may be at a disadvantage when compared to students who chose to enroll at other institutions. Descriptive statistics showed that the mean grade on Principles of Microeconomics for those who completed the course was 3.30 points, which is over half a letter grade higher than the mean course grade for the Principles of Macroeconomics course at 2.87.

Table 10. Transfer of Core Courses Effects on MFT-B Performance

	B	(*t*-value)
(Constant)	90.91	(18.15)
MALE	3.78***	(5.11)
AGE	0.40***	(2.84)
WHITE	3.51**	(2.09)
ASIAN	–4.00 [c]	(–1.64)
ORIGIN	–11.88***	(–5.13)
SAT	0.04***	(13.79)
COREGPA	7.83***	(9.05)
TRANSFMACECON	–0.83	(–0.65)
TRANSFMICECON	2.45**	(1.89)
TRANSFACCG1	1.72*	(1.49)
TRANSFACCG2	–3.32***	(–2.98)
TRANSFBLAW	–1.54 [c]	(–1.69)
TRANSFMRKT	–0.18	(–0.17)
TRANSFSTATS	–2.71**	(–2.02)
R Square	0.49	
Adj. R Square	0.48	
F	46.18***	

*** significant at .01 level, ** significant at .05 level, * significant at .10 level (1-tailed).
[a] significant at .01 level, [b] significant at .05 level, [c] significant at .10 level (2-tailed).

In this case, grades may not be indicative of knowledge acquired by nontransfer students. When Model 3 was estimated with a dummy variable indicating the transfer of the economics sequence, the coefficient was found positive but insignificant, suggesting that transferring the principles sequence does not contribute to lower performance on the MFT-B.

Accounting also showed some mixed findings from transfer courses. The coefficient on the transfer of the first course in accounting was positive, which was unexpected, but it was significant only at the 0.1 level. Students who transferred Principles of Accounting I were at a 1.72-point advantage on the MFT-B. The coefficient on the transfer of the second course in accounting was highly significant, with a negative value of 3.32 points. This result was the only highly significant coefficient found out of the 11 transferred courses in Model 3. Descriptive statistics showed that the second course in accounting exhibited the lowest mean grade from the 11 courses examined and was transferred by almost one third of students in the sample. A likely cause for the negative and highly significant coefficient of *TRANSFACCG2* in explaining student achievement on the MFT-B test is the difficulty level of the course, as shown by the average course grade, which may incite students to take the course at a community college or other junior institution. In this case, students will be at a disadvantage if the rigor and materials presented at other institutions are inferior to the materials used at UNL. Another likely explanation is the possibility that students enroll in the first accounting course at UNL and perceive its difficulty level, and then choose to take the second course at another institution [5].

Transferring Business Law from an outside institution was associated with a negative and significant coefficient at the 0.1 level. The estimated coefficients seem to suggest that students who transferred this course were at an MFT-B-score disadvantage when compared to those who enrolled and completed the course at UNL. It was previously hypothesized that intellectually able students, both in verbal and mathematical skills, are more likely to do well on the MFT-B and that the performance on the law course was most likely a proxy for able students. Students may chose to take this course at outside institutions for other than financial reasons (i.e., grading rigor). In this case, and given the coefficient found on transferring this course, lower ability students would choose to take the course at outside institutions. It is the intellectual ability of those who transfer the course, however, and not the fact that they chose to take the course somewhere else, that seems to be manifested on the statistically lower MFT-B scores.

Transferring statistics from an outside institution was also associated with a negative and significant coefficient at the .05 level. Students who transferred statistics were at a 2.71-point disadvantage when compared to those students who enrolled and completed the class at UNL.

Model 4: Transfer Course and Major Interaction

Model 4 examines the effect on MFT-B performance of interaction terms between the transfer of core courses and the choice of major after controlling for demographic characteristics and student ability. Table 11 reports the *B* coefficients and t-values. The regression model was highly significant and explained 48 percent of the variation in MFT-B scores. The coefficient signs and significance of the demographic and ability variables were similar to those found in the first three models examined in this study. The coefficient on Asian students, however, was negative but insignificant.

Table 11. Choice of Major and Transfer Interaction Effects

	B	(*t*-value)
(Constant)	91.61	(18.04)
MALE	3.59***	(4.82)
AGE	0.44***	(3.05)
WHITE	3.13**	(1.87)
ASIAN	–3.90	(–1.61)
ORIGIN	–11.64***	(–5.05)
SAT	0.04***	(14.15)
COREGPA	7.49***	(8.42)
ACCGMJRSTRANSFCORE	–3.15**	(–1.77)
BSADMJRSTRANSFCORE	–3.04***	(–3.00)
ECONMJRSTRANSFCORE	–2.65	(–0.94)
FINAMJRSTRANSFCORE	–1.58*	(–1.41)
MNGTMJRSTRANSFCORE	–2.89**	(–2.21)
MRKTMJRSTRANSFCORE	–3.98***	(–3.37)
R-Square	0.49	
Adj. R-Square	0.48	
F	49.43***	

*** significant at .01 level, ** significant at .05 level, * significant at .10 level (1-tailed).
[a] significant at .01 level, [b] significant at .05 level, [c] significant at .10 level (2-tailed).

As it was expected, the *B* coefficients for the six interaction terms in Model 4 were found to be negative, although the coefficient for economics majors was not significant. This finding, however, strongly suggests that students across majors who transfer core courses tend to perform worse than those who complete their entire core course training at UNL. Students who majored in business or marketing and transferred at least one core course from an outside institution were at a highly significant 3- to 4-point disadvantage when compared to other students in the sample. The coefficients on accounting and management students who transferred at least one core course from an outside institution were negative, significant at the .05 level and equal to 3.15 and 2.89 points, respectively. Finally, finance students who transferred core courses were at a 1.58-point disadvantage on the MFT-B, a significant result at the 0.1 level.

CONCLUSIONS AND IMPLICATIONS

The analysis conducted in this study revealed that performance on the Major Field Test in Business (MFT-B) of graduating seniors was consistently determined by a number of demographic, ability and transfer status variables. Male students outperformed females in all MFT-B models, suggesting that gender is a significant factor in the production of core business knowledge. Age was also found to positively influence MFT-B performance, with older students producing a significantly higher level of core business knowledge before graduation. Consistent with previous research findings in the economics and business literature were the results suggesting that white students are more efficient at producing business knowledge than students from other ethnicities/races. Foreign students were expected to perform significantly better than U.S. citizens on the MFT-B for two reasons, one being their basic ability improvements over the past 10 years and the other being their socioeconomic backgrounds. Foreign business students were found to significantly outscore U.S. business students by about 11 MFT-B points in each of the core business knowledge models.

SAT scores and core GPAs were positive and highly significant determining factors on the MFT-B performance of seniors in the sample. These findings suggest that students with high entry SAT scores are more likely to produce large amounts of core business knowledge before graduation, while their overall achievement in core business courses significantly contributes to their retention of basic business skills. The positive and significant nature of a student's core GPA on MFT-B scores indicates that the MFT-B test is a consistent good measure of core business knowledge.

Interestingly, the transfer of at least one core business course from an outside institution exhibited negative and significant coefficients in all of the MFT-B models, although the analysis by major showed that the effect of transferring core business courses on the MFT-B performance of management and marketing students was insignificant after controlling for demographic characteristics, student ability and course grades. This finding indicates that the quality of the course work students complete at other institutions may be insufficient in providing the basic business skills that students are required to learn before graduation at UNL.

The choice of major mattered in explaining the performance of senior students on the MFT-B. Examination of the results from Model 1 revealed that economics students were the only majors to exhibit a positive and highly significant MFT-B-point advantage after controlling for demographic, ability and transfer characteristics. This finding seems to indicate that economists are more efficient than students from other business majors at producing and retaining core business knowledge. Marketing students were the only major to score significantly lower than their other business peers and were found to be at about a 2-point disadvantage on the MFT-B, a value significant at the .05 level. Consistent with previous findings on the production of core business knowledge literature was the insignificant but positive coefficient exhibited by accounting majors.

The results from Model 2 showed that a total of five core business courses significantly influenced the production of core business knowledge, although only three exhibited highly significant coefficients. The performance of students in the Principles of Macroeconomics, Business Law, and Principles of Finance courses was associated with positive and significantly higher achievement levels on the MFT-B, with the finance course making the largest 1-point marginal contribution to an MFT-B score at about 2.2 points. Surprisingly, students who did well in the Marketing or Management Information Systems course scored significantly lower than other business students. Student achievement in the Operations and Resource Management principles course positively influenced MFT-B scores at the 0.1 level.

In Model 3, the transfer of specific core business courses had differential effects. The transfer of the Principles of Microeconomics and the Principles of Accounting I courses seemed to benefit the production of core business knowledge. Although the coefficient exhibited by the microeconomics course seems to be explained by specific instructor effects at UNL, the significant coefficient on the first accounting course presents a more complex finding because the Accounting Department at UNL offers this core course in a consistent and standardized way across sections. The transfer of the Principles of Accounting II course was the only highly significant core business course transfer found in Model 3, suggesting that students who complete this course at other institutions are at a significant disadvantage. The Business Law and statistics courses were also associated with a negative and significant impact on the MFT-B performance of students, with the coefficient on the statistics course being relatively large and significant. Their specific marginal effects and significance, however, varied by major.

The interaction effects between majors and the transfer of at least one core business course on the MFT-B achievement of graduating seniors were examined in Model 4. The findings indicate, after controlling for the demographic and ability characteristics of the student sample, that all majors but economics tend to be less efficient at retaining core business knowledge when they transfer at least one core business course from an outside institution. The largest and most significant interaction coefficients were exhibited by general business, international business, and marketing students, suggesting that their production of business knowledge is significantly impaired by transferring core business courses from other institutions.

Several policy implications emerge from this study. First, it is clear that higher SAT entry scores are associated with success on the MFT-B. This study showed that students with high entry SAT or ACT scores are more efficient at producing and retaining core business knowledge than students of lower basic academic ability. This study is not the first one to find a strong and significant relationship between a student's basic ability and college performance in business. In fact, the positive and significant effect of better SAT and ACT scores on student performance is the only significant and consistent finding in the economics and business literature.

Second, the negative and highly statistically significant impact of transferring core business courses on the production of core business knowledge should be of concern to credit validation administrators and university policy makers. It is not advisable for students enrolled in a four-year institution to complete courses at a community college to fulfill their core business requirements and continue with their programs of study. Students who transfer their core courses from community colleges are more likely to struggle at the intermediate level because they seem to lack the necessary building blocks to further improve their business and economic knowledge. The results presented in this study suggest that the requirements for credit validation and transfer student acceptance should be revised to produce more competent business students.

In this respect, several actions could be taken. For example, in economics, a department could develop an in-house principles test or use a nationally normed economics exam such as the Test of Understanding College Economics (TUCE) (Walstad, Watts, and Rebeck, 2007) to check whether transfer students acquired the basic economic knowledge needed to continue their education. Another plausible option would include a detailed examination of the syllabus from other institutions and possible communication with the outside institutions to get an idea of the material covered in their courses. These procedures, although time consuming, should provide for a better selection process and success rate of students transferring from outside institutions.

Third, faculty members teaching business and economics courses should emphasize student learning in specific core areas to improve the overall business performance and basic abilities of their students. The results presented in this study indicated that the production of core business knowledge by graduating seniors was positively influenced by their education and achievement in the Principles of Macroeconomics, Principles of Finance, Operations and Resource Management, and Business Law courses. Students majoring in business or economics should be made aware of the general importance of such core courses and their relative contributions to their production of core business knowledge.

Fourth, majoring in economics had the only positive and significant effect on the MFT-B score among the other business majors after controlling for demographic, ability and transfer characteristics. Unfortunately, only about 4 percent of the sample majored in economics, perhaps because of the difficulty of the major or because the relative attraction of other business majors for work or careers. Whatever the reason, the results from this study indicate that there are positive benefits to business colleges of having more students major in economics because such students tend to perform better on the MFT-B. Students should be made more aware of the benefits of studying economics by promoting the major and by motivating students at the principles level so they enroll in intermediate and advanced economics courses.

No study such as this one is without its limitations, so several of these should be kept in mind to qualify the conclusions and implications. The authors doubt such factors would make substantive changes in the findings but they may be worth addressing by other researchers with different data sets. First, the study would benefit from the inclusion of control variables for time spent studying and financial costs. Second, using course grades as a measure of achievement may be subject to measurement error because of the different ways that instructors calculate grades. Of course, this problem is a general one with the use of any aggregate grade measure such as a GPA, but it also applies to the use of grades for the specific course data used for this study. Third, the data set used for the cross-sectional analysis lacked the course sections and names of the professors or instructors who taught the different core business courses examined, making it impossible to control for specific instructor effects. Fourth, although graduating seniors were made aware of the importance of performing well on the MFT-B exam for personal (i.e., vitae) and institutional (i.e., accreditation) purposes, and are required to retake the test in extreme situations, there are no strong academic incentives to encourage student performance.

NOTES

[1] The mean SAT entry scores of foreign students attending UNL increased by approximately 15 percent between the 1999 and 2007 academic years.

[2] A similar result was found when model 1 was estimated with the variable *TRANSFCORECR*. The size and significance of the *B* coefficients decreased as the number course transfers increased.

[3] Because collinearity has an adverse effect on the standard errors of regression coefficients and the accuracy of computations due to rounding errors, a tolerance value of .0001 was used to identify highly correlated variables. Tolerance=1-R_i^2=1/VIF_i (Pedhazur, 1997).

[4] The group of Asian students was removed from the model due to its reduced sample size for certain majors.

[5] Model 3 was estimated with a dummy variable for those students who completed *ACCGI* at UNL and then transferred the second course from an outside institution. The coefficient found was large, negative and highly significant at the .01 level, with a value of -4.17 points.

REFERENCES

Allen, S.J., and Bycio, P. 1997. An Evaluation of the Educational Testing Service Major Field Achievement Test in Business. *Journal of Accounting Education,* 15(4): 503-14.

Allgood, S., and Walstad, W.B. 2002. The Economics and Business Knowledge of College Seniors in Schools of Business. Unpublished manuscript.

Arias, J.J., and Walker, D.M. 2004. Additional Evidence on the Relationship between Class Size and Student Performance. *Journal of Economic Education,* 35(4): 311-29.

Attiyeh, R.E., Bach, G.L., and Lumsden, K.G. 1970. Factors Affecting Student Learning of Elementary Economics. In K.G. Lumsden, (Ed.), *Rt Research in Economics Education.* Englewood Cliffs, N.J.: Prentice-Hall, Inc., 67-79.

Bagamery, B.D., Lasik, J.J., and Nixon, D.R. 2005. Determinants of Success on the ETS Business Major Field Exam for Students in an Undergraduate Multisite Regional University Business Program. *Journal of Education for Business,* 81(1): 55-63.

Ballard, L.B., and Johnson, M.F. 2004. Basic Math Skills and Performance in an Introductory Economics Class. *Journal of Economic Education,* 35(1): 3-23.

Barr, S.Z., and Carr, G.D. 1980. Improving Economic Understanding in Junior College Economics Principles Courses. *Community/Junior Research Quarterly,* 4(3): 219-24.

Bean, F.D., and Bernardi, R.A. 2002. Performance on the Major Field Test in Business: The Explanatory Power of SAT Scores and Gender. *Journal of Private Enterprise,* 17(2): 172-78.

Becker, W.E. 1997. Teaching Economics to Undergraduates. *Journal of Economic Literature,* 35(2): 1347-73.

Bellico, R. 1972. Prediction of Undergraduate Achievement in Economics. *Journal of Economic Education,* 4(1): 54-55.

Black, H.T., and Duhon, D.L. 2003. Evaluating and Improving Student Achievement in Business Programs: The Effective Use of Standardized Assessment Tests. *Journal of Education for Business,* 79(2): 91-98.

Bolch, B.W., and Fels, R. 1974. A Note on Sex and Economic Education. *Journal of Economic Education,* 6(1): 64-67.

Bonello, F., Swartz, T.R., and Davisson, W.I. 1984. Freshman-Sophomore Learning Differential: A Comment. *Journal of Economic Education*, 14(3): 205-10.

Borde, S.F. 1998. Predictors of Student Academic Performance in the Introductory Marketing Course. *Journal of Education for Business*, 73(5): 302-06.

Borde, S.F., Byrd, A.K., and Modani, N.K. 1996. Determinants of Student Performance in Introductory Corporate Finance Courses. Unpublished manuscript presented at the Southern Finance Association (SFA) Annual Meeting, Key West, Florida.

Borg, M.O., Mason, P.M., and Shapiro, S.L. 1989. The Case of Effort Variables in Student Performance. *Journal of Economic Education,* 20(3): 309-13.

Borg, M.O., and Shapiro, S.L. 1996. Personality Type and Student Performance in Principles of Economics. *Journal of Economic Education,* 27(1): 3-25.

Borg, M.O., and Stranahan, H.A. 2002. Personality Type and Student Performance in Upper-Level Economics Courses: The Importance of Race and Gender. *Journal of Economic Education,* 33(1): 3-14.

Bosshardt, W., and Watts, M. 2005. Teachers' Undergraduate Coursework in Economics in the Baccalaureate and Beyond Longitudinal Survey. *Journal of Economic Education,* 36(4): 400-06.

Bouillon, M.L., Doran, B.M., and Smith, C.G. 1990. Factors that Predict Success in Principles of Accounting Classes. *Journal of Education for Business,* 66(1): 23-27.

Brahmasrene, T., and Whitten, D. 2001. Assessing Success on the Uniform CPA Exam: A Logit Approach. *Journal of Education for Business,* 77(1): 45-50.

Brown, R.O. 1964. College Entrance Tests and Accounting Grades. *The Accounting Review* 39(2): 481-86.

Brown, R.O. 1966. Predictions of Accounting Grades. *The Accounting Review,* 41(2): 340-43.

Clayton, G.E., and Cate, T. 2004. Predicting MBA No-Shows and Graduation Success with Discriminate Analysis. *International Advances in Economic Research,* 10(3): 235-43.

Cohn, E. 1972. Student Characteristics and Performance in Economic Statistics. *Journal of Economic Education,* 3(2): 106-11.

Cohn, E., Cohn, S., and Bradley, J. 1995. Notetaking, Working Memory, and Learning in Principles of Economics. *Journal of Economic Education,* 26(4): 291-307.

Cohn, E., and Geske, T. 1990. *The Economics of Education* (3rd edition). Oxford, England: Pergamon Press.
Colley, J.R., and Volkan, A.G. 1996. Evaluating the Quality of Transfer versus Nontransfer Accounting Principles Grades. *Journal of Education for Business,* 71(6): 359-62.
Dal, D., and Baban, H. 1998. The Determinant of Performance in the University Introductory Finance Course. *Financial Practice and Education,* 8(1): 102-07.
Dockweiler, R.C., and Willis, C.G. 1984. On the Use of Entry Requirements for Undergraduate Accounting Programs. *The Accounting Review,* 59(3): 496-504.
Eckel, N., and Johnson, W.A. 1983. A Model for Screening and Classifying Potential Accounting Majors. *Journal of Accounting Education,* 1(1): 57-65.
Educational Testing Service (ETS), Higher Education Assessment. 1994. *Major Field Test: Content Description*. Princeton, NJ: ETS.
Educational Testing Service (ETS), Higher Education Assessment. 2006. *Description of Test Results*. http://www.ets.org (retrieved October 3, 2006). Princeton, NJ: ETS.
Educational Testing Service (ETS), Higher Education Assessment. 2006. *Test Description.* http://www.ets.org (retrieved October 3, 2006). Princeton, NJ: ETS.
Erlach, D. 2000. Hispanics and Higher Education: Multicultural Myopia. *Journal of Education for Business,* 75(5): 283-85.
Grove, W.A., Wasserman, T., and Grodner, A. 2006. Choosing a Proxy for Academic Aptitude. *Journal of Economic Education,* 37(2): 131-47.
Hirschfeld, M., Moore, R.L., and Brown, E. 1995. Exploring the Gender Gap on the GRE Subject Test in Economics. *Journal of Economic Education,* 26(1): 41-48.
Jonas, P.M., and Weiner, D. 1995. Core Curriculum Assessment Program: A Case Study. Association of Institutional Research Forum, 1-13.
Karathanos, D. 1991a. Outcome Measures of Collegiate Business Curricula. *Journal of Education for Business,* 66(3): 186-89.
Karathanos, D. 1991b. Outcome Measures of Collegiate Business Curricula: A Comparison of Two Instruments. *Journal of Education for Business,* 67(2): 100-04.
Korte, L., and Rosacker, R. 1994. A Preliminary Analysis of Student Performance in Business Core Courses. *Business Trends for the 21st Century,* 1(1): 15-22.
Laband, D.N., and Piette, M.J. 1995. Does Who Teaches Principles of Economics Matter? *American Economic Review* (Papers and Proceedings), 85(20): 335-38.
Leppel, K. 2001. Race, Hispanic Ethnicity, and the Future of the College Business Major in the United States. *Journal of Education for Business,* 76(4): 209-15.
Lipe, M.G. 1989. Further Evidence on the Performance of Female versus Male Accounting Students. *Issues in Accounting Education,* 4(1): 144-52.
Lopus, J.S., and Maxwell, N.L. 1993. Ethnic Differences in Learning College Economics: An Empirical Analysis. Unpublished manuscript presented at the Allied Social Science Association.
Manahan, J. 1983. An Educational Production Function for Principles of Economics. *Journal of Economic Education,* 14(2): 11-16.
Mirchandani, D., Lynch, R., and Hamilton, D. 2001. Using the ETS Major Field Test in Business: Implications for Assessment. *Journal of Education for Business,* 77(1): 51-56.
Mutchler, J.F., Turner, J.H., and Williams, D.D. 1987. The Performance of Female versus Male Accounting Students. *Issues in Accounting Education,* 2(1) : 103-11.

National Center for Education Statistics (NCES). 1996. Baccalaureate and Beyond Longitudinal Survey. *First Follow Up Methodology Report*. Chicago: National Opinion Research Center.

National Center for Education Statistics (NCES). 2003. Community College Students: Goals, Academic Preparation and Outcomes. *Postsecondary Education Descriptive Analysis Reports*. U.S. Department of Education.

Nichols, J.O., and Nichols, K.W. 2000. *The Departmental Guide and Record Book for Student Outcomes Assessment and Institutional Effectiveness*. New York: Agathon Press.

Nonis, S.A., Philhours, M.J., and Hudson, G.I. 2006. Where Does the Time Go? A Diary Approach to Business and Marketing Student's Time Use. *Journal of Marketing Education,* 28(2): 121-34.

Park, J.H., and Hayes, R.S. 1994. Men and Women: Equal in Accounting? *Journal of Education for Business,* 69(6): 349-53.

Pedhazur, E.J. 1997. Multiple Regression in Behavioral Research: Explanation and Prediction (3rd edition). Fort Worth, Texas: Harcourt College Publishers.

Reid, R. 1983. A Note on the Environment as a Factor Affecting Student Performance in Principles of Economics. *Journal of Economic Education,* 14(4): 18-22.

Rosacker, R.E., Rosacker, K.M., and Lau, R.S.M. 1995. Achievement in Business Core Courses: The Academic Quality of Accounting Majors. *Journal of Education for Business,* 71(2): 102-06.

Sacks, P. 1997. Standardized Testing: Meritocracy's Crocked Yardstick. *Change,* 29: 24-32.

Sauter, V.L. 1984. MS/OR Education: Quality of an Operations Management Course: An Examination of the Effects of Prerequisites and Their Transfer. *Interfaces,* 14(4): 88-92.

Schaffer, B.F., and Calkins, D.O. 1980. An Appraisal of Prerequisites to Business Finance. *Journal of Financial Education,* 9(2): 1-11.

Siegfried, J.J. 1979. Male-Female Differences in Economic Education: A Survey. *Journal of Economic Education,* 10(2): 1-11.

Siegfried, J.J., and Fels, R. 1979. Research on Teaching College Economics: A Survey. *Journal of Economic Literature,* 17(3): 923-69.

Siegfried, J.J., and Walstad, W.B. 1998. Research on Teaching College Economics. In W.B. Walstad and P. Saunders, (Eds.), *Teaching Undergraduate Economics: A Handbook for Instructors*. New York: McGraw-Hill, 141–66.

Simpson, W.G., and Sumrall, B.P. 1979. The Determinants of Objective Test Scores by Finance Students. *Journal of Financial Education,* 8(4): 58-62.

Tompson, H.B., and Tompson, G.H. 1996. Confronting Diversity Issues in the Classroom with Strategies to Improve Satisfaction and Retention of International Students. *Journal of Education for Business,* 72(1): 53-57.

Walstad, W.B., Watts, M., and Rebeck, K. 2007. *Test of Understanding of College Economics (TUCE): Examiner's manual* (4th edition). New York: Council for Economic Education.

Ward, D.R., Wilson, J.R., and Thomas, E. 1994. A Common Business and Accounting Vocabulary Base: Are Black Students Adequately Prepared? *Journal of Education for Business,* 69(5): 267-72.

Watts, M., and Bosshardt, W. 1991. How Instructors Make a Difference: Panel Data Estimates from Principles of Economics Courses. *Review of Economics and Statistics,* 73(2): 336-40.

Watts, M., and Lynch, G.J. 1989. The Principles Course Revisited. *American Economic Review,* 79(2): 236-41.

Westerman, J.W., Nowicki, M.D., and Plante, D. 2002. Fit in the Classroom: Predictors of Student Performance and Satisfaction in Management Education. *Journal of Management Education,* 26(1): 5-18.

Wetzel, J.N., O'Toole, D.M., and Millner, E.L. 1991. A Qualitative Response Model of Student Performance on a Standardized Test. *Atlantic Economic Journal,* 19(3): 8-25.

Williams, M.L., Waldauer, C., and Duggal, V.C. 1992. Gender Differences in Economic Knowledge: an Extension of the Analysis. *Journal of Economic Education,* 23(3): 219-31.

Ziegert, A.L. 2000. The Role of Personality Temperament and Student Learning in Principles of Economics. *Journal of Economics Education,* 31(4): 307-22.

In: Expanding Teaching and Learning Horizons
Editors: F. G. Mixon, Jr. and R. J. Cebula
ISBN 978-1-60741-971-6

Chapter 2

CHICKS DON'T DIG IT: GENDER, ATTITUDE AND PERFORMANCE IN PRINCIPLES OF ECONOMICS CLASSES

Christopher R. Bollinger, Gail Mitchell Hoyt and KimMarie McGoldrick

INTRODUCTION

There have been many attempts at understanding why women are less likely than men to major in economics. Although trends suggest that women are better represented among students graduating with a major in economics than in the past, they still constitute a minority with estimates for the 2003 -2004 academic year ranging from 30.3 percent in public institutions to 34.1 percent in private schools. (Siegfried, 2006: 378) Investigations into the impact of pedagogical practices (Jensen and Owen, 2001), learning styles (Borg and Stranahan, 2000a, 2000b; Ziegert 2000), faculty as role models (Robb and Robb, 1999; Rask and Bailey, 2002; Ashworth and Evans, 2001), math skills and interest in subject (Dynan and Rouse, 1997), and attitude (Jensen and Owen, 2001) all provide contributions to understanding why women are less likely to continue in economics. This paper contributes to this literature as it provides a more comprehensive study of attitude differences by gender through the inclusion of a larger number of attitude statements. Second, we link performance and attitude to show gender differences before and after taking a principles course.

In this paper we describe two surveys administered to approximately 2,200 students across 28 instructors at the beginning and end of the spring semester of 2003. We describe the measurement and construction of the economic knowledge and attitude variables used in the study. Preliminary results describing differences in attitude and knowledge suggest that men have more knowledge of and a better attitude towards economics than women prior to taking the course but that there is no difference in the gain in knowledge over the semester. We also present results which indicate that there is little or no difference in knowledge, pre- or post-test, between men and women who have not had a previous economics course. Attitudes between men and women (in both samples), however, are strikingly different with women viewing economics less favorably and even more so after taking a course.

Next, we present the models to be estimated and discuss potential specification and selection issues. The results in this section confirm initial findings. While women appear likely to appreciate the value of economics, they are not as likely to indicate liking economics. Our final section summarizes these conclusions and suggests that differences in attitudes may be the core problem in attracting more women to the major.

DATA AND METHODOLOGY

During the fall semester, 2002, the authors designed, tested and revised a survey focused on measuring both knowledge of and attitudes towards economics. The final version of the survey solicited information on student demographics and academic background including gender, age, race, GPA, economics course background (in both high school and college), and time use in activities such as studying. In order to gauge knowledge of economics, the survey included a series of fourteen content-oriented questions (specific to either the microeconomics or macroeconomics course in which the students were currently enrolled) based on a subset of the questions developed for the TUCE. Student attitudes towards the discipline are queried using fourteen statements consistent with Hodgin and Manahan (1978) and the Attitude Towards Economics section of the Survey on Economic Attitudes (Soper and Walstad 1983). A companion survey that elicited demographic information was administered to the instructors whose students participated in the survey.

The survey was administered at the beginning and at the end of each course (typically at the first and last class meeting) by twenty-eight different instructors (faculty members as well as graduate teaching assistants) at twelve institutions. We refer to the survey administered at the beginning of the course as the "pre-test" and the survey administered at the end of the course as the "post-test." Students were asked to supply an identifying code (typically the last four digits of their social security number) and the pre and post surveys were then matched. The final sample contains 2,159 students, 807 of whom completed both surveys [1].

Table 1 provides a summary of sample characteristics. The sample is nearly equally comprised of males and females. Approximately fifty percent of the students in the sample are sophomores, as would be expected given that the survey was administered in principles of economics courses. Because the number of nontraditional students at the surveyed schools skews the mean age of the sample, a variable measuring whether the student was above or below the typical age in the class was constructed and this further indicates a homogeneous sample in that only about 13 percent are either above or below the typically aged student. The sample is primarily Caucasian, spends nearly 10 hours a week studying, works nearly the same amount of hours, and participated in very little volunteer activity. The self-reported GPA was just under a 3.0. Many students had a background in economics either at the high school level (32 percent) or as a previous college course although as a result of the typical sequencing of courses this was more likely to be a microeconomics course (45 percent) than a macroeconomics course (8 percent). The typical class size was 190 and 60% were enrolled in a small economics class (defined as <100 students).

Table 1. Demographic characteristics

Variable	Overall Sample Mean	Standard Deviation
Female	0.483	0.500
Under Typical Age for Class	0.055	0.227
Over Typical Age for Class	0.074	0.263
African American	0.030	0.170
Asian American	0.014	0.116
Sophomore	0.494	0.500
Junior	0.171	0.377
Senior	0.042	0.201
Father's Education	14.937	2.705
College Cumulative GPA	2.989	0.827
Previous College Micro Class	0.445	0.497
Previous College Macro Class	0.082	0.274
High School Economics Class	0.320	0.467
Microeconomics Course	0.529	0.499
No Opinion	0.245	0.432
Hours Worked in Typical Week	9.955	11.473
Hours Studying in Typical Week	9.871	7.136
Volunteer Hours in Typical Week	0.776	2.042
Extracurricular Activities Hours in Typical Week	8.483	7.326
Number of Students in Class	190.999	182.916
Small Class Size (< 100 students)	0.601	0.490
Instructor Female	0.555	0.497
Instructor has Ph.D.	0.180	0.384
School has State Funding (=1)	0.820	0.384
Sample size	807	

Interest in the subject of economics is proxied by the response of "I have no opinion on this statement" to the request that students report their level of agreement with the statement "The redistribution of income through taxes and welfare payments is a legitimate role for government." Although a lack of opinion does not explicitly indicate a lack of interest in economics (and may also imply a lack of confidence in stating an opinion), those who state an opinion are expected to be more engaged in the subject in order to form such an opinion.

The main variables of interest in this study are the measures of economic knowledge and attitude obtained in both the pre and post-surveys which are described in Table 2. As one would hope, average knowledge rose as indicated by 9.27 (out of fourteen) questions answered correctly after taking an economics course compared to 7.67 questions prior. Since the sample consists of the same 807 students, this represents a gain for these students and is highly statistically significant [2]. The aggregate attitude variable consists of the sum of fourteen statements. If the student agrees with a positive statement about economics, the aggregate score is increased by one point. If the student agrees with a negative statement about economics the score is decreased by one. There are eight positive statements and six negative ones; hence the scores can range from -6 to +8. Unlike the literacy results, attitudes remain largely unchanged after taking an economics course with averages of 2.27 and 2.26 and the difference is not statistically significant.

Table 2 also presents economic knowledge and attitude scores by gender. Perhaps the most striking aspect of the table is the fact that both attitude and knowledge scores are higher for men than for women. On average, men score 0.404 points higher on the knowledge post-test than their female counterparts. While statistically significant, this represents only 4% of the mean and only 18% of the standard deviation of the full sample knowledge post-test. Indeed, the correlation between gender and the knowledge post-test is only 0.09. Perhaps more important is the comparison of the gain in knowledge from the pre-test to the post-test. Men gained an average of 1.54 points, while women gained an average of 1.67. While both genders have statistically significant gains in knowledge over the course, the gender difference in these gains is not statistically significant. Note that women score 0.54 points lower than men on the knowledge pre-test, suggesting that women enter these courses at a disadvantage. There is no evidence that women are poorer economics students than men. However there is some evidence that the typical woman starts an economics course with a weaker background than her male counterpart.

The comparison of results on attitude by gender also suggests that women score less than their male counterparts. Women score an average 1.34 points lower on the attitude pre-test. This statistically significant difference is also substantial in that it represents 59% of the mean and 52% of the standard deviation of the full sample attitude pre-test. Similarly, women score an average 1.75 points lower than men on the attitude post-test. Indeed, while men's attitude about economics appears to improve as a result of the course, women's attitude actually declines. The change in the differences is, in fact, statistically significant.

The attitude measure is the summation of fourteen different attitude statements. As noted earlier, six of the statements can be view as negative (for example "I hate Economics") and eight of the statements can be viewed as positive (for example "I enjoy reading articles about economic topics"). In order to better understand the underlying causes for the above described attitude differences, we disaggregate the attitude measure and report the proportion of students agreeing with each statement on the pre and post-test (see Table 3). We first present a summary of general differences before turning to gender specific differences.

In all but two questions, the proportion of students agreeing with the statement rose after taking an economics course. The two statements which had falling proportions were "On occasion I read an unassigned book in economics" and "I would be willing to attend a lecture by an economist." All other statements saw an increase from the pre to the post-test. This implies an interesting polarization. In the pre-test, only 4.1% of students agreed with the statement "I hate economics." In the post-test that proportion had risen to 9.5%. However, in the pre-test 40% of students agreed with the statement "I enjoy economics" and that proportion also rose to 46% by the post-test. Prior to an economics class, approximately 55.9% of students neither enjoy nor hate economics. After the economics class only 44.5% did not feel strongly one way or another. In general, having an economics class seems to polarize students across all but two of these indicators. The two statements that were not significant include "Studying economics is a waste of time" and "Economic ideas are dumb" each category having less than one percent agreement in the pre-test. These last two statements compared to other statements are fairly extreme and it is not surprising students would not agree as that would reflect negatively on the student.

Table 2. Gender Differences in Knowledge and Attitude Scores

	Full Sample		Women		Men		Gender Difference	Diff Test
Variable	Mean	Std. Dev.	Mean	Std. Dev.	Mean	Std. Dev.		
Pretest Knowledge Score	7.672	2.004	7.395	1.926	7.930	2.042	-0.536	-3.834*
Post-test Knowledge Score	9.270	2.177	9.062	2.199	9.465	2.141	-0.404	-2.639*
Pretest Attitude Score	2.271	2.555	1.579	2.435	2.918	2.497	-1.339	-7.712*
Post-test Attitude Score	2.259	2.946	1.356	2.934	3.103	2.699	-1.747	-8.783*
Change in knowledge	1.599*	2.451	1.667*	2.536	1.535*	2.371	0.132	0.762
Change in attitude	-0.012	2 556	-0.223	2.526	0.185	2.571	-0.408	-2.272*
Sample size	807		390		417			

*Denotes significantly different than zero at 5% level, calculated for differences (last column) and changes (last two rows).

Table 3. Gender Differences in Disaggregated Attitude Measurement

	Percentage on Pre test			Diff test	Percentage on Post test			Diff test
Student Indicates Agreement with	Total	Male	Female	Female-Male	Total	Male	Female	Female-Male
I enjoy reading articles about economic topics	34.9	43.2	26.2	-4.23*	33.7	42.2	24.6	-4.92*
I hate economics	4.1	2.2	6.2	2.43**	9.5	5.5	13.9	4.76*
Economics is easy for me to understand	29.5	38.6	19.7	-7.55*	34.3	45.3	22.6	-5.28*
Economics is dull	17	15.6	18.5	1.11	21.2	18.2	24.4	2.13**
I enjoy economics	40.6	48.7	32.1	-4.27*	46	54.7	36.7	-5.74*
Studying economics is a waste of time	0.5	0.2	0.8	1.03	2.9	2.6	3.1	0.54
Economics is one of my most dreaded subjects	10.9	6.0	16.2	5.33*	16.9	8.9	25.4	5.91*
On occasion I read an unassigned book in economics	6.6	9.6	3.3	-3.53*	5.8	8.4	3.1	-3.94*
I would be willing to attend a lecture by an economist	48.1	51.3	44.6	-2.05**	39.9	47.2	32.1	-4.04*
Economics is a very difficult subject for me	17.5	9.8	25.6	6.08*	26.6	16.3	37.7	5.04*
Economics is one of my favorite subjects	12.4	17.3	7.2	-5.54*	21.8	28.5	14.6	-6.85*
I use economic concepts to analyze situations	29.4	36.9	21.3	-5.63*	43.4	52.8	33.3	-5.18*
Economics is practical	76.3	80.6	71.8	-3.66*	79.2	83.5	74.6	-2.03*
Economic ideas are dumb	0.7	0.5	1.0	0.88	1.1	0.7	1.5	1.19
Sample Size	807	417	390		807	417	390	

Table 4. Gender Differences in Knowledge and Attitude Scores First economics class sub sample

	Full Sample		Women		Men		Gender Difference	Diff Test
Variable	Mean	Std. Dev.	Mean	Std. Dev.	Mean	Std. Dev.		
Pretest knowledge score	7.149	1.946	7.050	1.878	7.273	2.031	-0.222	-1.616
Post-test knowledge score	8.803	2.273	8.683	2.256	8.955	2.296	-0.271	-1.691*
Pretest attitude score	1.803	2.829	1.496	2.027	2.309	2.274	-0.813	-5.367*
Post-test attitude score	1.952	2.829	1.065	2.738	3.073	2.540	-2.008	-10.780*
Change in knowledge	1.655*	2.595	1.633*	2.577	1.682*	2.630	-0.049	-0.266
Change in attitude	0.096	2.703	-0.432	2.721	0.764	2.538	-1.195	-6.442*
Sample size	249		139		110			

* Denotes significantly different than zero at 5% level, calculated for differences (last column) and changes (last two rows).

Table 3 also indicates significant differences by gender in twelve of the fourteen attitudinal statements. What is interesting, however, is the direction of those differences. In every significant case, women have a more negative attitude than their male counterparts across both pre and post-test results. For example, women are less likely to agree with statements such as "I enjoy reading articles about economics," that "economics is easy for me to understand," or that "economics is one of my favorite subjects." Alternatively, women are more likely to agree with statements such as "I hate economics," "economics is one of my most dreaded subjects," and "economics is a difficult subject for me." Taking a course in economics also appears to exacerbate these differences across all statements. Thus, disaggregated results suggest that the overall gender differences in attitude are not driven by any particular statement [3].

It appears that women's positive attitudes about economics decline after having taken a course, while the positive attitudes of men increase. In order to examine and isolate these differences in attitudes we also consider students who have never had any formal exposure to economics and thus should not have any predispositions to be biased in their attitudes towards economics as a result of the course material. The initial survey asks students if they have had a previous college level or high school level course in economics. Table 4 presents the two attitude and two knowledge test scores by gender for students who have never had a formal economics course before this one. It is interesting to note that in Table 2, there are more males than females, while in Table 4 there are more females than males. Indeed, of the 417 males in our survey, only 26% of them are enrolled in their first economics course. In contrast 36% of the 390 women are enrolled in their first economics course. Men are more likely to be enrolled in a second economics course than their female counterparts. The knowledge and attitude patterns demonstrated in Table 2 appear to persist, but with much weaker pre-test differentials. Indeed, the difference between men and women in pre-test knowledge in Table 4 is only 0.22, and is not statistically significant. Similarly, the post-test difference between gender is only 0.27 and is also not statistically significant. The difference in gains is only 0.05. There is little or no difference in knowledge, pre- or post-test, between men and women who have not had a previous economics course.

The attitude scores, however, tell a much different story. Women who have never taken a formal economics course have a statistically significant 0.81 point lower attitude score than their male counterparts. After completing their first course, the difference in attitude scores more than doubles, to a 2 point difference which is highly significant. As with Table 2, women's positive attitudes fall (although not statistically significantly), while men's positive attitudes rise after the course. Like those for the total sample, these results are not driven by any single attitudinal statement [4]. Clearly, even though women appear to gain in understanding, they do not like the subject. Exposure simply exacerbates this important difference between men and women.

One interesting result appears to be that students in general think highly of the discipline. Attitudes at the end of the economics course indicate that only 2.9% of students agreed with the statement that "economics is a waste of time" (see Table 3). Similarly, 79.2% of students agreed with the statement "economics is practical." The two cases where the gender difference was insignificant represent questions about the value of economics in general. Women are not more likely to find studying economics as a waste of time than men (and contrary to folk wisdom, only 21% of students think economics is dull). Only 1.1% of all students think "economic ideas are dumb," and the difference between men and women is so small as to be zero.

Estimation Models

Previous research suggests that there are two ways to assess economic learning and, by extension, attitudinal changes. (Becker, Greene, and Rosen, 1990, p. 232) The first is a 'change-score model' in which the dependent variable is specified as the difference between the post-test and pre-test values. Alternatively, in the 'attainment model' post-test values are regressed on pre-test measures. In either case, the attempt to measure changes over the course of a semester is not without problems including sample selection bias (resulting from the lack of some students taking the post-test), missing observations (as a result of incomplete surveys), and self-selection into a course. (Becker, Greene, and Rosen, p. 239) [5]. Additional issues arise in the interpretation of results associated with many specifications previously estimated. Missing previous period values for key variables typically requires change score models to make restrictive assumptions that are not intuitively appealing in order to circumvent the associated modeling problems. Furthermore, problems associated with unobserved heterogeneity still exist [6].

Because we are interested in the impact of demographic variables (in our case, gender) on knowledge attainment and attitudes, we consider the following structural break model:

$$(1) K_{it} = x_i'(\beta+\theta) + (\rho+\tau)K_{it-1} + (\gamma+\kappa)A_{it} + (\delta+\eta)A_{it-1} + u_{it}$$
$$(2) A_{it} = z_i'(\alpha+\omega) + (\varphi+\psi)A_{it-1} + (\lambda+\xi)K_{it} + (\pi+\zeta)K_{it-1} + v_{it}$$

$$(3) K_{it-1} = x_i'\beta + \rho K_{it-2} + \gamma A_{it-1} + \delta A_{it-2} + u_{it-1}$$
$$(4) A_{it-1} = z_i'\alpha + \varphi A_{it-2} + \lambda L_{it-1} + \pi K_{it-2} + v_{it-1}.$$

The variables A_{it} and K_{it} are the post–test attitude and knowledge scores, while A_{it-1} and K_{it-1} are the pre-test attitude and knowledge scores. The vectors x_i and z_i contain demographic characteristics and may contain common elements but have sufficient exclusion restrictions to allow identification. Only the composite parameters of the model (those in the K_{it} and A_{it} model) are identified. It is, in general, impossible to identify all of the parameters of the model without at least one additional time period of observation (t-2). The intuition for why only the composite variables are identified is rather straightforward. Consider the term ($\beta+\theta$) and suppose that x_i only contains gender. The coefficient β measures how gender affects knowledge growth prior to the time period in which the class is taken (it is not difficult to show that the growth rate is determined by $\beta/(1-\rho)$ in equation (3) above). The term θ measures the difference in growth rates (or knowledge accumulation) that is specific to the course. Without multiple periods prior to the course, it is impossible to tell how growth occurred prior to the course. Hence it is impossible to tell how the course specifically effects growth. Thus all that can be identified is the composite $\beta+\theta$ term.

Vectors x_i and z_i contain variables chosen, to the extent possible, for consistency with previous research. Manahan (1983) proposed an "educational production function for principles of economics" and serves as a departure point for our variable inclusion strategy. That model suggests that post-course knowledge (TUCE) is a function of demographic characteristics of the student, measures of the student's academic ability, the student's effort, a pre-course measure of knowledge, and a post-course measure of the student's attitude. Attitude was modeled as a function of demographic characteristics, the student's effort, a pre-course measure of attitude, and the post-course knowledge score. Similar models have been estimated subsequently, most recently by Grimes et al (1989) for a sample of college students and Walstad and Soper (1989) using a sample of high school students.

Estimation equations based on the structural change model described above and including variables consistent with previous literature are based on the following general specification:

(5) knowledge attainment:

$$K_{it} = \beta_0 + \beta_1 K_{it-1} + \beta_2 A_{it} + \beta_4 Acad_{it-1} + \beta_5 Dem_{it-1} + \beta_7 Time_{it-1} + \beta_8 Inst + \varepsilon_{it}$$

(6) attitude attainment:

$$A_{it} = \beta_0 + \beta_1 K_{it} + \beta_2 A_{it-1} + \beta_4 Acad_{it-1} + \beta_5 Dem_{it-1} + \beta_7 Time_{it-1} + \beta_8 Inst + \varepsilon_{it}$$

The vector "Acad" represents variables measuring academic characteristics of the student including cumulative GPA, three indicators for previous micro, macro or high school economics courses, an indicator for whether the current course is microeconomics or macroeconomics, and a proxy for interest in subject. The subscript t-1 denotes that these variables were taken from the survey administered at the beginning of the course. The vector "Dem" represents demographic variables including gender, race, and father's education. It also includes a set of indicators for class standing (sophomore, junior and senior) and a pair of indicators for whether the student was younger or older than typical students of the class standing (e.g. a freshman is typically eighteen or nineteen, while a senior is typically twenty-one or twenty-two). The vector "Time" measures the number of hours per week the student spends working, studying, volunteering and participating in extracurricular activities. The vector "Inst" contains information about the instructor (gender and an indicator for Ph.D.) and institution (whether the institution receives state funding and course class size).

The instrumental variables estimation of the simultaneous system requires exclusion restrictions. Excluding pre-test knowledge from the attitude equation is consistent with the work of Grimes et al. (1989). The exclusion of father's education from the attitude equation is motivated by recent work of Altonji and Dunn (1996), while GPA is expected to affect performance but not necessarily attitude. Exclusions from the knowledge equation are also motivated by previous research. Excluding pre-test attitude is consistent with the work of Grimes et al. (1989). The variable no opinion identifies students who have no a-priori opinion on a subjective economic statement and is used to proxy general interest in (attitude towards) the topic but should have no effect on the students overall ability. Younger students are expected to be more enthusiastic (attitude), but are not expected to have differences in ability [7].

Overall, we find evidence that post-test attitude affects post-test knowledge. (See Table 5.) The coefficient on post-test attitude in the post-test knowledge equation is about 0.10 test units. A one standard deviation difference in attitude (2.94 units) will result in a 0.294 unit difference in knowledge scores. While not an overwhelming determinant of knowledge, it

Table 5. Simultaneous Equation Estimation of Attitude and Knowledge

	Eq. 6	Eq. 5
	IV-attitude	IV-knowledge
Posttest Knowledge Score	0.178	
	(0.133)	
Posttest Attitude Score		0.101
		(0.046)*
Pretest Knowledge Score		0.252
		(0.038)**
Pretest Attitude Score	0.579	
	(0.037)**	
Female	-0.872	-0.025
	(0.174)**	(0.161)
Under Typical Age for Class	1.058	
	(0.367)**	
Over Typical Age for Class	0.092	0.982
	(0.364)	(0.278)**
African American	-0.005	0.007
	(0.484)	(0.405)
Asian American	0.842	-0.806
	(0.729)	(0.603)
Junior	-0.235	-0.316
	(0.235)	(0.194)
Senior	0.545	0.139
	(0.423)	(0.350)
Father's Education		0.058
		(0.026)*
College Cumulative GPA		0.376
		(0.084)**
Previous College Micro Class	0.170	0.273
	(0.306)	(0.253)
Previous College Macro Class	0.547	-0.304
	(0.316)	(0.266)
High School Economics Class	-0.265	-0.111
	(0.179)	(0.148)
Microeconomics Course	0.494	-0.710
	(0.328)	(0.255)**
No opinion	-0.443	
	(0.199)*	
Hours Worked in Typical Week	0.009	0.000004
	(0.008)	(0.007)
Hours Studying in Typical Week	0.026	0.016
	(0.012)*	(0.010)
Hours Volunteering in Typical Week	-0.029	-0.045
	(0.041)	(0.034)
Hours in Extracurricular Activities per Week	0.004	-0.019
	(0.012)	(0.010)*
Instructor Female	0.228	0.016
	(0.337)	(0.282)
Instructor has Ph.D.	-0.693	-0.194
	(0.267)**	(0.222)
School has State Funding (=1)	0.724	-0.424
	(0.367)*	(0.300)
Small Class	0.389	-0.330
	(0.398)	(0.331)
Constant	-1.721	6.040
	(1.544)	(0.821)**
Observations	807	807
Standard errors in parentheses		

* significant at 5%; ** significant at 1%.

will clearly have the largest impact of all policy relevant variables included in the model (GPA and prior knowledge both have a larger impact, but in general are not under the control of the instructor).

The coefficient on post-test knowledge in the attitude equation is positive, but not statistically significant. We conclude that while it is possible that the system is simultaneous, we do not have strong evidence for knowledge affecting attitude. We continue to interpret the system as simultaneous since the coefficient is positive and of a large enough magnitude.

An important finding is the large and negative coefficient on attitude for women: on average women have a 0.87 lower attitude score on the post-test than do their male counterparts. Since attitude has an effect upon knowledge (on the order of .10), the effect of gender on knowledge, through attitude is -.087. We can use gender differences in important X variables to determine which factors contribute the most to the 0.405 unit gender difference in post-test knowledge. As noted above (Table 2), overall women score 1.75 units lower on the post-test attitude than their male counterparts: thus, approximately 43% of the post-test knowledge differential can be accounted for by post-test attitude differential. We also note that women have a 0.444 unit lower pre-test knowledge score, thus women's post-test knowledge score will be 0.11 units lower (0.444*0.25) than their male counterparts through the pre-test effect on post-test knowledge. This difference accounts for 27% of the difference in gender attainment on post-test scores. Finally, we note that men are twice as likely to be older than women, which accounts for 0.06 points difference in the overall post-test knowledge average. Overall, initial conditions and the attitude variable account for 70% of the relatively small gender differential in post-test knowledge.

Similarly, we note that the coefficient on gender in the post-test attitude equation implies that 50% of the post-test attitude gender differential is due simply to gender. We also find that 44% of gender differential in post-test attitude is due to the gender differential in pre-test attitude. Over 90% of the gender difference in post-test attitude is explained by the gender difference in pre-test attitude combined with the gender difference in the growth rate. Since much of the knowledge difference is due to either attitude or to the initial condition of knowledge (which should have been affected by gender differences in attitude in similar ways), we can conclude that the small gender differential in knowledge in primarily explained by attitudes about the course.

Disaggregating the Attitude Measurement

Again, to determine whether the impact of attitude is driven by a particular statement, we test the impact of the disaggregated measure. Table 6 presents the marginal effect (differential) from gender in the estimates of probit models on the response to the individual statements. The linear probability model responses were nearly identical (and are available upon request). The covariates included in the model are similar to those in the first column of Table 5 and include pre-test attitude (disaggregated and statement specific), pre-test knowledge, demographic, academic, time, and instructor/institutional characteristics. Consistent with aggregate results, post-test knowledge does not have a significant impact on attitude. As expected, pre-test attitude is a significant determinant of post-test attitude. The third column of Table 6 presents the difference in probability (marginal effect) of agreeing with the statement if you are a woman. For example women are 9.5% less likely to agree with the statement "I enjoy reading articles about economic topics."

Table 6. Predicted Probability Change Associated with Female Gender (Probit Models)

Dependent Variable: Student Indicates Agreement with	Pretest Knowledge Score Coefficient	Pretest Statement Coefficient	Gender Coefficient
I enjoy reading articles about economic topics	0.013	0.429**	-0.095**
I hate economics	0.002	0.221**	0.070**
Economics is easy for me to understand	0.035**	0.355**	-0.189**
Economics is dull	0.007	0.400**	0.053
I enjoy economics	-0.001	0.372**	-0.131**
Studying economics is a waste of time	0.000	0.461**	0.000
Economics is one of my most dreaded subjects	-0.013	0.325**	0.122**
On occasion I read an unassigned book in economics	0.001	0.262**	-0.021
I would be willing to attend a lecture by an economist	-0.002	0.406**	-0.127**
Economics is a very difficult subject for me	-0.012	0.382**	0.166**
Economics is one of my favorite subjects	0.004	0.514**	-0.102**
I use economic concepts to analyze situations	0.017	0.403**	-0.145**
Economics is practical	0.017*	0.242**	-0.054
Economic ideas are dumb	0.000	0.033*	0.000

*=significant at 5% level, **=significant at 1% level. Sample Size 807. Controls include all Demographic, Academic, Time and Instructor Variables.

Models for the statements "Studying economics is a waste of time" and "Economic ideas are dumb" were unstable and had no significant explanatory variables, largely due to the lack of variation in the response.

Results from Table 6 suggest that the aggregate results presented in Table 5 do not appear to be driven by any one particular statement. Although in 5 cases (rows 4, 6, 8, 13, and 14) the coefficient on gender was statistically insignificant, without exception, the coefficients imply that women are more likely to agree with negative statements about economics (rows 2,4,7, and 10) and less likely to agree with positive statements about economics (rows 1,3,5,8,9,11,12, and 13) than their male counterparts. In many cases, the coefficient on gender is quite large in magnitude relative to the overall probability of agreeing with the statement. For example, 16.6% of all students agree with the statement "Economics is a very difficult subject for me" (row 10). The coefficient implies that women are 16.6% more likely to agree with this statement than men. 34.3% of all students agree with the statement "Economics is easy for me to understand" (row 3), and the gender coefficient implies that women are 18.9% less likely to agree with this statement than men.

The question-specific results presented here further strengthen the results in the previous section. Women do not view economics favorably. While in general they do see the value of economics, they are less likely to enjoy it and are more likely to claim that they find it difficult to understand. Perhaps most importantly, it is not simply that women arrive at their first economics class with a bad attitude. The strength of their dislike for the subject grows with exposure. It is something about how economics is taught and the subject itself that they appear to dislike.

Conclusion

Gender differences in the probability of majoring in economics have received a great deal of attention in the literature. Potential explanations for these differences have included pedagogical practices, learning styles, role model effects, and quantitative skills. Little has been done to investigate how gender differences in attitudes play a role. We add to this body of literature by first establishing that there is no significant gender difference in performance in principles of economics courses. We then investigate the degree to which attitudes towards economics differ by gender and find that women have significantly more negative attitudes (in the aggregate and across disaggregated measures). Furthermore, these significant differences do not disappear with controls for performance in the course, academic and demographic characteristics, time use allocations, and instructor/institutional characteristics.

The significant gender differences in attitude found above are unlikely to simply measure dissatisfaction with their grades. They are also unlikely to be measures of some innate lack of ability. In fact, taking an economics course tends to polarize attitudes, strengthening women's negative and men's positive attitude toward the subject. This last point leads one to wonder if there is some commonality in our content selection, course structure, or teaching style that is less amenable to women. If women start out as skeptics, do our courses confirm their worst suspicions? Given the strong indication that women's attitudes are negatively affected by a principles course in economics, future research should place added emphasis on *why* women do not like economics as much. Furthermore, research should investigate whether the differences in attitude are the causal "smoking gun" for why women are less likely to major in economics and pursue graduate work in economics.

Notes

[1] The large discrepancy between the number of students completing the pre-test (2116) and the ultimate sample on which matches could be identified for this analysis (807) may raise concern over possible self selection biases. In order to address this, we use the two step Heckman sample selection correction in our estimation as described in Appendix 2.

[2] The gain is statistically significant at all conventional levels. The standard error of the difference is 0.086 and the test that the difference is zero yields a test statistic of 18.54.

[3] It is important to note that these differences do not account for student characteristics that may contribute to such differences but more sophisticated tests (reported below) confirm these results.

[4] Results from Table 3 were replicated for the sample of first economics course subsample and are available upon request.

[5] A test for sample selection for the final model specified below was conducted. Results suggest no evidence of sample selection bias. Appendix section 2B and Table 3 provides additional details of this test and the associated results.

[6] A more detailed explanation of the underlying models and required restrictive assumptions is provided in Appendix 1.

[7] Standard tests for over-identifying restrictions (see Wooldridge, p. 508) fail to reject the null hypothesis that these variables may excluded from the relevant equations (see Appendix 2 Table 1 for a further explanation and results of these tests). These variables are generally significant predictors of the variables they instrument (GPA, father's education and pre-knowledge are all significant at the 5% or higher level for post-knowledge; pre-attitude, no opinion and under typical age for class are all significant at the 5% or higher level for post attitude).

APPENDIX 1: MODEL AND SPECIFICATION

Simultaneous dynamic systems, such as typically estimated in this literature are complicated and difficult to consistently estimate. We begin, as a departure point with a relatively general model similar to that proposed by Grimes et al. (1989):

$$L_{it} = x_i'\beta + \rho L_{it-1} + \gamma A_{it} + \delta A_{it-1} + u_{it}$$
$$A_{it} = z_i'\alpha + \varphi A_{it-1} + \lambda L_{it} + \pi L_{it-1} + v_{it}$$

The variables A_{it} and L_{it} are the post test attitude and literacy scores, while A_{it-1} and L_{it-1} are the pre test attitude and literacy scores. The vectors x_i and z_i contain demographic characteristics and may contain common elements but have sufficient exclusion restrictions to allow identification. A variety of authors have included additional restrictions by assuming δ and π are both zero. Provided sufficient exclusion restrictions exist, this assumption can be tested. The above model can be consistently estimated provided that random or fixed effects do not exist. In the presence of random or fixed effects, coefficients will be biased.

Some authors estimate the above system in first differences. If the above system is the underlying data generating process, then the first difference specification is given as

$$\Delta L_{it} = \Delta x_i'\beta + \rho\Delta L_{it-1} + \gamma\Delta A_{it} + \delta\Delta A_{it-1} + \Delta u_{it}$$
$$\Delta A_{it} = \Delta z_i'\alpha + \varphi A A_{it-1} + \lambda\Delta L_{it} + \pi\Delta L_{it-1} + \Delta v_{it}$$

In practice, because only a pre- and post-test are given, the terms ΔL_{it-1} and ΔA_{it-1} are unavailable. This first difference specification does have the advantage that any unobserved heterogeneity (random or fixed effects) will be differenced out. However, because most of the demographic variables in x_i and z_i do not vary over time for individuals (for example age and gender) these would also be differenced out. For some characteristics, such as cumulative GPA, which do change over time, two concerns arise. First, the intra-semester timing of the two surveys should result in no change in cumulative GPA and so in practice this difference should drop out. Empirically, of course, we see changes in reported cumulative GPA within the semester: likely due to measurement error which will more significantly bias results in first difference than in level equations. Finally, even if ΔL_{it-1} and ΔA_{it-1} are available, problems in estimation arise since Δu_{it} is correlated with Δu_{it-1} and so ΔL_{it-1} is correlated with Δu_{it} (similarly for ΔA_{it-1} and Δv_{it}). These are typically solved by using ΔL_{it-s} and ΔA_{it-s}, (further lags) as instruments, requiring even more periods of observation. These approaches are not available for most applications since sufficient lags are not typically available.

Instead many authors, such as Grimes et al., estimate a hybrid specification: they regress ΔL_{it} on x_i, L_{it-1} and ΔA_{it} and they regress ΔA_{it} on z_i, A_{it-1} (possibly) and ΔL_{it}. Using our original model, this hybrid difference equation can be written as

$$\Delta L_{it} = x_i'\beta + (\rho - 1)L_{it-1} + \gamma \Delta A_{it} + (\delta + \gamma)A_{it-1} + u_{it}$$
$$\Delta A_{it} = z_i'\alpha + (\varphi - 1)A_{it-1} + \lambda \Delta L_{it} + (\pi + \lambda)L_{it-1} + v_{it}$$

It is important to note that this approach will not address unobserved heterogeneity. If $u_{it} = \mu_i + \varepsilon_{it}$ for all t, then the inclusion of lagged level variables biases the estimated results, in a similar way as the level equations above, through the common error term μ_i. It is also important to note that in this model, exclusion of A_{it-1} from the ΔL_{it} equation (for example) imposes not only the restriction that δ is zero, but also the restriction that γ is zero which would then suggest the equations are not simultaneous (alternatively, one would have to believe that $\delta = -\gamma$: which seems unlikely). Omission of this variable would bias coefficients. An important point here is that there is no difference in the results from either the first difference or the level specification; the same coefficients are identified under the same assumptions: no unobserved heterogeneity and sufficient exclusion restrictions. The first differencing does not identify an unidentified model.

The above model, however, does not address the fact that the class itself is hypothesized to change parameters in the model. One parameterization of this type of structural break model is

$$L_{it} = x_i'(\beta + \theta) + (\rho + \tau)L_{it-1} + (\gamma + \kappa)A_{it} + (\delta + \eta)A_{it-1} + u_{it}$$
$$A_{it} = z_i'(\alpha + \omega) + (\varphi + \psi)A_{it-1} + (\lambda + \xi)L_{it} + (\pi + \zeta)L_{it-1} + v_{it}$$
$$L_{it-1} = x_i'\beta + \rho L_{it-2} + \gamma A_{it-1} + \delta A_{it-2} + u_{it-1}$$
$$A_{it-1} = z_i'\alpha + \varphi A_{it-2} + \lambda L_{it-1} + \pi L_{it-2} + v_{it-1}$$

Only the composite parameters of the structural break model (those in the L_{it} and A_{it} model) are identified. It is, in general, impossible to identify all of the parameters of the model without at least one additional time period of observation. The first difference specification is given as

$$\Delta L_{it} = \Delta x_i'\beta + x_i'\theta + \rho \Delta L_{it-1} + \tau L_{it-1} + \gamma \Delta A_{it} + \kappa A_{it} + \delta \Delta A_{it-1} + \eta A_{it-1} + \Delta u_{it}$$
$$\Delta A_{it} = \Delta z_i'\alpha + z_i'\omega + \varphi \Delta A_{it-1} + \psi A_{it-1} + \lambda \Delta L_{it} + \xi L_{it} + \pi \Delta L_{it-1} + \zeta L_{it-1} + \Delta v_{it}$$

We note again that estimation of this model would require observation on L_{it-2} and A_{it-2} as well as the other issued noted above. The hybrid specification favored by Grimes et al. and others can be expressed as

$$\Delta L_{it} = x_i'(\beta+\theta) + (\rho+\tau-1)L_{it-1} + (\gamma+\kappa)\Delta A_{it} + (\delta+\eta+\gamma+\kappa)A_{it-1} + u_{it}$$
$$\Delta A_{it} = z_i'(\alpha+\omega) + (\varphi+\psi-1)A_{it-1} + (\lambda+\xi)\Delta L_{it} + (\pi+\zeta+\lambda+\xi)L_{it-1} + v_{it}$$

Again, this specification can only identify composite coefficients and does not clearly address any unobserved heterogeneity. Omission of A_{it-1} and L_{it-1} would result in biased coefficients unless one believed that $(\delta+\eta)$, the coefficient on A_{it-1}, and $(\gamma+\kappa)$ the coefficient on A_{it}, were both zero. One must assume that there is no simultaneity to drop A_{it-1} from the difference specification. Clearly, if one wishes to estimate these models using first difference dependent variables all lagged levels must be included to estimate the coefficients of interest.

APPENDIX 2: SPECIFICATION TESTING

A. Testing Validity of Instruments for IV estimation

Instrumental Variables estimation requires two assumptions be met (see Bound et al 1995 and Wooldridge 2003 for complete discussions): the identifying instruments need to be significant predictors of the endogenous variable while being uncorrelated with the dependent variable. We have two endogenous variables: L_{it} and A_{it}. We have chosen GPA, father's education and L_{it-1} as instruments for L_{it}. We have chosen A_{it-1}, no-opinion and younger as instruments for A_{it}.

Appendix Table 1 presents the reduced from (the first stage for the IV estimation) equations where the first assumption is tested. Column 1 presents the post-test attitude equation. We note that pre-test attitude, younger and no-opinion are all highly significant. The F-test for joint significance has a value of 102.9 and so the null hypothesis of jointly insignificant is rejected at all conventional levels. It should also be noted that these three coefficients are significant in the structural equation as well (see Table 5 in the text).

When IV estimation has multiple instruments for each endogenous variable, the hypothesis that the instruments are uncorrelated with the residual in the structural equation can be tested. Wooldridge (2003, p. 508) recommends the following procedure. Construct the residuals using the actual endogenous variable (rather than the predictions) and the IV estimated coefficients. Regress this 2SLS residual on all explanatory variables and the instruments. The joint test for significance of the instruments is distributed chi-squared(r-1) where r is the number of instruments (in our models r = 3). Appendix Table 2 presents these results. We note that both individually and jointly the instruments are not significant and thus the null that they are valid instruments is supported. Hence discussion about whether these are valid cross equation restrictions is not necessary as it has been formally tested and the assumption is not rejected.

Appendix Table 1. Reduced Form (First Stage) Regressions

	(1)	(2)
	Post-Test Attitude	Post-Test Literacy
Pretest Knowledge Score	0.053	0.258
	(0.045)	(0.038)**
Pretest Attitude Score	0.590	0.061
	(0.036)**	(0.030)*
Female	-0.895	-0.113
	(0.177)**	(0.148)
Under Typical Age for Class	1.065	0.041
	(0.372)**	(0.311)
Over Typical Age for Class	0.256	1.003
	(0.346)	(0.289)**
African American	-0.034	0.006
	(0.493)	(0.412)
Asian American	0.749	-0.724
	(0.727)	(0.609)
Junior	-0.298	-0.341
	(0.238)	(0.199)
Senior	0.576	0.201
	(0.427)	(0.358)
Father's Education	-0.011	0.057
	(0.032)	(0.026)*
College Cumulative GPA	0.081	0.385
	(0.103)	(0.086)**
Previous College Micro Class	0.217	0.294
	(0.310)	(0.260)
Previous College Macro Class	0.490	-0.253
	(0.322)	(0.269)
High School Economics Class	-0.294	-0.140
	(0.182)	(0.152)
Microeconomics Course	0.379	-0.671
	(0.310)	(0.259)**
No Opinion	-0.447	-0.047
	(0.201)*	(0.168)
Hours Worked in Typical Week	0.009	0.001
	(0.008)	(0.007)
Hours Studying in Typical Week	0.030	0.019
	(0.012)*	(0.010)
Hours Volunteering in Typical Week	-0.039	-0.049
	(0.042)	(0.035)
Hours in Extracurricular Activities per Week	0.001	-0.019
	(0.012)	(0.010)
Instructor Female	0.247	0.040
	(0.343)	(0.287)
Instructor has Ph.D.	-0.734	-0.269
	(0.271)**	(0.227)
School has State Funding (=1)	0.655	-0.357
	(0.367)	(0.307)
Small Class	0.335	-0.296
	(0.404)	(0.338)
Constant	-0.433	5.990
	(1.002)	(0.838)**
Observations	807	807
R-squared	0.39	0.22
Valid Instruments F-Test(3,783)	102.91	26.20
Standard errors in parentheses		

* significant at 5%; ** significant at 1%

Appendix Table 2. Test of Over-identifying Restrictions

	(1)	(2)
	attitude error regression	literacy error regression
Pretest Knowledge Score	0.007	0.000
	(0.045)	(0.037)
Pretest Attitude Score	-0.001	0.001
	(0.035)	(0.030)
Female	-0.002	0.002
	(0.175)	(0.146)
Under Typical Age for Class	-0.000	-0.066
	(0.367)	(0.307)
Over Typical Age for Class	-0.015	-0.005
	(0.341)	(0.286)
African American	-0.031	0.002
	(0.486)	(0.407)
Asian American	0.036	0.007
	(0.718)	(0.601)
Junior	-0.002	0.004
	(0.235)	(0.197)
Senior	-0.005	0.004
	(0.422)	(0.353)
Father's Education	-0.021	0.000
	(0.031)	(0.026)
College Cumulative GPA	0.012	0.001
	(0.101)	(0.085)
Previous College Micro Class	-0.006	-0.001
	(0.306)	(0.256)
Previous College Macro Class	-0.012	0.001
	(0.318)	(0.266)
High School Economics Class	-0.004	0.001
	(0.180)	(0.151)
Microeconomics Course	0.005	0.000
	(0.306)	(0.256)
No Opinion	0.004	-0.002
	(0.199)	(0.166)
Hours Worked in Typical Week	-0.000	-0.000
	(0.008)	(0.007)
Hours Studying in Typical Week	0.000	-0.000
	(0.012)	(0.010)
Hours Volunteering in Typical Week	-0.001	0.000
	(0.041)	(0.034)
Hours in Extracurricular Activities per Week	0.001	-0.000
	(0.012)	(0.010)
Instructor Female	0.012	-0.001
	(0.339)	(0.284)
Instructor has Ph.D.	0.007	-0.000
	(0.267)	(0.224)
School Has State Funding (=1)	-0.006	0.001
	(0.362)	(0.303)
Small Class	-0.001	-0.000
	(0.399)	(0.334)
Constant	0.219	-0.005
	(0.988)	(0.828)
Observations	807	807
Over-Identifying Restrictions Test F(2,783)	0.48	0.05
Standard errors in parentheses		

* significant at 5%; ** significant at 1%.

B. Testing for Sample Selection

Concern arises over possible self selection for the models using the post-test literacy and attitude variables. The original pre-test was administered to 2116 students, 807 of whom completed the post-test. In order to address this, we use the two step Heckman sample selection correction.

We have chosen two variables which enter the selection equation but do not determine post-test literacy or attitude. The first variable, credit hours taken, is believed to affect selection through two avenues. Students who are "course shopping" generally have higher credit hour enrollment to allow them to drop courses after the first week (or perhaps longer) if they don't like it or are finding it difficult. Students who are full time, but taking fewer courses must remain in those courses to maintain full time status which is important for scholarships, student loans, athletic eligibility, and health insurance. Hence, we would expect the probability of remaining in the course through the semester to be lower for students with more credit hours. Yet, there should be little correlation between learning and credit hours.

The second variable is an indicator for college athlete. Because of NCAA rules, athletes are more likely to remain in classes in which they have enrolled. However, conditional upon GPA, prior literacy and attitude, and other characteristics, it would be surprising if being an athlete was related to post-test scores.

Appendix Table 3. IV Sample Selection Regression

	(1)	(2)	(3)	(4)
	Selection Attitude	Selection Knowledge	Attitude IV (selection corrected)	Knowledge IV (selection corrected)
Mills Ratio			-0.609	0.688
			(1.564)	(1.308)
Posttest Knowledge Score	0.149		0.114	
	(0.045)**		(0.204)	
Posttest Attitude Score		0.076		0.135
		(0.020)**		(0.079)
Pretest Knowledge Score		0.018		0.261
		(0.015)		(0.042)**
Pretest Attitude Score	0.030		0.569	
	(0.013)*		(0.048)**	
Female	0.169	0.216	-0.935	0.075
	(0.061)**	(0.066)**	(0.246)**	(0.246)
Under Typical Age for Class	0.323		0.947	
	(0.145)*		(0.471)*	
Over Typical Age for Class	-0.380	-0.247	0.234	0.889
	(0.119)**	(0.109)*	(0.507)	(0.338)**
African American	-0.009	0.031	-0.004	0.027
	(0.164)	(0.165)	(0.488)	(0.413)
Asian American	-0.072	-0.245	0.878	-0.926

Appendix Table 3. (Continued)

	(0.240)	(0.237)	(0.742)	(0.653)
Junior	-0.106	-0.122	-0.184	-0.378
	(0.078)	(0.078)	(0.269)	(0.234)
Senior	-0.320	-0.331	0.673	-0.003
	(0.130)*	(0.129)*	(0.532)	(0.449)
Father's Education		0.090		0.069
		(0.036)*		(0.034)*
College Cumulative GPA		0.026		0.412
		(0.011)*		(0.111)**
Previous College Micro Class	-0.007	0.008	0.162	0.290
	(0.100)	(0.099)	(0.309)	(0.261)
Previous College Macro Class	0.117	0.048	0.497	-0.277
	(0.113)	(0.113)	(0.346)	(0.276)
High School Economics Class	-0.045	-0.044	-0.244	-0.131
	(0.062)	(0.062)	(0.187)	(0.157)
Microeconomics Course	0.258	0.114	0.380	-0.648
	(0.107)*	(0.100)	(0.437)	(0.285)*
No Opinion	-0.045		-0.425	
	(0.067)		(0.205)*	
Hours Worked in Typical Week	-0.006	-0.006	0.011	-0.003
	(0.003)*	(0.003)*	(0.010)	(0.009)
Hours Studying in Typical Week	0.001	0.001	0.026	0.015
	(0.004)	(0.004)	(0.013)*	(0.011)
Hours Volunteering in Typical Week	-0.009	-0.012	-0.025	-0.053
	(0.012)	(0.012)	(0.044)	(0.037)
Hours in Extracurricular Activities in Typical Week	-0.005	-0.008	0.004	-0.021
	(0.004)	(0.004)	(0.012)	(0.011)*
Instructor Female	-0.165	-0.185	0.290	-0.076
	(0.106)	(0.106)	(0.384)	(0.332)
Instructor has Ph.D.	-0.376	-0.365	-0.535	-0.368
	(0.090)**	(0.090)**	(0.488)	(0.402)
School Has State Funding (=1)	-0.175	-0.284	0.808	-0.566
	(0.125)	(0.123)*	(0.428)	(0.408)
Small Class	-0.012	-0.075	0.388	-0.372
	(0.128)	(0.128)	(0.402)	(0.344)
Credit Hours Registered	-0.031	-0.031		
	(0.017)†	(0.017)†		
Member Athletic Team	0.207	0.211		
	(0.114)†	(0.114)†		
Constant	-0.985	-0.268	-0.619	5.194
	(0.565)	(0.416)	(3.121)	(1.840)**
Observations			2118	2118
†significant at 7%; * significant at 5%; ** significant at 1%				

Column 1 and 2 of appendix Table 3 present the selection equations, while columns 3 and 4 present estimates from the Heckman two step correction for the IV estimates of the simultaneous system. In both cases, the coefficients on the Mills ratio are statistically insignificant. Qualitatively, the significant variables in the main model presented in Table 5 in the text are quite similar to the selection correction estimates. Hence there is no evidence for selection and little concern that the results in the text are biased because of selection.

REFERENCES

Altonji, J. G. and T.A. Dunn. 1996. Effects of Family Characteristics on the Returns to Education. *Review of Economics and Statistics.* Vol. 78(4) pp. 692-704.

Ashworth, J. and J.L. Evans. 2001. Modeling Student Subject Choice at Secondary and Tertiary Level: A Cross-Section Study. *Journal of Economic* Education. Vol. 32 (4). p 311-20.

Becker, W.E., W. Greene, and S. Rosen. 1990. Research on High School Economic Education. *Journal of Economic Education*, Vol. 21 (3). P. 231-245.

Becker, W.E. and W.B. Walstad. 1990. Data Loss from Pretest to Posttest as a Sample Selection Problem. *Review of Economics and Statistics*, Vol. 72 (1). P. 184-188.

Borg, M. and H. Stranahan. 2002a. The Effect of Gender and Race on Student Performance in Principles of Economics: The Importance of Personality Type. *Applied Economics.* Vol. 34 (5). p 589-98.

Borg, M. and H. Stranahan. 2002b. Personality Type and Student Performance in Upper-Level Economics Courses: The Importance of Race and Gender. *Journal of Economic Education.* Vol. 33 (1). p 3-14.

Bound, J.,D.A. Jaeger, R.M. Baker. 1995. Problems with Instrumental Variables Estimation When the Correlation between the Instruments and the Endogenous Explanatory Variable Is Weak. *Journal of the American Statistical Society*, Vol 90 (430) pp. 443-450.

Dynan, K. and C. Rouse. 1997. The Underrepresentation of Women in Economics: A Study of Undergraduate Economics Students. *Journal of Economic Education.* Vol. 28 (4). p 350-68.

Grimes, P. W., T. L. Krehbiel, J. E. Nielsen and J. F. Niss. 1989. The Effectiveness of Economics U$A on Learning and Attitudes. *Journal of Economic Education*, Vol.20, No. 2, pp. 139-152.

Heckman, J.J. 1979. Sample Selection Bias as a Specification Error, *Econometrica*, 47, 153-161.

Hodgin, R.F. and J. Manahan. 1978. Attitudes toward Economics and Student Cognitive Performance, *Economics: Innovations in Teaching the Introductory Course*, Conference Proceedings of a Symposium at VPI, Blacksburg, Virginia, April.

Jensen, E.J. and A.L. Owen. 2001. Pedagogy, Gender, and Interest in Economics. *Journal of Economic Education.* Vol. 32 (4). P 323-43.

Manahan, J. 1983. An Educational Production Function For Principles Of Economics. *Journal of Economic Education*, Vol. 14(spring): pp. 11-16.

Rask, K.N. and E. Bailey. 2002. Are Faculty Role Models? Evidence from Major Choice in an Undergraduate Institution. *Journal of Economic Education.* Vol. 33 (2). p 99-124.

Robb, R.E. and A.L. Robb. 1999. Gender and the Study of Economics: The Role of Gender of the Instructor. *Journal of Economic Education.* Vol. 30 (1). p 3-19.

Siegfried, J.J. 2006. Trends in Undergraduate Economics Degrees, 1991-2005. *Journal of Economic Education*, vol. 37(3): 376-381.

Soper, J.C. and W.B. Walstad. 1983. On Measuring Economic Attitudes. *Journal of Economic Education.* Vol. 14 (4). p 4-17.

Walstad, W.B. and J.C. Soper. 1989. What is High School Economics? Factors Contributing to Student Achievement and Attitudes. *Journal of Economic Education*, Vol. 20 (winter), pp. 23-38.

Wooldridge, J.M 2003. *Introductory Econometrics: A Modern Approach.* United States: Thompson-SouthWestern Publishing.

Ziegert, A.L. 2000. The Role of Personality Temperament and Student Learning in Principles of Economics: Further Evidence. *Journal of Economic Education.* Vol. 31 (4). p 307-22.

In: Expanding Teaching and Learning Horizons
Editors: F. G. Mixon, Jr. and R. J. Cebula ISBN 978-1-60741-971-6

Chapter 3

EXPERIENCES WITH, AND ATTITUDES TOWARDS, CHEATING AMONG BUSINESS STUDENTS AND THEIR PEERS

Charles O. Kroncke, Lynnette S. Smyth and James R. Davis

INTRODUCTION

Experience with academic cheating is an unfortunate part of college life. Students feel pressure from their family, peers, and from themselves to make good grades. Students know the right thing to do is to study hard and accept the grade earned. However, the temptation to improve a one's grade by cheating is always present. It is easy for the casual cheater to glace at a peer's exam, and it is getting easier for the more organized cheater to use technology for an unfair advantage. Media reports of business leaders amassing fortunes with illicit behavior and shady accounting practices often give the impression that cheating is only wrong if you get caught. Thus, educators should be aware of the amount and forms of cheating that are being used by students. This is particularly interesting to business educators as one recent report indicates that MBA students are more likely to cheat than other graduate students. Many business schools recognized that including an ethics component in the curriculum is a necessity. The leaders of tomorrow must learn that ethical behavior is needed for advancement and success.

AACSB accreditation requires that business schools have an ethics component in their curriculum. Schools must address such issues as corporate responsibility and governance in order to receive and maintain accreditation. Most large US schools are currently accredited and many medium-size schools are interested in AACSB accreditation while many smaller schools are interested in ACBSP accreditation. ACBSP puts more emphasis on teaching and less on research than AACSB. Thus, for accreditation reasons alone business programs are including ethics as part of their curriculum. Community colleges, not seeking business school accreditation, may also be interested in promoting business ethics in the curriculum as they are feeder schools for four-year accredited programs.

Accreditation is not the only motivation fueling the drive for an increasing role of ethics in business curriculums. Legislation such as the Sarbanes-Oxley Act is creating ethics standards that must be followed by accounting and business professionals. In addition, many private businesses have social responsibility codes that state the environmental and other non-economic goals of the corporation. These self-created and self-enforced codes may improve the image of a corporation among consumers and civic leaders. The private sector needs and desires ethical leaders and employees.

In this paper, we examine the experiences of with academic cheating of 786 students at 3 colleges. We look correlations between gender, enrolment status, on or off campus domicile, students with children, business major, a self-assessment of spirituality and academic cheating. We also examine attitudes toward cheating. We observe that over half the respondents have cheated, and we ask them whether or not they think such behavior is ethically wrong and socially acceptable. The survey was administered at three different colleges in three different states.

BACKGROUND

Cheating is fraudulent behavior involving deception in which ones own efforts or the efforts of others are misrepresented (Prescot, 1989). Academic cheating often involves cheat sheets used during exams, copying from others during a test, the use of cell phones or other electronic devices to help student find answers during tests, and plagiarism on writing assignments. Small and smaller devices connected to the internet and wireless internet access on college campuses will make electronic cheating easier and more tempting as technology progresses. Undoubtedly, there will be forms of academic cheating in the future that are unimaginable today.

Smyth and Davis (2003) analyzed student attitudes toward cheating at a two year college. They found that men are more likely to cheat than women. They found that while respondents agree that cheating is ethically wrong, most of the students find it socially acceptable. They also found evidence that business student cheat more than other majors. Smith, Davy, Rosenberg and Haight (2002) suggest that unethical classroom behavior is likely to be associated with unethical behavior in the work place. Our study extents the analysis of Smyth and Davis to two private colleges and new data from the two year school examined in their paper.

DATA AND METHODOLOGY

During the spring semester of 2006, 786 students were surveyed regarding their experiences with cheating at three colleges with enrollments less than 3500 students: Anderson University, a private Baptist Affiliated College in Anderson South Carolina; Gordon College, a two-year public school in the University of Georgia System located in Barnesville; and the College of Mount Saint Joseph, a Catholic college in Cincinnati, Ohio. A broad cross section of students was given the survey instrument during classroom time in selected courses representing various majors at each institution. The sample size roughly equals 10% of the student body at each institution. All respondents were assured with confidentiality and anonymity of their responses. Students were given the opportunity to decline participation. Less than one percent declined.

Students were given a set of questions regarding generalized inquires into how often they have cheated in college, how often they have observed cheating and its detection, their willingness to participate in cheating, and their sense of ethics and acceptability of cheating. In addition, a number of demographic variables were collected for each respondent to see how experiences of cheating may differ by demographic grouping.

Anderson University has ethics modules formally embedded in sophomore, junior, and senior courses. Mount Saint Joseph has one ethics course as part of the core curriculum and business ethics is a required course for business students. Gordon College does not formally have an ethics component in its curriculum. Individual professors at all three schools may informally put an ethics component into a course. Ethical issues are commonly discussed in management, marketing, economics, finance and accounting textbooks, so such issues are likely to be incorporated into the courses.

RESULTS

Table 1 summarized students experiences with cheating collectively at all three institutions; 1a summarized that data from Anderson University; 1b from Gordon College; and 1c from the College of Mount Saint Joseph. The questionnaire was worded so a respondent is reporting his or her individual behavior and the behavior of peers. Thus, one event of cheating may be reported by more than one respondent. For example one student may have used a cell phone to cheat, but this incident may be recorded and an observed experience with cheating by several survey respondents. The question require that the respondent only report experiences with college cheating, so high school cheating should not be reported.

Table 1. Three Institutions

	Valid %responding		
Experiences with Cheating	Never	1 – 10 times	More than 10 times
How often have you observed cheating in college?	23.3%	60.9%	15.7%
How often have you seen or known of faculty detection of cheating in college?	56.9	41.6	1.5
If you have observed cheating, how often have you observed the following types of cheating?			
• Use of a Cheat Sheet	37.2	57.6	5.2
• Copying from others during exams	31.2	60.4	8.4
• Plagiarism	49.1	45.8	5.1
• Use of cell phones during exams	83.8	14.9	1.3
• Use of PDAs, headphones, or other electronic devices during exams	87.0	12.3	0.7

Table 1a. Anderson University

	Valid %responding		
Experiences with Cheating	Never	1 – 10 times	More than 10 times
How often have you observed cheating in college?	23.3%	55.8%	20.9%
How often have you seen or known of faculty detection of cheating in college?	56.9	41.1	2.0
If you have observed cheating, how often have you observed the following types of cheating?			
• Use of a Cheat Sheet	42.4	51.5	6.1
• Copying from others during exams	34.5	55.6	9.9
• Plagiarism	51.1	43.2	5.7
• Use of cell phones during exams	83.8	14.5	1.8
• Use of PDAs, headphones, or other electronic devices during exams	85.9	13.7	0.4

Table 1b. Gordon College

	Valid %responding		
Experiences with Cheating	Never	1 – 10 times	More than 10 times
How often have you observed cheating in college?	25.3%	64.8%	9.9%
How often have you seen or known of faculty detection of cheating in college?	58.1	40.5	1.4
If you have observed cheating, how often have you observed the following types of cheating?			
• Use of a Cheat Sheet	34.2	61.0	4.8
• Copying from others during exams	31.5	61.1	7.3
• Plagiarism	51.6	44.9	3.5
• Use of cell phones during exams	82.2	16.4	1.3
• Use of PDAs, headphones, or other electronic devices during exams	88.0	11.3	0.7

Approximately 76% of students at all three institutions have observed some form of cheating, a majority of these respondents have observed less than 10 incidents of cheating. At the two four year schools about 21% of the student observed more than 10 instances of cheating; while only 9.9% of students at Gordon College witnessed 10 or more acts of cheating. This difference may be explained by the fact that students at a two year school have spent less time in college, and they have had fewer opportunities to experience cheating. The questionnaire intentionally does not define the word "cheating", students are able to decide for themselves what they consider cheating. The survey asks questions about types of cheating, but this is a non-exclusive list. There may be forms of cheating that we did not ask about.

A majority (56.9%) of students have never seen or known of faculty detecting cheating behavior. The survey question simply read "How often have you seen or known of faculty detection of cheating". Thus, rumors of detection may be included in the responses. Less than 2% of respondents knew of more than 10 incidents where faculty detected cheating.

Table 1c. Mount St Joseph College

	Valid %responding		
Experiences with Cheating	Never	1 – 10 times	More than 10 times
How often have you observed cheating in college?	19.0%	60.1%	20.8%
How often have you seen or known of faculty detection of cheating in college?	54.2	44.6	1.2
If you have observed cheating, how often have you observed the following types of cheating?			
• Use of a Cheat Sheet	35.3	60.0	4.7
• Copying from others during exams	25.5	66.0	8.5
• Plagiarism	40.8	51.7	7.5
• Use of cell phones during exams	86.9	12.4	0.7
• Use of PDAs, headphones, or other electronic devices during exams	86.5	12.2	1.4

The most common form of cheating experienced by the respondents is copying from others during an exam, 68.8% of all respondents witnessed this type of cheating behavior. The second most common form of cheating is the use of cheat sheets during exams with 62.8% of respondents witnessing such behavior. Almost 51% reported experience with plagiarism. Electronic cheating is less popular with 16.2% of student witnessing the use of cell-phones during exams and 13% witnessing other forms of electronic cheating. Simple copying behavior is likely the most popular as it requires no planning.

In addition to asking students about experiences with cheating, we also collected data concerning attitudes toward cheating. These data are reported in Tables 2, 2a, 2b, and 2c. Approximately 60% of males surveyed and 51% of women surveyed reported ever cheating. Fulltime students and residential students are more likely to cheat than part-time and off campus students. Having children and ones self assessment as "spiritual" does not significantly affect the likelihood of cheating.

About 60% of men and 57% of women have been asked to cheat. Full-time and residential students are more likely to have been asked to cheat. A large majority of students fear punishment associated with being caught in the act of cheating; 84% of men and 91% of women reported such fears. Likewise, a large majority of respondents consider academic cheating ethically wrong. It is interesting to note that while almost all students consider cheating ethically wrong, almost half of these same students think it is socially acceptable, even students who self-assess themselves as spiritual. However, only 37% of students with children feel that cheating is socially acceptable. People with children are also far less willing to assist others.

Table 2. t-test results for differences in means

		Ever Cheated	Been Asked to Cheat	Fear Punishment	Ethically Wrong	Socially Acceptable	Willing to Assist
Gender	Male	0.60	0.60	0.84	0.87	0.49	0.25
	Female	0.51	0.57	0.91	0.94	0.43	0.15
	t-stat	2.193	0.963	-2.995	-3.239	1.637	3.403
	p-value	(0.029)	(0.336)	(0.003)	(0.001)	(0.102)	(0.001)
Status	Part-time	0.32	0.39	0.84	0.95	0.32	0.05
	Full-time	0.58	0.61	0.89	0.91	0.47	0.21
	t-stat	-5.013	-4.212	-1.144	1.650	-2.878	-5.852
	p-value	(0.000)	(0.000)	(0.255)	(0.101)	(0.005)	(0.000)
Domicile	Off Campus	0.50	0.55	0.87	0.91	0.44	0.17
	Residential	0.67	0.65	0.91	0.90	0.48	0.26
	t-stat	-4.728	-2.655	-1.929	0.229	-1.087	-2.695
	p-value	(0.000)	(0.008)	(0.054)	(0.819)	(0.278)	(0.007)
Children	Without	0.59	0.62	0.89	0.90	0.46	0.21
	With	0.32	0.36	0.86	0.96	0.37	0.09
	t-stat	5.484	5.106	0.832	-2.853	1.755	3.780
	p-value	(0.000)	(0.000)	(0.407)	(0.005)	(0.081)	(0.000)
Self-assessed as "spiritual"	No	0.54	0.54	0.79	0.88	0.47	0.26
	Yes	0.56	0.58	0.90	0.91	0.45	0.19
	t-stat	-0.233	-0.748	-2.359	-0.893	0.442	1.561
	p-value	(0.816)	(0.455)	(0.020)	(0.374)	(0.658)	(0.121)
Business Major?	No	0.57	0.59	0.89	0.92	0.45	0.18
	Yes	0.54	0.56	0.87	0.90	0.44	0.22
	t-stat	0.818	0.744	0.697	0.636	0.252	-1.152
	p-value	(0.414)	(0.457)	(0.486)	(0.525)	(0.801)	(0.250)

Table 2a. Anderson University: t-test results for differences in means

		Ever Cheated	Been Asked to Cheat	Fear Punishment	Ethically Wrong	Socially Acceptable	Willing to Assist
Gender	Male	0.62	0.51	0.82	0.87	0.46	0.26
	Female	0.55	0.64	0.93	0.95	0.52	0.17
	t-stat	1.006	-1.964	-2.375	-1.967	-0.904	1.504
	p-value	(0.316)	(0.051)	(0.019)	(0.051)	(0.367)	(0.134)
Status	Part-time	0.21	0.33	0.96	1.00	0.17	0.04
	Full-time	0.63	0.60	0.88	0.91	0.53	0.22
	t-stat	-4.595	-2.580	1.677	4.675	-4.336	-3.637
	p-value	(0.000)	(0.010)	(0.102)	(0.000)	(0.000)	(0.001)
Domicile	Off Campus	0.45	0.49	0.85	0.92	0.46	0.14
	Residential	0.71	0.66	0.91	0.92	0.53	0.27
	t-stat	-4.135	-2.820	-1.490	-0.107	-1.160	-2.482
	p-value	(0.000)	(0.005)	(0.138)	(0.914)	(0.247)	(0.014)
Children	Without	0.63	0.63	0.89	0.91	0.52	0.24
	With	0.40	0.40	0.85	0.98	0.43	0.07
	t-stat	2.781	2.674	0.694	-2.221	1.103	3.330
	p-value	(0.006)	(0.008)	(0.489)	(0.028)	(0.271)	(0.001)
Self-assessed as "spiritual"	No	0.50	0.36	0.79	0.79	0.36	0.31
	Yes	0.59	0.59	0.89	0.93	0.51	0.20
	t-stat	-0.671	-1.740	-0.913	-1.222	-1.091	0.977
	p-value	(0.503)	(0.083)	(0.377)	(0.242)	(0.293)	(0.329)
Business Major?	No	0.68	0.60	0.88	0.91	0.56	0.20
	Yes	0.46	0.55	0.89	0.94	0.43	0.21
	t-stat	3.524	0.796	-0.247	-0.960	1.998	-0.178
	p-value	(0.001)	(0.427)	(0.805)	(0.338)	(0.047)	(0.859)

Table 2b. Gordon College: t-test results for differences in means

		Ever Cheated	Been Asked to Cheat	Fear Punishment	Ethically Wrong	Socially Acceptable	Willing to Assist
Gender	Male	0.59	0.67	0.83	0.86	0.45	0.22
	Female	0.50	0.54	0.93	0.94	0.40	0.14
	t-stat	1.478	2.360	-2.487	-2.528	1.000	1.695
	p-value	(0.141)	(0.019)	(0.014)	(0.012)	(0.318)	(0.091)
Status	Part-time	0.33	0.51	0.87	0.95	0.40	0.07
	Full-time	0.56	0.61	0.90	0.90	0.43	0.19
	t-stat	-2.931	-1.267	0.632	1.489	-0.350	-2.792
	p-value	(0.005)	(0.206)	(0.528)	(0.141)	(0.727)	(0.007)
Domicile	Off Campus	0.50	0.59	0.89	0.92	0.42	0.15
	Residential	0.64	0.60	0.90	0.87	0.44	0.26
	t-stat	-2.298	-0.085	-0.197	1.331	-0.402	-2.153
	p-value	(0.023)	(0.932)	(0.844)	(0.186)	(0.688)	(0.033)
Children	Without	0.57	0.62	0.89	0.90	0.42	0.18
	With	0.24	0.38	0.94	0.94	0.39	0.11
	t-stat	4.233	2.825	-1.230	-1.026	0.341	1.355
	p-value	(0.000)	(0.005)	(0.224)	(0.310)	(0.734)	(0.182)
Self-assessed as "spiritual"	No	0.48	0.63	0.80	0.89	0.49	0.15
	Yes	0.54	0.59	0.92	0.91	0.41	0.18
	t-stat	-0.825	0.516	-1.822	-0.393	0.945	-0.521
	p-value	(0.410)	(0.606)	(0.074)	(0.695)	(0.345)	(0.603)
Business Major?	No	0.50	0.59	0.90	0.92	0.40	0.18
	Yes	0.64	0.61	0.87	0.87	0.44	0.17
	t-stat	-2.203	-0.346	0.773	1.170	-0.620	0.353
	p-value	(0.029)	(0.730)	(0.440)	(0.245)	(0.536)	(0.724)

Table 2c. Mount St. Joseph College: t-test results for differences in means

		Ever Cheated	Been Asked to Cheat	Fear Punishment	Ethically Wrong	Socially Acceptable	Willing to Assist
Gender	Male	0.59	0.60	0.86	0.88	0.58	0.31
	Female	0.48	0.50	0.85	0.91	0.33	0.13
	t-stat	1.426	1.270	0.244	-0.766	3.263	2.891
	p-value	(0.156)	(0.206)	(0.823)	(0.445)	(0.001)	(0.004)
Status	Part-time	0.41	0.22	0.70	0.89	0.33	0.04
	Full-time	0.57	0.62	0.88	0.90	0.47	0.26
	t-stat	-1.513	-4.315	-1.906	-0.246	-1.346	-4.196
	p-value	(0.132)	(0.000)	(0.066)	(0.806)	(0.186)	(0.000)
Domicile	Off Campus	0.53	0.51	0.83	0.88	0.47	0.23
	Residential	0.63	0.71	0.94	0.94	0.37	0.20
	t-stat	-0.998	-2.272	-2.187	-1.210	1.036	0.428
	p-value	(0.323)	(0.027)	(0.031)	(0.230)	(0.305)	(0.669)
Children	Without	0.60	0.61	0.88	0.89	0.48	0.25
	With	0.29	0.29	0.79	0.96	0.25	0.07
	t-stat	3.206	3.362	1.064	-1.667	2.467	2.903
	p-value	(0.003)	(0.002)	(0.295)	(0.101)	(0.018)	(0.005)
Self-assessed as "spiritual"	No	0.66	0.50	0.78	0.91	0.50	0.41
	Yes	0.53	0.56	0.86	0.89	0.42	0.18
	t-stat	1.357	-0.572	-1.043	0.191	0.771	2.377
	p-value	(0.181)	(0.568)	(0.303)	(0.849)	(0.442)	(0.022)
Business Major?	No	0.61	0.55	0.81	0.94	0.39	0.10
	Yes	0.54	0.54	0.86	0.90	0.45	0.25
	t-stat	0.764	0.036	-0.721	0.674	-0.644	-2.285
	p-value	(0.449)	(0.972)	(0.472)	(0.501)	(0.521)	(0.026)

Approximately 40 percent of students surveyed are business student. Descriptive statistics can be found in the appendix. Our overall finding indicate that business majors are less likely to cheat and less likely to label cheating as socially acceptable, however this is not consistent across the three institutions. Similar to the finding of Smyth and Davis (2003), business students at Gordon are more likely to cheat than their non business peers. Business students at Anderson and MSJ are less likely to cheat than their non-business peers. Business majors are less likely to find cheating socially acceptable than their non-business peers only at Anderson.

A relatively small percentage of students are willing to assist other with cheating, with a higher percentage of men willing to do so. Residential and full-time student are more willing to assist other in their quest for assistance. People with children are fare less likely to assist others in the cheating process.

SUMMARY AND IMPLICATIONS

Our study analyzes student cheating and attitudes toward cheating at three different institutions, two religiously orientated private colleges and one public two year college. Our study confirms the findings of Smyth and Davis that men are more likely to cheat than women. While not consistent across institutions, we find that undergraduate business students are less likely to cheat than their non-business peers. The press article concerning academic cheating reported that MBA student are more likely to cheat than their non-MBA graduate student peers.

APPENDIX. DEMOGRAPHICS OF SURVEY RESPONDENTS

		Number	Percent
Class:	Freshman	239	30.4%
	Sophomore	318	40.5
	Junior	136	17.3
	Seniors	90	11.5
	No Response	3	0.4
	Total	786	100.0%
Major:	Business	316	40.2
	Other majors	453	57.6
	No response	17	2.2
	Total	786	100.0%
Gender:	Female	402	51.1
	Male	308	39.2
	No Response	76	9.7
	Total	786	100.0%
Cheated	Yes	402	55.1
	No	308	41.2
	No Response	76	3.7
	Total	786	100.0%

REFERENCES

Ethics Education Task Force, (2004) . Ethics in Education in Business Schools. AACSB International.

McCabe, D.L. and Trevino, L.K. (1993). "Academic Dishonesty: honor codes and other contextual influences". *Journal of Higher Education*, 63(5), 522-538.

Prescot, P.A. (1989), "Academic Misconduct: considerations for educational administrators". *Journal of Professional Nursing*, 5(5), 283-287.

Kostigen, T. (2006), "M.B.A.s: The Biggest Cheaters", Yahoo Finance.

Smith, K.L., Davy J.A., Rosenberg, D.L., and Haight, G.T., (2002). "A structural modeling investigation of the influence of demographic and attitudinal factors and in-class deterrents on cheating behavior among accounting majors". *Journal of Accounting Education,* 20(1), 45-65.

Smyth, L.S. , and Davis, J.R.,(2003) "An Examination of Cheating in the Two-year College", *Community College Review*, Vol.31, No1. 1-15.

Smyth L.S., Davis, J. R., and Kroncke, C.O. (2009) "Students Perceptions of Business Ethics: Using Cheating as a Surrogate for Business Situations", *Journal of Education for Business*", 84(4), 229-238.

In: Expanding Teaching and Learning Horizons
Editors: F. G. Mixon, Jr. and R. J. Cebula
ISBN 978-1-60741-971-6

Chapter 4

DO THEY, OR DON'T THEY? A REVIEW OF EVIDENCE ON CHEATING BY ECONOMICS MAJORS*

Patrick A. Taylor

INTRODUCTION

Most college students cheat; at least they say they do. Bowers (1964) found about three-fourths of college students in his very large sample self reported having cheated in one way or another at least once. Thirty years later, McCabe and Bowers (1994) found students were still saying they were cheating at about that same rate. McCabe, Trevino, and Butterfield (2001) continued to find much that same rate of cheating, though the preferred modes of cheating may have changed some since Bowers' 1964 study.

This chapter deals with students who choose the economics major and considers whether the probability they will cheat is different from that of other students. If economics majors are more prone to cheat, the implication is either studying economics actually teaches students to cheat or antecedent conditions that predispose students to choose economics also predispose them to cheat more.

The conventional wisdom regarding cheating by economics students seems to be that they are going to learn to be, or already were, strict maximizers of a utility function whose major component is monetary return. Furthermore, so the story seems to go, in so doing they are largely unconstrained by moral or ethical considerations. This seems to suggest studying economics somehow resets students' moral compass in such a way they deem morally acceptable a wider range of behaviors in pursuit of self interest than do other people. At least anecdotally, the question is generally phrased in the prejudicial, one-tailed form: Do economics majors cheat more than students who choose other majors? However, there is neither theoretical nor solid empirical evidence to support the conclusion they do cheat more.

* The author thanks the editor and publisher of the *Journal of Economics and Economic Education Research* for their kind permission to adapt for use here his article published in the *Journal of Economics and Economic Education Research*, vol. 8, no. 1, 2007, pp. 33-47.

In the absence of theory and evidence, there is no reason to believe economics students will be more (or less) likely to cheat than will other students. Hence, the conventional wisdom may be conventional but not wise.

Concerning cheating by economics majors, much of the work done to date condemns them through guilt by association with those highly suspect academic reprobates, business majors. In many studies of the possible determinants of cheating which consider academic major, beginning with Bowers (1994), economics majors and business majors are often tarred with the same brush. Bowers' choice to lump together business and economics majors apparently influenced many later researchers to do the same.

For those who teach economics it is important to look at economics majors alone in order to know whether they are more likely to cheat than are other students. Either students who we accept into the major are already more prone to cheat or we are somehow teaching them to cheat, however unintentionally, once they enter the major. Regardless of which is the case, we are doing something wrong. It might be worth investigating the source of the general perception that economics and business majors can be expected to be less honest than average. That investigation will have to wait for another day, however.

Mark Twain once said, "Supposing is good, but finding out is better." Economists both suppose and find out. Next I briefly deal with the supposing part before turning to what has been found out about economics majors' cheating so far.

A Very Short Course in the Economic Theory of Cheating

Homo economicus is self-interested and rational. At least as a first approximation, economists take that to mean people engage in behavior for which the additional benefits outweigh the additional cost. Making such choices increases the level of attainment of whatever objective one is pursuing. But knowing this does not go far in helping us understand why a particular student chooses to cheat. That is so because the choice to cheat involves an individual's assignment of costs and benefits the relative values of which we have little way of knowing. Beyond our saying, "Ah ha!" Student X cheated so for him, or her, the marginal benefits of cheating must have exceeded the marginal costs of doing so, we can not say much else.

Economists do have insight into what motivates all sorts of unsavory actions. Becker (1968) rigorously applied economic theory to the study of criminal behavior. As applied to academic honesty, Becker's analysis suggests *all* students will cheat more when the benefit - cost ratio increases and will cheat less when that ratio falls. As Kerkvliet (1994) put it so well, cheating is, ". . . a rational act of the expected-utility maximizing student." (p. 124). However, there is little in the literature reviewed below to lead one to believe economics majors assign benefits and costs differently than do other students. Hence, there is no reason to expect them to cheat at a rate different from other students. If students of economics are better informed about the nature of opportunity costs and are therefore better able to evaluate costs and benefits of choices then they will cheat more when the incentives favor that choice and cheat less when cheating is the higher opportunity cost option. The optimal level of any activity is seldom zero, after all.

On the cost side, according to Callahan (2004), the cost of cheating is low because cheaters are rarely punished, even if they are caught. He also notes the typical benefit-cost calculation for faculty members provides little incentive for them to take steps to deter, detect, and punish cheating. Furthermore, Callahan suggests administrators may be reluctant to back faculty members who bring cheating charges. He correctly notes the buyers' market nature of higher education for most undergraduate institutions. Administrators may be inclined to think of faculty members as hired help so, when balanced against the "customer is always right" attitude, they find it hard to back faculty attempts to get tough with cheaters.

Though there is much more economic theory relevant to the decision to cheat, for the present purpose, this is sufficient supposing. Now the question is: What has been found out about cheating by economics students?

The Literature on Cheating

This section provides details of previous work on cheating by college students focusing on students of economics. The main body of relevant literature can be loosely organized into three main categories: cost-benefit studies; self reported survey based studies including review articles, most of which are attributable to McCabe and his several colleagues; and what are referred to below as econometric studies. It is in that order those three tributaries, the confluence of which forms the river of cheating literature, are considered below. The section concludes with some discussion of the question whether economists' brains might work a bit differently than do the brains of "normal" people such that they are more apt to cheat.

Cost-Benefit Studies

Bunn, Caudill and Gropper (1992) and Kerkvliet (1994) estimate models which explicitly try to apply the benefit-cost approach to the study of student cheating. Neither study, however, singles out economics majors. In the case of the Kerkvliet study, measures of both the benefits and costs of cheating are mostly of the psychic sort. In fact, it is only by implication that one may be able to attach any monetary value to either study's measures. For example, Kerkvliet includes a dummy variable measuring whether a student's parents were college graduates. He finds that students with college educated parents tend to cheat more. Because college graduates ordinarily earn higher incomes than do those without degrees, one may conclude students from wealthy families tend to cheat more, regardless of their major.

Looking at the matter again later, Kerkvliet and Sigmund (1999) included in their model several individual characteristics such as; sex, grades, year in college, and level of alcohol consumption. None materially altered the benefit-cost ratio, hence were not shown to influence cheating behavior. Though Kerkvliet and Sigmund did not include academic major among their variables, as noted below, it seems unlikely that including major would significantly affect the benefit-cost ratio, therefore would have little, if any, impact on cheating behavior had they included it.

Several authors, Callahan (2004); Crown and Spiller (1998); and McCabe, Trevino, and Butterfield (2001) note an increase in professional rewards, financial and otherwise, that flow to those having a college degree. Therefore the returns to completing college with attractive grades is higher, meaning the net benefits of cheating will be higher, holding fixed the probability of being caught and sanctioned for cheating. But, as Callahan (2004) notes, cheaters are not likely to be sanctioned even if they are detected. These cost-benefit studies suggest why college students cheat. They do not suggest why economics majors may be more frequent offenders. Let's turn to the much larger body of survey-based work to see if there is a stronger indictment of economics majors.

Survey-Based and Review Studies

Since McCabe, Trevino, and Butterfield (2001) summarized the work McCabe several other colleagues did over the previous decade, there has not been much investigation of economics majors' cheating. As McCabe, *et al* (2001) note, most studies find contextual variables, factors related to students' surrounding circumstances, have the strongest influence upon students' attitudes and behavior regarding academic honesty. They find two factors are especially important; most importantly students' perceptions of the extent to which peers cheat and, secondarily, the presence of an effective honor system. However, neither McCabe and his colleagues nor others provide strong, direct evidence as to whether economics majors cheat more or less than do others. Furthermore, most of the evidence coming from analysis of self reported direct question survey data is suspect, as discussed below.

The main theme running through all of the work on cheating McCabe, *et al* have done is peer behavior is the most important determinant of how much cheating a student is likely to do. That in turn is most strongly influenced by the culture of the institution especially as it pertains to the deterrence, detection, and punishment of cheating. The lesson for economics departments is cheating deterrence is best achieved by making sure the department and the entire institution create and inculcate what students perceive to be a "just community" (McCabe, Trevino, and Butterfield, 1996, p. 461).

Students' attitudes about whether their campus is a "just community" is, of course, not related to academic major. Of the variables usually identify as playing significant roles in determining the probability a student will cheat, academic major is ordinarily thought of as an individual, rather than contextual, variable. While it is perfectly reasonable to think of one's choice of major as a purely individual trait, the milieu from which one comes is also likely to have some bearing upon that choice. Hence, looking at major choice only as an individual variable may misstate the problem to some degree. As Crown and Spiller (1998) note, it may be more appropriate to think of major choice as a composite variable, some of whose antecedents are contextual and some individual. In effect, this is the old nature versus nurture debate.

Table 1 lists some of the variables most often considered in studies of college student cheating. It also notes some of the authors who have employed particular variables in their work on cheating. As can be seen, there is a mix of contextual and individual variables. As discussed further below, not many of these variables pertain to either nature or nurture.

Previous work in the area strongly supports the primacy of contextual variables, over individual variables, as factors influencing whether and to what extent students cheat. McCabe, Trevino, and Butterfield (2001) reach that conclusion following their review of several studies from the decade ending in 2000. McCabe, *et al*, (1996, 1997, 1999, 2001) all find contextual variables, especially peer cheating and the existence of a credible honor system, are more important influences upon cheating than are individual variables.

Table 1. Variables Affecting Cheating

Variable	Studies
Contextual Variables	
Effective Honor Code	McCabe, *et al.*
Institutional/Faculty Diligence	McCabe, *et al.*
Seen (or think) peers cheat	McCabe, *et al.*; Bunn, *et al;* Mixon; Carrell, *et al.*
Full-time Faculty	Nowell and Laufer; Kerkvliet and Sigmund
In-class warnings	Kerkvliet and Sigmund
Size of institution	McCabe, *et al.*
Probability of detection	McCabe, *et al.*
Severity of Sanctions	McCabe, *et al.*
"Just community"	McCabe, *et al.*
Fraternity/Sorority membership	McCabe, *et al.*; Kerkvliet and Sigmund
Individual Variables	
Academic major	Nowell and Laufer, Bowers, Krikvliet and Sigmund, McCabe, *et al.*
Grades (GPA)	Many
Off campus work load	Kerkvliet; Kerkvliet and Sigmund; Nowell and Laufer
Year in college	Kerkvliet and Sigmund; Nowell and Laufer
Course load	Kerkvliet and Sigmund
Demographic variables-age, sex, race, etc.	Many
Religious practice of student	Nowell and Laufer
Extra Curricular Activities	McCabe, *et al.*
Socio-economic group	McCabe, *et al.*
Alcohol Consumption	Kerkvliet
Student contribution to cost	Diekhoff, *et al.*

The first of the McCabe studies, McCabe and Trevino (1993), found the single most important influence upon the probability a student will cheat is the student's perception of the extent to which her or his peers are cheating. In that study, no consideration was given to what sort of influence the student's major choice might have, however. In their 1997 study, McCabe and Trevino again find factors surrounding peer behavior to be the most important influences upon the decision to cheat. They go on to say contextual variables as a whole account for more than twice as much of the variation in cheating behavior (21% versus only 9%) as do several individual variables. Of course, that means the remaining 70 percent of variation is explained by neither contextual nor individual variables.

To the extent McCabe and Trevino's numbers are accurate, the upper limit of the possible power of academic major to explain variation in cheating behavior is only nine percent. Because there are several other individual variables which have been found to play at least some role; gender, age, grades, for example, the share of variation for which academic major can be responsible must be quite small. That does not mean, however, it is not worth knowing whether students who choose the economics major are systematically more (or less) inclined to cheat. It would also be interesting and valuable to know what factors account for the other seventy percent of variation, a point to which the chapter returns later.

Baird (1980) found business majors tend to cheat more. He did not separate economics and business majors. But he also found males tend to cheat more than females. Though he did not report the gender mix among the business majors in his sample, during the time when his study was done, business majors were predominately male. If that was true of his sample, males were over-represented in his sample, hence we can not be sure his finding is due to the fact that business majors cheat more or that males cheat more than females. However, there is evidence (Baird, 1980; Moffatt, 1990; and Roberts, Anderson, and Yanish, 1997) that students majoring in business, which may or may not include economics majors, tend to cheat more than do other students. Baird's evidence is weak, however. Of the twenty three questions on his survey, the effect of major was statistically insignificant for nineteen of the questions.

Looking specifically at economics majors, Moffatt (1990) found 87 percent of economics majors self reported having cheated at least once, which was the largest percentage of four groups of majors at which he looked. His other three groups included students from several majors. His first group included students majoring in communications, political science, and psychology. The second combined English and history majors. And the third included majors in several disciplines in the physical sciences. Moffatt found students in those three groups cheated at the rates of 80 percent, 65 percent, and 60 percent, respectively. It is not clear why Moffatt looked at economics majors by themselves and combined several other majors in his other three groups. His having done so makes it difficult to know what to make of his survey results. Furthermore, it is not possible to say whether the 87 percent of economics major respondents who reported having cheated is statistically different from the responses of his other groups of majors or the roughly 75 percent Bowers (1994) and McCabe and Bowers (1994) found.

There are other, survey-based studies but the gist of the matter is such studies are unconvincing if one is looking for reasons to pillory economics majors. There is a little econometric evidence about that question to which I now turn.

Econometric Studies

Since Bowers' 1964 study, only Kerkvliet (1994), Nowell and Laufer (1997), and Carrell, Malmstron and West (2005) have done quantitative analyses of factors influencing cheating. Kerkvliet's study looked at students in principles of economics classes but not specifically at economics majors. And he included only individual variables excluding major. Of factors at which he looked, he found a student's alcohol consumption was most likely to be linked to cheating behavior.

To corroborate what McCabe and his colleagues find about cheating, Carrell, *et al*, (2005) examined the relationship between peer cheating and the probability a student will cheat. Various versions of their model, none of which included major, estimated using both logit and two-stage least squares techniques explained only between 7.5 and 11 percent of the total variation in cheating behavior.

Nowell and Laufer's (1997) logit study added an interesting twist to the study of cheating. Their study has an advantage compared to studies whose conclusions are based upon direct question survey results. They combined researcher observed experimental data with students' responses to a random response type questionnaire. Nowell and Laufer make the case that random response type instruments produce more honest responses than do direct question instruments because they insure respondents' anonymity. Concerning self-reported survey data and observed behavior data, while each has its advantages (Kerkvliet, 1994) and disadvantages (Umeseh and Peterson 1991), using the two methods together strengthens the conclusions one might be able to draw from Nowell and Laufer.

They found economics majors are no more likely to cheat than are students pursuing other majors. The logit model Nowell and Laufer estimate found being an economics major increases the odds of cheating by only between two and four percent. That finding, however, was not nearly statistically significant, in addition to being absolutely small.

The only other major for which Nowell and Laufer tested was computer information systems. They found CIS majors had a 28 percent higher probability of cheating. Hence, their results do not tend to ratify the findings of Bowers and others whose findings tend to support the conclusion that business and economics majors are more likely than average to cheat.

As for the random response portion of their study, Nowell and Laufer found instances of cheating were twice as numerous as their survey responses suggested. This raises serious questions about the validity of any study based upon survey data, be it a direct question or random response type survey. More is said about survey issues below.

Do Economists Think Differently?

Some people appear to believe economists think differently than do other people. In fact, Carter and Irons (1991) find economics majors are different from other students in that they appear to be better at behaving rationally, in the economic sense of the word. They also find economists tend to be born, not made. Their work suggests students who choose the discipline come to economics because of predispositions developed before reaching college. However, that does not mean economics majors cheat more and Carter and Irons present no evidence they do. Furthermore, of the differences between economics and other majors, their model explains little of total variation (between 5 and 17 percent) in cheating behavior.

Frank, Gilovich, and Regan (1993) found economics majors are more self-interested and less likely to behave cooperatively the more courses in economics they have taken. They also suggest economics majors may be less honest than other students, though they do not systematically investigate that question. Frank (2004) believes students of economics are less cooperative specifically because they have studied economics rather than being predisposed to behave more self-interestedly. Furthermore, he finds a little evidence that studying microeconomics in certain ways might cause students to be more accepting of dishonesty in others, if not in themselves. However, Frank draws no conclusions as to what this might mean for the likelihood that economics majors will cheat.

The literature discussed above answers some important questions about cheating, though not about economics majors specifically. But it leaves important questions unanswered and raises new ones. Some of those questions are below.

Some Unresolved Questions

As noted above, much of the literature categorizes as either individual or contextual variables thought to influence cheating behavior. This raises the question as to the extent to which economics majors may be affected by both contextual and individual variables. It also raises the question whether the effects of individual and contextual variables are structurally different for economics majors from their effects upon the general population of college students.

The literature to date also begs the question whether there may be circularity between influences of individual and contextual variables. For instance, college students self select into major fields of study. Are there common antecedent influences predisposing students to choose economics which also predispose them to cheat more than their peers? And are there contextual influences that either increase or decrease the rate of cheating by economics majors (McCabe, Trevino and Butterfield, 2001)? If so, does this mean those directing economics major programs should try to identify informal leaders among their group of majors and try to influence them to model academic honesty?

Going part way down the road toward including such other variables, McCabe and Trevino (1997) discuss some sources of influences upon cheating that do not fit conveniently into the individual-contextual dichotomy. Using a concept from psychology, they mention variables of either sort may affect students differently depending upon the individual's locus of control. One who believes life outcomes are under his or her own control has an internal locus of control. One who believes life outcomes are largely determined by forces beyond his or her control has an external locus of control. McCabe and Trevino find little evidence to support the notion that cheating behavior is related to locus of control. McCabe, Trevino, and Butterfield (1999) do mention in passing the potential role of one's upbringing as an influence upon her or his likelihood to cheat.

Otherwise the entire matter of circumstances under which a student grew up is essentially absent from the literature on cheating. In fact, there is perhaps an entire array of variables composing the circumstances of one's upbringing that may be important in shaping cheating behavior. These influences may help form moral and ethical predilections which in turn shape the ways in which one finally solves moral and ethical dilemmas, such as whether to cheat. To date, there have been no attempts to incorporate such information in models of student cheating behavior.

Problems with Survey Data

The empirical work reviewed here, indeed nearly all of the empirical work on the subject, is based upon self reported data, usually in the form of direct question survey responses. While surveys certainly have their place in social science research, as Kerkvliet (1994); Kerkvliet and Sigmund (1999), and Sudman and Bradburn (1974) point out, there are reasons to exercise caution when searching survey data for meaning. Other than perhaps Frank, *et al*, (2004), no one argues that students of economics are systematically more or less inclined to respond truthfully to surveys asking about their own cheating behavior. Furthermore, neither is there theory suggesting economics majors will respond less or more honestly than will be others. Using a random response type instrument in concert with direct questions, as did Nowell and Laufer (1993), may help in this regard. Nevertheless, there remain concerns that students will respond untruthfully to randomized response type surveys as well.

There is some reason to be optimistic about our chances of getting better at determining when respondents are being truthful. Recently two interesting ways to deal with the likelihood of misclassified responses (a polite term for lies) to direct question instruments have been proposed. The first is the work of King, *et a*l (2004), the second by Caudill and Mixon (2005). Though an ingenious and potentially rich solution to the misclassification problem, the King, *et al* "vignette" (p. 192) method requires considerably more development, testing, administration, and analysis time than do direct question instruments. In addition, the vignette scheme would have to be adapted from its original purpose if it is to be useful to ferret out truthful responses to questions about cheating. Because the King, *et al* approach is a more costly solution, it remains to be seen if the added insight potentially available from that method is worth the added costs.

Perhaps the more promising of the two research innovations is the Caudill and Mixon approach. Using a logit model, based upon pioneering work of Hausman, Abrevaya, and Scott-Morton (1998), Caudill and Mixon have been able, at a statistically significant level, to tease out the proportion of truthful responses in student direct question responses about their own and peers' cheating behavior. Their method must be less costly because it requires nothing new, other than the way in which responses are analyzed. There are no additional costs of writing, testing, administering and analyzing more complex survey instruments and responses.

To test their idea, Caudill and Mixon applied the HAS method, as they call it, to the same set of data Bunn, *et al* (1992) collected using a direct question instrument. In that survey, about half of respondents (51 percent) indicated they had cheated at least once. When Caudill and Mixon submitted the data to HAS analysis, they found just over 70 percent had in fact cheated, tantalizingly close to the proportion of cheaters Bowers (1964) and McCabe and Bowers (1994) found. In other words, about 19 percent of students misrepresented their cheating behavior when they said they had not cheated. As Caudill and Mixon point out, we probably do not have to worry about misclassification in the other direction; students who do not cheat are unlike to say they do.

If others are able to replicate the Caudill and Mixon results using other data, their innovation will provide a powerful tool in the ongoing research into students' cheating. It will mean simple, relatively inexpensive surveys, of which many already exist, can be used to gain insight into the what, why, when and wherefore of student cheating.

Until such time as we design better experiments, invent survey instruments that are better at eliciting truthful responses, perhaps along the King, *et al* line, or perfect analytical methods such as the one Caudill and Mixon suggest, we are going to have to be very careful interpreting self reported data.

Are We Missing Something? The Case for Missing Variables

Based upon the results of research reviewed here, particularly the work of McCabe and his colleagues, it seems fair to say contextual variables are likely to play the largest role in the cheat/don't cheat decision. McCabe, Trevino and Butterfield (1996) find students are less likely to cheat if they perceive their campuses to be "ethical communities" (p. 461). This raises the question whether students who have been raised in an "ethical community" are less likely to cheat. The literature so far does not address that question. As noted below, designing questions and a survey format to get at that question may not be easy, however.

According to Frank, Gilovich, and Regan (1993) students of economics are more self interested and tend to cooperate less with others than students pursuing other academic majors. If true, that may mean economics majors are influenced by what their peers do to a lesser degree than are other students. As related to the dichotomy between individual and contextual variables, this would mean economics majors are perhaps more driven by the effects of individual variables. That argues for including in the examination more extensive measurement of individual variables, such as family background and other early life influences.

Here are some other questions about the influences upon cheating behavior the literature has yet to address very well, or at all. While this set of questions is merely suggestive, it may include the more important heretofore unmeasured influences. How would parents react to their student being charged with cheating? Did parents ever discuss cheating as unacceptable behavior? Did parents (or teachers) cheat in college? At what age did the student first notice peers cheating? Does the student have plans for graduate study? How risk averse is the student? What is the student's expected income in his or her first job? How large is the earnings gap between college graduates and non-graduates? Does the student find the institution to be a "just community"? How frequently does the student's family attend religious services? Several of these questions have been at least implied by others, but none of them have been specifically included in empirical work to date.

Some of these influences could be easily measured. For example, it would be relatively easy to find data as to the size of the income gap between college graduates and those without degrees. Other variables, however, would only be measurable through self-reported survey responses, the veracity of which is suspect, as noted above. It would be informative to see which, if any, of these would improve the power of statistical models to predict cheating behavior.

CONCLUSIONS

Considering the body of work so far, it appears applying economic models to the study of student behavior does not lead to the conclusion that economics majors are more likely than average to cheat. There is neither theory nor convincing empirical evidence sufficient to support the argument *homo economicus* is more inclined to cheat than are her or his peers. Additionally empirical studies are able to explain a relatively small part of total variation in measured cheating differences, regardless of whether academic major is included as an explanatory variable. Of those studies for which it is possible to determine the size of explained variation, shares range from about 7.5 percent (Carrell, *et al*, 2005) to a high of about 30 percent (McCabe and Trevino, 1997). Therefore, statistical work to date leaves unexplained a rather large share of total variation in the data. Furthermore, there are methodological issues with self-reported survey data.

To address some of the shortcoming of the present state of the literature on cheating further work will have to be done. In addition there are important influences upon students' decision to cheat that are not investigated in the existing literature. In particular, we have yet to systematically include data from the pre-college stage of students' development, including the influences of their upbringing and family background. Controlling for other influences, if economics majors cheat differently than does the average student, we need to know why, if we are to find ways to improve the situation.

Scholars have made good progress investigating the antecedents of cheating behavior so the state of the art is not deplorable. However, heretofore unexplored territory exists and covering that ground holds the promise of advancing the state of the art. We may find, to paraphrase Pogo, we have met *homo economics* and he is all of us!

REFERENCES

Baird, John. S. (1980). Current Trends in College Teaching, *Psychology in the Schools*, 17, 515-522.

Becker, Gary S. (1968). Crime and Punishment: An Economic Approach, *Journal of Political Economy*, 76(2), 169-217.

Bowers, William J. (1964). *Student Dishonesty and its Control in College*, New York, Bureau of Applied Social Research, Columbia University.

Bowers, William J. and Donald L. McCabe. (1994). Academic Dishonesty Among Males in College: A Thirty Year Perspective, *Journal of College Student Development*, 35, 5-10.

Bunn, Douglas N., Steven B. Caudill, and Daniel M. Gropper. (1992). Crime in the Classroom: An Economic Analysis of Undergraduate Student Cheating Behavior, *Journal of Economic Education*, 23, 197-207.

Callahan, David. (2004). *The Cheating Culture: Why More Americans Are Doing Wrong to Get Ahead.* Orlando: Harcourt.

Carrell, Scott E., Frederick V. Malmstrom, and James E. West. (2006). Peer Effects in Academic Cheating, www.dartmouth.edu/~scottcarrell/Cheating.pdf.

Carter, John R. and Michael D. Irons. (1991). Are Economists Different, and If So, Why? *Journal of Economic Perspectives*, 5(2), 171-177.

Caudill, Steven B. and Franklin G. Mixon, Jr. (2005). Analysing Misleading Discrete Responses: A Logit Model Based on Misclassified Data, *Oxford Bulletin of Economics and Statistics*, 67(1), 105-113.

Crown, Deborah F. and M. Shane Spiller. (1998). Learning from the Literature on Collegiate Cheating: A Review of Empirical Research, *Journal of Business Ethics*, 17(6), 683-700.

Diekhoff, George M., Emily E. LaBeff, Robert E. Clark, Larry E. Williams, Billy Francis, and Valerie J. Haines. (1996). College Cheating: Ten Years Later, *Research in Higher Education*, 37(4), 487-502.

Frank, Robert H. (2004). *What Price the Moral High Ground: Ethical Dilemmas in Competitive Environments*. Princeton: Princeton University Press.

Frank, Robert H. and Thomas Gilovich, and Dennis T. Regan. (1993). Does Studying Economics Inhibit Cooperation? *Journal of Economic Perspectives*, 7(2), 159-171.

Hausman, J. A., J. Abrevaya, and F. M. Scott-Morton. (1998). Missclassification of a dependent variable in a discrete-response setting, *Journal of Econometrics*, 87, 239-269.

Kerkvliet, Joe. (1994). Cheating by Economics Students: A Comparison of Survey Results, *Journal of Economic Education*, 25(2), 121-133.

Kerkvliet, Joe and Charles L. Sigmund. (1999). Can We Control Cheating in the Classroom? *Journal of Economic Education*, 30(4), 331-343.

King, Gary, Christopher J. L. Murray, Joshua A. Salomon, and Ajay Tandon. (2004). Enhancing the Validity and Cross-Cultural Comparability of Measurement in Survey Research, *American Political Science Review*, 98(1), 191-207.

McCabe, Donald L. and Linda K. Trevino. (1993). Academic Dishonesty: Honor Codes and Other Contextual Influences, *Journal of Higher Education*, 64(5), 520-538.

McCabe, Donald L. and Linda K. Trevino. (1996). What We Know About Cheating in College, *Change,* 28(1), 28-33.

McCabe, Donald L. and Linda K. Trevino. (1997). Individual and Contextual Influences on Academic Dishonesty, *Research in Higher Education*, 38(3), 379-396.

McCabe, Donald L., Linda K. Trevino and Kenneth D. Butterfield. (1996). The Influence of Collegiate and Corporate Codes of Conduct on Ethics-Related Behavior in the Workplace, *Business Ethics Quarterly*, 6(4), 461-476.

McCabe, Donald L., Linda K. Trevino and Kenneth D. Butterfield. (1999). Academic Integrity in Honor Code and Non-Honor Code Environments, *Journal of Higher Education*, 70(2), 211-234.

McCabe, Donald L., Linda K. Trevino and Kenneth D. Butterfield. (1996). The Influence of Collegiate and Corporate Codes of Conduct on Ethics-Related Behavior in the Workplace, *Business Ethics Quarterly*, 6(4), 461-476.

McCabe, Donald L., Linda K. Trevino and Kenneth D. Butterfield. (2001). Cheating in Academic Institutions: A Decade of Research, *Ethics and Behavior*, 11(3), 219-232.

Mixon, Franklin G., Jr. (1996). Crime in the Classroom: An Extension, *Journal of Economic Education*, 27(3), 195-201.

Moffatt, Michael. (1990). Undergraduate Cheating, mimeograph, Rutgers University.

Nowell, Clifford and Doug Laufer. (1997). Undergraduate Student Cheating in the Fields of Business and Economics, *Journal of Economic Education*, 28(1), 3-12.

Roberts, Patty, Janet Anderson, and Paula Yanish. (1997). Academic Misconduct: Where Do We Start? EDRS: Microfiche, 317-324.

Sudman, Seymour and Norman M. Bradburn. (1974). *Response Effects in Surveys*, National Opinion Research Center. Chicago: Aldine Publishing Co.

Umeseh, U. N. and R. A. Peterson. (1991). A Critical Evaluation of the Randomized Response Method, *Sociological Methods and Research*, 20(1), 104-137.

In: Expanding Teaching and Learning Horizons
Editors: F. G. Mixon, Jr. and R. J. Cebula
ISBN 978-1-60741-971-6

Chapter 5

Economic Literacy, Attitudes and Opinions of Adults*

Kenneth C. Rebeck

Introduction

Economics is taught in many U.S. primary schools, middle schools and high schools to prepare future adults for making informed decisions. In an economic system where markets allocate most resources, many opportunities arise for policies to be proposed that are intended to counteract the negative effects that market forces deal some individuals. An understanding of economics provides the tools for identifying the good and the bad consequences of these policies. As the economics education profession continues to seek better technologies and greater access to pre-college students, "it doesn't hurt to remind ourselves," writes Minneapolis Federal Reserve President Gary Stern, that "economics has a lot to say about important issues" (2002).

This study examines the factors that affect adult economic literacy and attitudes regarding economic issues. Data was gathered from a sample of adults in Minnesota using a survey that contained a 20-item version of the Test of Economic Literacy (Walstad and Rebeck 2000; Saunders, Rebeck and Saunders 2004), and, for the first time, the Economic Attitude Sophistication survey (Soper and Walstad 1983). Unlike prior studies, the influence of economic knowledge on attitudes of the general public was estimated with an established, reliable *attitude* index rather than individual survey items concerned with *opinions* on selected issues. Also unlike many prior studies, economic knowledge was measured with an established and reliable test instrument that adults were allowed to read rather than respond to over the phone. With the use of these instruments, adult knowledge of economics and the sophistication of their attitudes were able to be compared to that of high school and college students. Also, with the use of an attitude index rather than responses to individual items,

* This essay was repared originally for presentation at the National Council on Economic Education/National Association of Economic Educators (NCEE/NAEE) annual meetings, San Antonio, 2005. The author wishes to thank John Guck for assistance with data collection and coding.

factors, including economics knowledge, previously found to influence *opinions* on specific issues were tested in a model explaining an adult's broader *attitude* toward economic issues.

THE DATA AND INSTRUMENTS

Data were collected using a small-scale version of the creative and inexpensive approach used in a study of adults in Wisconsin by Gleason and Van Scyoc (1995). College students, specifically students taking a principles of microeconomics course at St. Cloud State University (SCSU), were given extra credit for administering a survey to seven to ten anonymous adults age 18 or older. Students were directed to give the survey to no more than three adults from any one family, and to no students at any level.

Table 1. Profile of Adults (n=267)

		Mean or Percent	S.D
Knowledge & Attitudes:	20-Item TEL Score	11.60	3.52
	EAS Index Score	3.61	0.49
Prior Former Econs. Study:	High School	50%	
	# College Courses	0.92	1.38
Gender:	Male	47%	
	Female	53%	
Age:	18 or 19	4%	
	20 to 29	31%	
	30 to 39	18%	
	40 to 49	26%	
	50 to 59	16%	
	60 or older	5%	
Income:	Low ($29,999 or less)	25%	
	Middle ($30,000 to $69,999)	56%	
	High ($70,000 or more)	19%	
Occupation:	Blue Collar or Farmer	22%	
	Other (Profession/Self -Employed, etc.)	78%	
Party Affiliation:	Democrat	39%	
	Republican	29%	
	Libertarian	1%	
	Independent	12%	
	Other	18%	
Education:	Less than High School	3%	
	High School Graduate	21%	
	Some College	23%	
	College Graduate	38%	
	Advanced Degree	6%	

College faculty were also not allowed to be surveyed. Of the 69 students completing the course, 36 completed the extra-credit assignment. This process resulted in 293 adult respondents. Table 1 presents the background characteristics of the sample of 267 adults for which complete data was available.

The survey contained a 20-item version of the Test of Economic Literacy (TEL III). The 20 items were selected by a committee made up of economic education research fellows from the Developing Skills in Evaluation Workshop held at Indiana University during the summer of 2000. Committee members rated the 40 individual TEL III items within each category (fundamental, microeconomics, macroeconomics and international economics) and from this rating the 20 items were chosen. For a description of the 20-item TEL and its use in eastern Europe, see Saunders, Rebeck and Saunders (2004).

The last section of the survey contained the Economics Attitude Sophistication survey (EAS), one of two instruments contained in the Survey of Economic Attitudes (SEA). The EAS examines a respondent's agreement or disagreement (on a 5-point Likert-scale ranging from "strongly disagree" to "strongly agree", with "undecided" the middle option) with the consensus position of economics professionals on 14 statements. For details regarding the creation, validity and reliability of the EAS, see Soper and Walstad (1983) and Phipps and Clark (1993).

ATTITUDES

Table 2 presents the average response from the 267 adults to each item on the EAS. For 12 of the 14 items, "strongly disagree" was considered the sophisticated response, while 2 items, items 10 and 12, had "strongly agree" as the sophisticated response (Soper and Walstad 1983). With the sophisticated response given the value of 5, the average response to each item could range from 1, representing complete disagreement with economics professionals, to 5, complete consensus. Following Soper and Walstad, and index was computed by combining the 14 responses into an average attitude toward markets, economic freedom and government intervention.

Alone, the EAS index and responses to individual items by the adults are hard to interpret, so for comparison purposes Table 2 also includes the responses to the EAS by 22 SCSU economics majors taking the final capstone course for their degree. Also included are the responses by the original 2,048 high school students used to norm the SEA. The average EAS index score for the adults was 3.61, a value closer to agreement than disagreement with that of professional economists. This adult index value fell between that of high school students (3.39) and that of college economics majors (3.79). Adults would be expected to have more sophisticated attitudes toward economic issues than teenagers, yet less sophisticated than soon-to-be college graduates who selected for themselves economics as their major of study.

The average responses for the adults were between that of economics majors and high school students for 9 of the 14 EAS items. Adults showed slightly greater agreement with economists regarding statements that suggest unemployment does not imply laziness (items 7 and 13), people should not be told how to spend their money (10), profits should not be regulated (12) and that government should not settle disputes during strikes (14). Adults showed less agreement with economists than the high school or college economics majors regarding free medical care (5) and the notion that everyone would be better off if everyone had more money (11).

Table 2. EAS Index Scores

	MN Adults (n=267)	SCSU Econ Majors (n=22)	High School Students (n=2,048)
1. (-) Government should control the price of gasoline.	3.23	4.05	2.53
2. (-) Inflation is caused by greedy business & union leaders.	3.34	4.00	2.96
3. (-) Business makes too much profit.	3.46	4.18	3.08
4. (-) People should not have to pay taxes.	3.95	4.13	3.84
5. (-) Free medical care should be provided for all all Americans.	3.12	3.45	3.28
6. (-) Banks should not charge interest on loans to customers.	3.94	4.36	3.77
7. (-) Most people who don't have jobs are too lazy to work.	3.36	3.14	3.23
8. (-) When a business gets big, it should be controlled by government.	4.00	4.27	3.62
9. (-) New factories are not needed.	4.07	4.23	3.87
10. (+) People should not be told how to spend their money.*	4.21	3.86	4.11
11. (-) If everybody had more money, we'd all be better off	3.50	3.64	3.61
12. (+) Profits should not be regulated by government.*	3.41	3.41	3.14
13. (-) Most unemployed people are lazy.	3.57	3.05	3.44
14. (-) When a strike occurs, government should settle the dispute.	3.45	3.32	3.02
EAS Index Score	*3.61*	*3.79*	*3.39*

1=Strongly Agree; 2=Agree; 3=Undecided; 4=Disagree; 5=Strongly Disagree. * denotes reverse-coded item; (-) indicates the sophisticated EAS response is to strongly disagree; (+) indicates the sophisticated EAS response is to strongly agree.

KNOWLEDGE

Table 3 presents the average score (percent correct) achieved by the adult sample on the 20-item TEL. The adults averaged a 58 percent on the test, but the score varied when broken down by content. Adults scored higher on fundamental and microeconomic concepts (60 and 61 percent), and a bit lower on international economic concepts (57 percent). The least understanding appeared for macroeconomic concepts (51 percent). Interpreting these average scores is difficult in that the TEL III was developed as a norm-referenced, rather than criterion-referenced, instrument, so a 58 percent correct on the entire test does not necessarily imply a low level of knowledge for the adults in the sample. For comparison purposes scores achieved on the 20-items were computed for three groups that took form A of the TEL III and included in Table 3: the sub-sample of the TEL III high school students who had completed a regular economics course, and the sub-sample who had completed an AP or honors level course, and also students beginning an introductory or principles-level college economics course at SCSU or the University of Minnesota-Duluth.

Table 3. 20-Item TEL Scores (Percent)

	MN Adults (n=267)	MN University[1] (n=813)	*U.S. High School Economics*[2] Regular (n=2,124)	AP/Honors (n=495)
20-item TEL	58%	63%	59%	72%
Fundamental: 1-5	60%	63%	61%	74%
Micro: 6-12	61%	72%	66%	76%
Macro: 13-163	51%	53%	52%	69%
International: 17-20	57%	57%	53%	64%

1. St. Cloud State University and University of Minnesota – Duluth students; freshman (28%), sophomore (41%), junior (25%), seniors and graduate students (5%); 39% had taken at least one economics course.
2. U.S. norming of the TELIII, 1999-2000.
3. Item 15 is from B of the TEL. For the high school sample, ne-2,718 (regular) and 293 (AP/Honors); for MN university students, the average percent correct between regular and AP/Honors from the form B high school U.S. norming sample was used.

The adult sample's scores were most like that of the high school students finishing a regular economics course (58 compared to 59 percent, respectively). Compared to this regular economics high school group, adults showed less knowledge of microeconomics but more knowledge of international economics. Compared to university students and advanced high school students, adults scored lower on the 20-items (58 compared to 63 and 72 percent, respectively) and in every category with the exception of international concepts, where adult and college student understanding were equal at 57 percent. Gleason and Van Scyoc's (1995) results using the second edition of the TEL found adults scored higher than regular economics high school students (55 percent compared to 51 percent).

KNOWLEDGE AND ATTITUDE FORMATION

Recent studies of adults were rich in the sense that a variety of background factors were tested to study the influence of adult characteristics on knowledge of economics and opinions concerning economic issues. One shortcoming of these studies was that opinions on specific issues, although important, were captured with specific questions (see Gleason and Van Scyoc 1995, Walstad 1997, Walstad and Rebeck 2002), but no measure of the general public's broad attitude toward markets, government and economic freedom was utilized. This study filled this gap by utilizing the EAS index as a measure of the broader attitudinal outlook of adults.

The model developed and tested in this study combined the models of adult literacy and opinions used in the studies above with models of student outcomes, where a reciprocal association was allowed between knowledge and attitudes. Walstad (1987) discusses in detail the application of two-stage least squares (2SLS) to knowledge and attitude formation. To explain attitudes, the following model was used:

Attitudes = f(Knowledge, Gender, Age, Education, Income, Occupation, Political Party)

To explain economic knowledge, the following model was used:

Economic Knowledge = f(Attitudes, Course-work, Gender, Age, Education, Income)

Following Walstad (1997) course-work in economics was excluded from the function explaining attitudes. (Course-work in economics was found to be an insignificant factor when included (with the insignificant variable MALE removed for identification of the knowledge equation).) In turn, an adult's occupation and political affiliation are expected to influence his or her attitudes toward economic issues, but neither is assumed to directly influence knowledge of economics.

RESULTS

Table 4 presents the two-stage least squares estimation results. The descriptive statistics of the variables are included in brackets, but a more detailed description of these variables can be found in Table 1. The variable EAS SCORE, the adult's EAS index score, represents the measure of the adult's attitude sophistication level, and TEL20 SCORE, the adult's raw score on the 20-item TEL, is the measure of the adult's economic knowledge; both are discussed in previous sections. Results for the equation explaining attitudes are found in the first column of numbers. The variables included in the equation explained about 21 percent of the variance in the dependent variable EAS SCORE.

As expected, holding other factors constant, TEL20 SCORE (now proxied by its predicted value using all exogenous variables) was found to significantly influence an adult's attitudes, with each additional point scored on the 20-item TEL adding .118 points to the EAS index (scaled from 1 to 5). Although similar to past results of adult opinions, this is the first estimate of the effect of economic knowledge on a broad index of attitudes of the general public. Past studies have shown similar results using attitude indices, but these studies typically measured student knowledge and attitudes directly after course-work at some level of economic education. The results of this study suggest that this influence of knowledge on attitudes continues into adult life.

Other factors were also found to influence adult attitudes after controlling for the effect of economic knowledge. The age of the adult was found to positively influence the attitude index score, suggesting that experience at work, raising a family and making a living affects attitudes of adults such that they become more in agreement with economists. This influence was also found to be non-linear — the first few years of an adult's life influence attitudes more than later years, as would be expected.

Categorizing adults by their occupation, the 22 percent of the sample that worked in either blue-collar jobs or were farmers showed less agreement with economists than adults in non-blue-collar occupations. This might suggest that blue-collar workers see unionization and government programs beneficial to their job security and earning potential. Compared to adults identifying themselves as democrats, neither republicans (which included 3 libertarians) or independents showed attitudes significantly more or less in agreement with economists.

Table 4. Two-Stage Least Squares Regression Results (n=267 adults)

Variable	*Dependent Variable* EAS SCORE	TEL20 SCORE
TEL20 SCORE	0.118***	---
[Mean=11.60; S.D.=3.52]	(3.229)	
EAS SCORE	---	-0.454
[Mean=3.61; S.D.=0.49]		(0.206)
MALE	-0.055	1.344***
[47%]	(0.665)	(2.856)
AGE	0.032**	-0.043
[Mean=38.39; S.D.=13.61]	(2.447)	(0.425)
AGE2	-0.0003**	0.0008
[Mean=1658.52; S.D.=1148.86]	(2.161)	(0.709)
HIGH SCHOOL ECONOMICS	---	-0.571
[50%]		(1.251)
# COLLEGE ECONOMICS COURSES	---	0.742***
[Mean=0.92; S.D.=1.38]		(3.057)
SOME COLLEGE	-0.068	0.843
[31%]	(0.685)	(1.498)
COLLEGE GRAD	0.022	0.787
[38%]	(0.216)	(1.247)
ADVANCED DEGREE	0.033	2.236***
[6%]	(0.181)	(2.053)
MID INCOME ($39 -$69k)	0.024	0.891
[56%]	(0.271)	(1.561)
HIGH INCOME (>$70k)	-0.010	2.667***
[19%]	(0.070)	(2.904)
BLUE COLLAR/FARMER	-0.140*	---
[22%]	(1.739)	
REPUBLICAN/LIBERTARIAN	0.040	---
[40%]	(0.520)	
INDEPENDENT	0.008	---
[30%]	(0.074)	
OTHER PARTY	0.230**	---
[18%]	(1.952)	
Constant	1.557	10.865
Adjusted R^2	*.207*	*.243*
F	*6.350****	*8.763****

Note: *, **, and *** denote significantly different than zero at the .10, .05 and .01 levels, respectively (2-tailed test).

However, those identifying themselves with another party (OTHER PARTY) showed significantly more agreement with economists than any other group. Further study would be interesting on the topic of political views and attitudes on economic issues to identify what characteristics were related to OTHER PARTY, but nevertheless this result suggests that political views are related to attitudes.

Factors found not to influence attitudes after controlling for knowledge, age, occupation and political affiliation were an adult's gender and income. Walstad and Rebeck (2001) examined five different adult data sets and found gender and income to have no consistent, significant influence on adult opinions on specific economic issues using probit analysis.

Results for the equation explaining knowledge are found in the second column of numbers. The variables included in the equation explained about 24 percent of the variance in the dependent variable TEL20 SCORE. Consistent with studies of student outcomes (see, for example, Grimes 1995) attitudes did not significantly affect knowledge when the endogeneity of attitudes (and knowledge) was assumed. Controlling for other factors, the estimated coefficient on EAS SCORE (now proxied by its predicted value using all exogenous variables) was negative (-0.454) but not significantly different than zero. This supports findings that the causality flows from knowledge to attitudes, but not vise versa. When the same equation was estimated with OLS, EAS SCORE appeared to positively influence knowledge, and this shows the bias that will result when it is wrongly assumed that the error term and attitude variable are independent. (See the appendix for estimates of the model when OLS is used in place of 2SLS.)

Other factors were found to influence knowledge. Consistent with other studies examining economic knowledge of almost any sub-sample of the population (students, adults, etc.; see Walstad and Robson 1997) males showed a higher level of knowledge than females, with an estimated coefficient on MALE of 1.344 points, significant at the .01 level.

Unlike other recent studies of adults, age did not significantly influence knowledge after controlling for other factors. While controlling for many of the same variables, age was found to positively influence knowledge in four of the five data sets examined by Walstad and Rebeck (2001), and in Gleason's and Van Scyoc's (1995) study of Wisconsin adults. One explanation might be the differences in instruments used to measure knowledge in the different data sets. For the 267 adults in this study, age and TEL20 SCORE had a positive correlation coefficient of .163, significantly different than zero at the .01 level. But after controlling for factors, age did not appear to influence the knowledge of adults in this study.

Formal course-work in economics at the college level positively influenced adult knowledge, with each additional economics course taken at college adding .742 points, an estimate significantly different than zero at the .01 level. This estimate controls for education level attained by the adults as well as other factors that one might hypothesize is correlated with college course-work in economics, suggesting that course-work in economics does effectively increase the economic knowledge of adults later in life, and that the 20-item TEL can capture this influence. Whether or not an adult took economics in high school was also included, but like other studies, the nature of this variable is vague in that a high school economics course taken in 1975 might be quite different than one taken today. Adults might also remember consumer economics or personal finance courses and consider these courses "economics." Like these other studies, this variable showed no influence on economic knowledge.

Controlling for college course-work in economics, simply graduating college showed no effect on economic knowledge, with estimates on the coefficients on SOME COLLEGE and COLLEGE GRAD being insignificantly different from zero (the omitted group being high school graduates and those not finishing high school). Although this result is inconsistent with the results of Gleason and Van Scyoc (1995) and Walstad and Rebeck (2001), when the number of college courses in economics is removed from the equation and OLS is applied rather than 2SLS, SOME COLLEGE and COLLEGE GRAD become positive and significantly different than zero at the .01 level. The 2SLS results in this study seem more reasonable. The results from the other studies mentioned above either did not control for economics course-work (two of the 5 regressions in Walstad and Rebeck (2001)), used adults who had not finished high school as the omitted group by which to compare (all 5 regressions in Walstad and Rebeck), or used a dummy variable for college economics course-work (1=yes; 0=no), while the influence of each additional course is modeled in the present study. It is difficult to make a strong case that taking some college classes other than economics, or even graduating college, has an effect on economic knowledge beyond that of the number of economics courses taken while attending college. However, consistent with other studies, the estimated coefficient on ADVANCED DEGREE in this study was positive and statistically different than zero at the .05 level. Finally, those adults categorized as having a high income ($70,000 or higher) showed a greater understanding of economics, with an estimated coefficient on HIGH INCOME of 2.667 points, significantly different than zero at the 01 level. Income was also found to be associated with knowledge of economics in the previous studies mentioned above.

CONCLUSION

This study sought to further investigate the general public's level of economic understanding, attitudes concerning economic issues, and factors that influence each. Measuring attitudes with an index rather than capturing opinions on specific issues, attitudes of adults were able to be compared with that of high school and college economics majors, and it was found that the average adult in the study had a slightly lower level of agreement with economists on economic issues than did economics majors, but a slightly greater level than high school students. The adults in the sample showed a knowledge level comparable to that of high school students finishing a regular course in economics, but lower than that of high school students finishing an advanced economics course and lower than college students (of which about 40 percent had taken at least one course in economics). Lastly, a knowledge of economics was found to positively influence attitudes of adults toward that of economists, as well as other factors such as age, occupation and political affiliation. Attitudes were not found to influence knowledge, while gender, college course-work in economics, holding an advanced degree and having a high income did have an effect.

The 20-item version of the TEL was used as a measure of adult understanding, and a quasi-Gleason/Van Scyoc (1995) method was used to gather data on the sample of adults. Both were inexpensive and provided results that appeared quite reasonable. One might argue, for example, that sample selection bias might be *less* in a sample of adults when adults are asked to complete a survey to help a college student receive extra credit than it would be in a sample of adults willing to participate in a rather long phone survey. Further, the adults in this study were allowed to sit down and take the survey at their leisure, re-reading options to make the best choices on the survey, again a potentially better situation than a phone survey. On the other hand, one might argue that without supervision, adults might look up answers they did not know, or that the students seeking extra credit did not follow the directions concerning selection of potential adults. Also, the reliability of the 20-item TEL was lower than that of the full 40-item version.

Overall, the results of this study added to the research literature on adult economic literacy. The slight differences in the results found in this study with past studies seem just as interpretable as the alternative findings. Further study of the factors influencing the general public's economic knowledge and attitudes might examine the robustness of these findings.

APPENDIX: OLS REGRESSION RESULTS (N=267 ADULTS)

	Dependent Variable	
Variable	EAS SCORE	TEL20 SCORE
TEL20 SCORE	0.035***	---
[Mean=11.60; S.D.=3.52]	(4.276)	
EAS SCORE	---	1.449***
[Mean=3.61; S.D.=0.49]		(3.317)
MALE	-0.067	1.118***
[47%]	(1.240)	(2.936)
AGE	0.026**	-0.094
[Mean=38.39; S.D.=13.61]	(2.350)	(1.186)
AGE2	-0.0002*	0.001
[Mean=1658.52; S.D.=1148.86]	(1.869)	(1.357)
HIGH SCHOOL ECONOMICS	---	-0.402
[50%]		(1.005)
# COLLEGE ECONOMICS COURSES	---	0.582***
[Mean=0.92; S.D.=1.38]		(3.740)
SOME COLLEGE	-0.044	0.768
[31%]	(0.599)	(1.431)
COLLEGE GRAD	0.149**	0.529
[38%]	(2.071)	(0.981)
ADVANCED DEGREE	0.291**	1.763*
[6%]	(2.334)	(1.960)
MID INCOME ($39 -$69k)	0.105	0.673
[56%]	(1.510)	(1.355)
HIGH INCOME (>$70k)	0.219**	2.128***
[19%]	(2.272)	(3.218)
BLUE COLLAR/FARMER	-0.181***	---
[22%]	(2.713)	
REPUBLICAN/LIBERTARIAN	0.033	---
[40%]	(0.503)	
INDEPENDENT	0.021	---
[30%]	(0.238)	
OTHER PARTY	0.174*	---
[18%]	(1.778)	
Constant	2.375	5.725
Adjusted R^2	*.284*	*.280*
F	*9.126****	*10.411****

Note: *, **, and *** denote significantly different than zero at the .10, .05 and .01 levels, respectively (2-tailed test).

REFERENCES

Gleason, J. And L. J. Van Scyoc. 1995. A report on the economic literacy of adults. *Journal of Economic Education* 26 (Summer): 203-210.

Grimes, P. W. 1995. Economic education for at-risk students: an evaluation of Choices and Changes. *American Economist* 39 (Spring): 71-83.

Phipps, B. J. and J. E. Clark. 1993. Attitudes toward economics: uni- or multidimensional? *Journal of Economic Education* 24 (Summer): 195-212.

Saunders, P., K. Rebeck and K. T. Saunders. 2004. High school economic education in eastern Europe: findings from five nations. *Journal of Economics and Economic Education Research* 5(1): 49-64.

Soper, J. C. and W. B. Walstad. 1983. Measuring economic attitudes in high school. *Journal of Economic Education* 11 (Spring): 41-54.

Stern, G. 2002. Economic literacy leads to better grasp of public policy issues. *The Region* (December).

Walstad, W. B. 1987. Applying two-stage least squares. In Becker, W. E. and William B. W. (Eds.) *Econometric Modeling in Economic Education Research*. Boston: Kluwer-Nijhoff Publishing.

Walstad, W. B. 1997. The effect of economic knowledge on public opinion of economic issues. *Journal of Economic Education* 28 (Summer): 195-205.

Walstad, W. B. and K. Rebeck. 2000. Test of Economic Literacy: Forms A and B (3rd Ed.). New York: National Council on Economic Education.

Walstad, W. B. and K. Rebeck, 2001. Assessing the economic knowledge and economic opinions of adults. *The Quarterly Review of Economics and Finance* 42: 921-935.

Walstad, W. B. and D. Robson. 1997. Differential item functioning and male-female differences on multiple-choice tests in economics. *Journal of Economic Education* 28 (Spring): 155-172.

In: Expanding Teaching and Learning Horizons
Editors: F. G. Mixon, Jr. and R. J. Cebula
ISBN 978-1-60741-971-6

Chapter 6

HOMEWORK, PRACTICE AND PERFORMANCE IN PRINCIPLES OF MICROECONOMICS

Steven B. Caudill and James E. Long

INTRODUCTION

As enrollment in college-level economics classes has risen, with an increasing number of students taking micro- and macro-principles courses in large auditoriums, experts have devoted more attention to alternative teaching methods and their effects on student learning. For years the annual meeting of the American Economic Association has regularly included multiple sessions on the teaching of economics, and several academic journals devoted to this topic have been established in the recent past (Lo, Wong and Mixon, 2008; Mixon and Upadhyaya, 2008). The present paper's primary contribution to the growing literature is an empirical analysis of how students' grades on in-class exams are affected by their scores on out-of-class homework assignments. Our major finding, that exam grades and homework scores are positively related, is what educators might have anticipated (hoped for?), yet surprisingly there is little published research that has documented a link between student learning and out-of-class exercises [1]. Our study's results justify the suggestions of Grove and Wasserman (2006) and Hansen, Salemi, and Siegfried (2002) that principles students be given more opportunity to practice economic analysis.

A description of the analysis and data utilized in our study is presented in the next section. Regression results describing the relationship between homework and exam performance appear in the following section of the paper. This is followed by an investigation of the link between "practice" exercises and graded homework assignments. A "differences in differences" analysis of the effects of economics homework and practice on student performance is then presented. A summary and concluding comments appear in the last section of the paper.

ANALYSIS AND DATA

Data for the study consist of exam grades, homework scores, completion of practice exercises, and academic and personal characteristics of about 700 students who were enrolled in micro-economics principles classes taught by one of the authors during the Fall 2006 and Spring 2007 semesters of Auburn University. There were four classes overall, two in a lecture hall seating around 250 students, and two classes taught in a smaller auditorium with maximum capacity of 100 seats. The homework assignments consisted of short-answer questions and problems (mainly graphical exercises that required students to draw and shift demand, supply, cost, product, and revenue curves) created by Aplia [2] and customized for the assigned textbook, *Microeconomics: Private and Public Choice*, 11 ed., authored by Gwartney, Stroup, Sobel, and Macpherson. In addition to economics questions and problems accompanying each chapter, some Aplia homeworks instructed students to read an attached article that had appeared in a newspaper or other outlet and answer economic questions relating to the article's content.

Each one-semester course was structured identically in that one and sometimes two Aplia homework assignments were due each week. These homeworks were completed on-line and students could submit their answers as many times as desired, prior to the assignment's "due date" (usually Thursday or Sunday at 11 pm). The answers that had been submitted when the due date arrived were computer-graded and the results then reported to students and professor.

In each class from which data were obtained, a student's final letter grade was based on a weighted average of performance on Aplia homeworks (measured as an overall average score for graded exercises and problems) and scores on three in-class exams (denoted EXAM1, EXAM2, and EXAM3 in the empirical analyses.) EXAM1 and EXAM2 covered approximately the first five and second five chapters of the textbook, respectively. Students were assigned about seven graded homeworks prior to taking each in-class exam. EXAM3 was a considerably longer test that was administered during the final exam period; it covered four chapters of new material assigned after the second test as well as the introductory supply and demand chapters. Grades for EXAM1, EXAM2, and EXAM3 are reported on a 0 to 100 scale. In the empirical analyses to follow, GHW1, GHW2, and GHW3 refer to the simple average of scores (0 to 100) on all graded Aplia homework assignments from chapters covered preceding EXAM1, EXAM2, and EXAM3, respectively.

In the next section we empirically estimate the relationship between (1) EXAM1 and GHW1, (2) EXAM2 and GHW2, and (3) EXAM3 and GHW3. In other words, we seek to determine whether success on graded homework exercises translates into higher grades on in-class exams. At the outset, it should be stressed that each in-class exam and the corresponding Aplia assignments cover the same content but their questions are distinctly different. The in-class exams consist of multiple-choice questions, over ninety percent of which are randomly selected from a computerized test bank that the textbook's publisher provides instructors.[3] The Aplia homework questions for each chapter are "customized" for the required textbook and make heavy use of graphical exercises and calculation problems. Consequently, if homework scores and exam grades are positively related it is not evidence of the impact of "teaching to the test", a behavior often attributed to elementary and secondary public school teachers whose classes must undergo standardized competency tests or graduation exams.

Instead, a direct link between homework and exam proficiency would be consistent with Aplia's goal of "engaging, preparing, and educating" students. The possibility that homework grades and exam performance might be negatively related is raised by recent research by Nowell and Alston (2007) on student overconfidence. Students earning high homework grades might perceive less need to study for in-class exams, with the result being lower test grades.

As control variables, our empirical models include several of the student characteristics found by previous studies to influence academic performance and college-student behavior. These are GPA, cumulative grade point average (0 to 4 scale) at the time the student was enrolled in the micro principles course; HOURS, earned semester hours prior to enrollment in microeconomics; FEMALE, a dummy variable to identify female students; TRANSFER, a dummy variable for transfer students; PREVIOUS, a dummy variable identifying students who had previously taken micro principles; and a series of six binary variables indicating the student's major field of study (such as business, education, or engineering.) Arguably, the most important control factor is GPA, as it reflects both previous academic achievement at the university level and the potential to excel in the classroom. Some researchers interpret GPA as a measure of effort if there is also a control for aptitude (e.g. SAT scores), and as a combined reflection of effort and aptitude otherwise. Not surprisingly, many researchers including Durden and Ellis (1995), Brown and Liedholm (2002), Sosin et al (2004), and Grove and Wasserman (2006) have found that GPA is positively related to performance in economics classes. However, since GPA might poorly proxy academic potential due to grade variations by course, curriculum, and instructor, in some of our empirical models EXAM1 or EXAM2 are included as additional control factors. Controlling for entering overall GPA, we find students who score highly on one in-class exam can be expected to possess greater ability or motivation which leads to higher grades on subsequent in-class exams.

DETERMINANTS OF IN-CLASS EXAM GRADES

Regression estimates of the determinants of students' grades on three in-class exams administered in selected micro principles classes at Auburn University during 2006-2007 are reported in Table 1. Performance on the assigned homework exercises preceding the first exam is positively related to the exam grade and the coefficient is significant at the α=.01 level. According to equation (1), a 10-point increase in GHW1 adds about 2.3 points to the EXAM1 grade, other factors constant. Females score about 2.5 points lower than males on the first exam, whereas more "senior" students (in terms of college credit) garner relatively higher exam grades. The effect of homework performance on the exam grade remains positive and highly significant, albeit about twenty percent smaller, when GPA is added in equation (2). Because effort (proxied by GPA) influences both homework and exam scores, the reduced coefficient of homework when GPA is included in the regression is not surprising. With GPA omitted, homework score probably reflects the conscientiousness of the student as well as the direct effect of out-of-class assignments on exam performance. As expected, students with high grades entering micro principles do better on EXAM1 than students with lower GPAs. Controlling for academic quality and potential of students eliminates the earned-hours effect but increases the gender disparity in exam success. Also, students with previous micro-economics class experience are found to score about 4 points higher on EXAM1 than "first-timers".

Table 1. Determinants of In-Class Exam Grades

Variable	Exam1	Exam1	Exam2	Exam2	Exam3	Exam3
GHW1	0.227***	0.175***				
	(12.14)	(8.87)				
GHW2			0.232***	0.181***		
			(9.21)	(7.82)		
GHW3					0.124***	0.073***
					(6.96)	(4.66)
GPA		4.434***	6.320***	3.631***	6.326***	2.604***
		(6.66)	(7.68)	(4.67)	(8.65)	(3.95)
Female	-2.480***	-3.133***	-3.985***	-2.361***	-4.673***	-2.485***
	(-3.08)	(-3.99)	(-4.19)	(-2.71)	(-5.48)	(-3.34)
Hours	0.054**	0.028	0.010	-0.007	0.022	0.012
	(2.47)	(1.32)	(0.38)	(-0.30)	(0.95)	(0.58)
Transfer	-0.499	-0.215	1.294	1.494	0.256	-0.623
	(-0.38)	(-0.17)	(0.85)	(1.09)	(0.19)	(-0.53)
Previous	1.109	3.561**	2.347	0.978	3.872**	3.026**
	(0.73)	(2.36)	(1.28)	(0.59)	(2.40)	(2.15)
Exam1				0.498***		
				(11.87)		
Exam2						0.455***
						(14.91)
Intercept	59.556***	52.322***	40.908***	13.034***	49.437***	30.229***
	(42.89)	(30.29)	(20.18)	(4.38)	(27.27)	(14.97)
Adj. R^2	0.2234	0.273	0.313	0.440	0.278	0.469
n	644	644	627	627	622	616

Notes. Regressions also include six dummy variables for College Major. T-values in parentheses: *p = .10, **p = .05, ***p = .01.

A similar story regarding the effect of homework on exam performance is told by equation (3), which analyzes the second in-class exam. A 10-point improvement on graded homework assignments raises the exam score by 2.3 points and this effect persists even after controlling for entering GPA, which directly affects exam performance. Female students score about 4 points lower than males on EXAM2, but no other listed variables are significant. Equation (4) adds the observed grade on the first exam which, for reasons noted earlier, may be a better proxy for academic ability than overall GPA. Students scoring highly on EXAM1 are more likely to also do well on the second exam, and this effect is significant at the α=.01 level. With EXAM1 in the model, the partial effects of GPA and gender are about half as large though still highly significant. More importantly, the coefficient of GHW2 retains its sign, significance, and approximate magnitude. Each 10-point improvement in scores on homeworks preceding the second exam adds about 2 points to the grade on EXAM2.

The positive and highly significant coefficients of the graded homework variables in Table 1 are consistent with the view that time and effort devoted to out-of-class exercises contribute to an improved understanding of economics that leads to higher exam grades. An alternative to the interpretation that doing well on homework causes students to do better on exams is that students with an unmeasured "knack" for economics score more highly on both assignments and tests. The positive signs on the *prior* exam grade in equations (4) and (6) are consistent with a "knack affects performance" perspective, but our results showing that current homework grades directly affect current exam score are evidence of a "knowledge and preparation affects performance" hypothesis.

According to equations (5) and (6), students who improve their homework grades by 10 points score from 0.7 to 1.2 points higher on the final exam in microeconomics. These relatively smaller impacts of homework success on exam performance (although still significant) are understandable since EXAM3 covered more material than just the last four chapters assigned after the second exam, which formed the basis for GHW3. Note that GPA, gender, and prior exam grade show approximately the same impacts on the final exam grade as were revealed in the case of EXAM2. Interestingly, students who had previously taken micro score over 3 points higher on the final exam than first-time micro students. The former group might have failed microeconomics the first time, but they retained some knowledge useful the second time around. Alternatively, these students might have initially passed micro principles but are re-taking the class to improve their grade point average as permitted under Auburn's "grade forgiveness" policy.

Although not reported in Table 1, there are a few interesting and statistically significant findings involving college major and exam performance. Education majors scored about 5 points lower on EXAM1, business majors about 2 points higher, and students planning to attend professional schools (e.g., medicine and law) after graduation scored about 4 points higher than the base category. On the second exam, only engineering majors exhibited a grade advantage (of about 4 points), whereas business majors scored about 2.5 points higher than other students on the final exams. This last finding might be explained by Auburn's requirement that students must earn a minimum GPA in order to enroll in any College of Business course other than Principles of Microeconomics, which counts as a University "Core Curriculum" course. Because the final exam counts more heavily in the letter grade determination than EXAM1 or EXAM2, students hoping to continue taking business classes have an additional incentive to score highly on EXAM3.

Does Practice Make Perfect?

An important feature of the Aplia instructional software used in these classes is that it provides students an opportunity to examine and answer "practice" questions that are comparable (but not identical) to each chapter's graded homework exercises. Students receive immediate feedback when answering a practice question, including a brief explanation of why the answer submitted might have been an incorrect answer. There is one set of practice problems and exercises corresponding to each chapter's graded homework questions. Using records of students' answers to the practice assignments, we created the variables PHW1, PHW2, and PHW3, which are the overall average grades (on a 0 to 100 scale) on the 4 to 5 practice problem sets that accompanied the graded homework exercises. In this section we investigate the relationship between (1) GHW1 and PHW1, (2) GHW2 and PHW2, and (3) GHW3 and PHW3. That is, how do completion and mastery of practice questions affect students' grades on assigned homework? Finding a positive relationship would point to an incentive for students to invest time and effort on the practice assignments, even though in the classes examined "practice" grades do not *directly* count in the final letter grade determination.

Table 2 reports our estimates of the determinants of homework grades of students who submitted the assignments. Equations (1), (3) and (5) reveal that practice "success" is positively related to homework grade at the α=.01 level.

Table 2. Determinants of Homework Grades

Variable	GHW1	GHW1	GHW2	GHW2	GHW3	GHW3
PHW1	0.317***	0.500***				
	(12.10)	(5.24)				
PHW2			0.448***	0.472***		
			(15.50)	(4.09)		
PHW3					0.459***	0.690***
					(13.69)	(5.01)
GPA	9.358***	12.484***	8.136***	8.113***	8.273***	10.401***
	(8.54)	(7.23)	(7.78)	(5.57)	(6.20)	(6.00)
Female	-3.913***	-7.789***	-4.244***	-2.262	-4.191***	-5.584***
	(-2.92)	(-3.36)	(-3.42)	(-1.28)	(-2.65)	(-2.66)
Hours	0.005	0.007	-0.005	-0.010	-0.004	-0.003
	(0.12)	(0.18)	(-0.14)	(-0.29)	(-0.08)	(-0.07)
Transfer	-0.814	-0.966	0.510	0.614	-1.007	-0.954
	(-0.38)	(-0.45)	(0.26)	(0.31)	(-0.40)	(-0.38)
Previous	-1.164	-1.333	-1.433	-1.050	1.054	0.631
	(-0.45)	(-0.52)	(-0.60)	(-0.43)	(0.34)	(0.20)
Practice*GPA		-0.087**		0.004		-0.093**
		(-2.42)		(0.09)		(-1.93)
Practice*Female		0.102**		-0.089		0.061
		(2.01)		(-1.58)		(0.93)
Intercept	26.624***	20.456***	14.356***	13.771***	15.915***	11.079**
	(9.43)	(4.79)	(5.25)	(3.67)	(4.50)	(2.48)
Adj. R^2	0.348	0.355	0.411	0.411	0.353	0.356
n	638	638	618	618	577	577

Notes: See Table 1.

Other factors constant, scoring 10 points higher on practice problems increases the homework grade by 3.2, 4.5, and 4.6 points, respectively. In each equation GPA carries a positive and highly significant coefficient, whereas the gender dummy variable's coefficient is negative and significant at the α=.01 level, revealing that female students score about 4 points lower than males. None of the other explanatory variables in these equations were significant at conventional levels except the dummies for engineering and business majors (not shown in the table) were found to increase GHW3.

As an alternative to the model shown in equations (1), (3) and (5) above, we replaced the actual practice grade variable with a dummy coded 1 for students who did any of the practice assignments preceding the corresponding graded homeworks, and coded 0 for students who did none of the practice problems before submitting answers to the graded homework assignments. The estimated coefficients (t values) of these dummy variables are 9.90 (5.06), 10.84 (6.39), and 11.74 (6.37), respectively. If, as discussed previously in this paper, some students have a knack for doing well on economics assignments and in-class exams, then it would seem not to matter if they "practiced" or not. We interpret the positive and highly significant practice dummy coefficients as evidence that practice, preparation, and effort – not merely a "knack for economics" – leads to higher grades.

Since virtually all studies -- including the present one -- find that females do more poorly in economics classes than males and that "better" students make higher economics grades than lower-GPA students, it seemed natural to test for differences by gender and GPA in the effect of practice on homework grades (and, indirectly, final course grade). Therefore, equations (2), (4), and (6) add terms that interact the appropriate practice score with gender and grade point average. The estimated coefficient of PRACTICE * FEMALE is statistically significant in equation (2) alone. All else constant, a 10-point increase in the average practice exercise score raises the first homework grade by 5 points for males and 6 points for females, but this small advantage for female students vanishes later in the semester. Two of the PRACTICE* GPA coefficients are negative, statistically significant, and of similar magnitude. Among students who devote enough time and effort to increase early-semester practice scores by 10 points, the boost to assigned homework grades is 4.1 points for "D" students compared to 1.6 points for students entering micro with 4.0 GPAs. For homework assignments during the final third of the term, a 10-point increase in practice "success" raises the average homework grade by 6 points for "D" students but only 3.1 points for "A" students. While "practice" may not yield perfection, in the case of students taking principles of microeconomics it is an avenue to higher scores on graded work. And the less-skilled students appear to benefit the most, grade-wise, from economics practice.

Alternative Tests of Homework and Practice Effects on Student Performance

In this section we report the results of a "differences in differences" approach that uses each student as his or her own control. This technique answers the question, "If homework grades improved over the course of the semester, did exam grades change in the same direction?" Likewise, we can investigate whether improvement in practice exercises results in higher grades on homework assignments.

Table 3. Differences in Differences Regression Results

Variable	EXAM2-1	EXAM2-1	EXAM3-2	EXAM3-2	GHW2-1	GHW2-1	GHW3-2	GHW3-2
GHW2-1	0.128*** (5.13)	0.091*** (3.92)						
GHW3-2			0.113*** (4.98)	0.087 (7.78)				
PHW2-1					0.328*** (9.84)	0.237*** (7.78)		
PHW3-2							0.462*** (10.72)	0.429*** (10.18)
GPA		5.398*** (7.19)		3.330*** (5.18)		6.639*** (6.29)		3.732*** (2.98)
Female		-2.938*** (-3.34)		-2.633*** (-3.61)		-2.193* (-1.84)		-1.544 (-1.10)
Base		-0.414*** (-9.71)		-0.507*** (-16.95)		-0.451*** (-13.19)		-0.269*** (-6.54)
Intercept	-5.725*** (-8.79)	11.686*** (3.85)	3.576*** (8.40)	29.468*** (14.80)	-13.491*** (-16.05)	-3.627 (-1.30)	2.287*** (3.21)	4.085 (1.31)
Adj. R^2	0.039	0.179	0.037	0.350	0.136	0.325	0.167	0.220
n	627	627	616	616	612	612	570	570

Notes: See Table 1.

Operationally, we calculate the following variables: (1) EXAM2-1 and EXAM3-2, which equal the difference between EXAM2 and EXAM1 and EXAM3 and EXAM2, respectively; (2) GHW2-1 and GHW3-2, which equal the difference between GHW2 and GHW1 and GHW3 and GHW2, respectively; and (3) PHW2-1 and PHW3-2, which equal the difference between PHW2 and PHW1 and PHW3 and PHW2, respectively. Each difference in exam grade (or assigned homework grade) is regressed on the corresponding difference in assigned homework grade (or practice exercise score).

The regression results are shown in Table 3. Equations (1) and (3) reveal that when the difference in homework grades rises by 10 points, the difference in exam grades expands by about 1 point, and this relationship is significant at the α=.01 level. The impact of homework on exam performance diminishes slightly but remains highly significant when several control variables are added to the regression, including the new term BASE, which refers to the initial exam or homework grade, i.e. EXAM1 in equation (2) and EXAM2 in equation (4). Students whose beginning exam grade is high cannot demonstrate as much improvement on the next exam as lower-scoring students can, so BASE carries the expected negative and significant coefficient in equations (2) and (4). Exam-to-exam grade changes are about 3 points lower for female than male students, and vary directly with grade point average. For example, other things the same, exam performance improvement is 3 to 5 points greater for "B" students than for students entering the class with 2.0 GPAs.

The remaining columns in Table 3 contain the results of analyzing changes in assigned homework grades during the semester. Equations (5) and (7) reveal that the "gross" effect of improvement in practice exercise scores is an increase in the homework grade difference in the range of 3.3 to 4.6 points per each 10-point improvement. The coefficients of PHW2-1 and PHW3-2 decline but remain highly significant when the initial or base-line assigned homework grade and other control variables are included in the regression. GPA carries a positive and highly significant coefficient in both equation (6) and (8), but the gender dummy is at best marginally significant in equation (6) alone.

SUMMARY AND CONCLUSIONS

With individual teaching careers spanning about 30 years, it becomes increasingly difficult to recall the time when our classes were small enough so that students' names could easily be memorized, exams could utilize both short-answer and essay-type questions, homework exercises and problem sets could be graded by hand, and we could readily identify and provide extra attention to those students most challenged by the complexity of introductory economics. Today in relatively large public universities like Auburn, small classes are generally reserved for teaching by graduate students and summer school sessions, and the microeconomics principles classes that we have personally taught over the last decade have almost always been offered in auditoriums seating 250 to 400 students. Often the only personal contact we have with students is when we verbally question whether the picture ID being presented with an exam scantron matches the "mug shot" on our class roll!

The introduction of computer-assisted instructional tools and Internet-based interactive student-study resources has brought relief to instructors concerned about the impact of larger class size on teacher work loads, and hope to professors worried that student learning suffers when larger classes contribute to depersonalized instruction and disengaged students. A recent survey by Schaur, Watts, and Becker (2008) reveals that the percentage of instructors assigning homework/problem sets in introductory economics classes increased between 2000 and 2005 from 51 to 63 percent. Because of their additional costs in terms of time and sometimes money, students are understandably reluctant to embrace Aplia and similar on-line instructional software providing homework exercises, practice exams, interactive tutorials and so forth. However, our study suggests that resources devoted to homework and out-of-class practice assignments yield returns in the form of increased student learning and higher exam (and course) grades. As long-time educators, we would be gratified if publication of our findings encourages college students to become more engaged in their economics courses via additional out-of-class study and practice.

Analysis of student data collected for our study reveals that lower-GPA students are relatively less likely to complete the Aplia practice exercises (and attend class lectures, for that matter) than higher-GPA students. Auburn microeconomics students may not be unique in this regard. The providers of Aplia instructional software have observed that students spend much more time working graded problem sets than practice ones, and that many Aplia users do not read the available feedback that might allow students to learn from their mistakes. In light of this, in Fall 2008 Aplia Economics introduced a new format (Grade It Now) in which separate "graded" and "practice" problem sets are not used. Under the new format, students can submit answers to graded problems and receive their scores as before, or they can click "Grade It Now" after submitting answers and receive immediate feedback. If students believe they can improve their performance after reading the feedback, they can click "Try Another Version" and attempt new (different) questions covering the same concept. Students are allowed to attempt a given page of questions up to three times, with the final score reported to instructors being the average of points received on each attempt. How students' in-class exam grades are related to homework success under the new Aplia format is a topic for future investigation.

NOTES

[1] Grove and Wasserman (2006) also note the paucity of research on the effectiveness of problem sets and practice exercises on student learning. Their research concludes that a grade incentive to practice economics raises exam scores for some but not all principles of micro students. Because of the nature of data they used, Grove and Wasserman were unable to estimate the effect of homework "performance" on student learning in micro principles classes. Pozo and Stull (2006) did have data on homework grades for principles of macro students, but their research did not address the linkage between exam scores and homework performance.

[2] Aplia is an educational technology company founded in 2000 by Stanford University economist Paul Romer. Aplia's on-line homework assignments, interactive tools, and experiments have been used at over 850 colleges and universities. Readers unfamiliar with the Aplia approach are encouraged to contact Aplia, Inc., 959 Skyway Rd., Suite 325, San Carlos, CA 94070 or visit their site www.Aplia.com for details and examples of Aplia products.

[3] The remaining questions are composed by the instructors and usually address a specific issue or concept covered during the class lectures.

REFERENCES

Ball, Sheryl; Eckel, Catherine and Rojas, Christian. "Technology Improves Learning in Large Principles of Economics Classes: Using Our WITS." *American Economic Review*, May 2006 (*Papers and Proceedings*), 96(2), pp. 442-46.

Brown, Bryon and Liedholm, Carl. "Can Web Courses Replace the Classroom in Principles of Microeconomics?" *American Economic Review*, May 2002 (*Papers and Proceedings*), 92(2), pp. 444-48.

Durden, Garey and Ellis, Larry. "The Effects of Attendance on Student Learning in Principles of Economics" *American Economic Review*, May 1995 (*Papers and Proceedings*), 85(2), pp. 343-46.

Grove, Wayne and Wasserman, Tim. "Incentives and Student Learning: A Natural Experiment with Economics Problem Sets" *American Economic Review,* May 2006 (*Papers and Proceedings*), 96(2), pp. 447-51.

Hansen, Lee; Salemi, Michael and Siegfried, John. "Use It or Lose It: Teaching Literacy in the Economics Principles Course" *American Economic Review*, May 2002 (*Papers and Proceedings*), 92(2), pp. 463-71.

Lo, Melody, Wong, Sunny and Mixon, Franklin. "Ranking Economics Journals, Economics Departments and Economists using Teaching-Focused Research Productivity" *Southern Economic Journal*, January 2008, 74(3), pp. 894-906.

Mixon, Franklin and Upadhyaya, Kamal. "A Citations-Based Appraisal of New Journals in Economics Education" *International Review of Economics Education*, June 2008, 7(1), pp. 36-46.

Nowell, Clifford and Alston, Richard. "I Thought I Got An A! Overconfidence Across The Economics Curriculum" *Journal of Economic Education*, Spring 2007, 38(2), pp. 131-42.

Pozo, Susan and Stull, Charles. "Requiring a Math Skills Unit: Results of a Randomized Experiment" *American Economic Review*, May 2006 (*Papers and Proceedings*), 96(2), pp. 437-41.

Schaur, Georg; Watts, Michael and Becker, William. "Assessment Practices and Trends in Undergraduate Economics Courses" *American Economic Review*, May 2008 (*Papers and Proceedings*), 98(2), pp. 552-56.

Sosin, Kim; Blecha, Betty; Agarwal, Rajshree; Bartlett, Robin and Daniel, Joseph. "Efficiency in the Use of Technology in Economic Education: Some Preliminary Results" *American Economic Review*, May 2004 (*Papers and Proceedings*), 94(2), pp. 253-58.

In: Expanding Teaching and Learning Horizons
Editors: F. G. Mixon, Jr. and R. J. Cebula
ISBN 978-1-60741-971-6

Chapter 7

STUDENT RESPONSE TO ATTENDANCE POLICIES IN PRINCIPLES COURSES: THE CARROT AND THE STICK

Linda S. Ghent and Marie Truesdell

INTRODUCTION

Economists believe that individuals respond to incentives. These incentives may be in the form of a reward for behavior that we wish to encourage or a punishment for behavior that is considered to be undesirable. In theory, these costs or benefits could be structured to achieve equal results. After all, the loss of potential benefits is an opportunity cost of the undesired behavior.

This paper examines the effects of two different policies on student attendance, one which provides a "reward" for attending class and one which "punishes" the student for not attending class. Two questions are addressed: (1) Do attendance policies in general alter student behavior? and (2) Is there a significant difference in the efficacy of each type of policy? The first question simply focuses on the strength of using an incentive structure to induce changes in classroom attendance. The second question allows us to see whether students can properly identify missed rewards as "costs" and respond in a manner similar to the way in which they would respond to a punishment policy.

BACKGROUND

Much of the literature on student behavior in courses with attendance policies can be found in psychology. Some economic studies look at the effects of attendance policies on student outcomes [see Marburger (2006) for example]. However, the focus in this study is on the difference in student response to rewards and punishments. If economists believe that individuals consider opportunity costs when making decisions, we should expect that our students respond to both positive and negative incentives in similar ways. Those responses are what are measured in this analysis.

Students may have distinct preferences concerning which types of policies that faculty members use to encourage them to attend class. Wilder et al. (2001) test what they call positive reinforcement methods to increase attendance where extra credit pop quizzes are offered in a psychology of learning course with 32 students. Since the quizzes were extra credit, there was no penalty for missing class [1]. Quizzes were randomly administered once a week for six weeks and then for two weeks no quizzes were given. Quizzes were then begun again for the final five weeks of the term. Students were informed of this plan at the beginning of the term. Attendance is measured as the number of students present during each class period. They find that attendance went from 63.4 percent in the first 6-week period to 52.1 percent for the two-week hiatus from quizzes and back up to 62.1 percent for the last 5-week period. A student survey was also administered concerning the students' opinions of the extra credit quizzes. Ninety-four percent of students stated that they liked the extra credit quizzes, with 69 percent reporting that they attended class more often because of the opportunity to gain extra credit points.

Hovell et al. (1979) also examines whether or not giving quizzes throughout the semester leads to increased attendance. Students from three different sections of an introductory child development course are studied. Each of the three classes had a different format to encourage attendance. One class was selected to take unit quizzes and four major exams, the second class reviewed graded quizzes and took four major exams, and the final group took only the four major exams.

Students who took quizzes were given credit based on their performance on the quiz, but those who just reviewed graded quizzes received full credit for that portion of their grade just by attending class. The other class was given credit only for their four exams. The results show that those in the class without quizzes had average attendance of 59 percent, those in the section which simply reviewed quizzes had an average attendance of 77 percent, and those who took the quizzes had an attendance average of 81 percent. An interesting fact that Hovell et al. report is that on days where there was not a quiz or test, attendance was significantly lower for all three groups; moreover, on these days the group taking only unit exams had the highest attendance. Additionally, they find a significantly lower attendance rate for all groups in the second half of the semester [2].

Shimoff and Catania (2001) investigate whether the simple act of recording attendance has positive effects even if the attendance is not included in the students' grade. In their study, an introductory psychology course with 132 students was split into two groups and students were assigned seats after the first quiz of the semester. Students were told that they were participating in an experiment testing attendance on quiz performance. Half of the students were told that their attendance would be recorded with a sign up sheet.

The other half of the students were counted each class period, but no record of individual attendance was made. Their results show that recording attendance on an individual basis increased attendance by approximately one third. On a survey asking students whether they thought that recording their presence had any affect on their attendance, both groups responded that they believed that recording attendance would have little or no effect on their actual attendance.

Again, in an attempt to find ways to increase attendance, McCutcheon (1988) ran three experiments in three sections of a general psychology course. In the first experiment, he had a cohort call a randomly selected group of students to let them know the professor wanted them to be successful in the course and to encourage their attendance.

Results show that the phone call had significant positive effects on attendance for those called. In the second experiment, the professor talked to selected students individually for 15 seconds to one minute. There was no significant difference in the attendance of these students when compared to a control group. The third experiment involved testing different attendance options on several sections to see their effects on attendance. One group was given six extra credit points at the beginning of the semester and one half of a point was taken away for each absence. Students in a second group were told that they could earn six extra credit points in increments of one half of a point for each day they attended class. Students in the third class were given three extra credit points to start and were told that they would be able to gain one quarter of a point for each day they were present. The fourth group (a control group) was told that attendance would be taken but these students were not given any opportunity for extra credit points.

All three groups were told of these attendance policies after the fifth meeting of the quarter. They were told that the instructor would be taking attendance randomly in 12 of remaining class periods. Group one had the lowest absence rate and group four had the highest, although the only significant difference was between groups one and four.

Some of the literature focuses on the different effects of positive (reward) and negative (punishment) reinforcement on attendance. Beaulieu and Sheffler (1988) compare attendance rates for students who are punished for not attending class with those who are rewarded for attending courses.

In two sections of an undergraduate business management course, 108 students were studied. In the first part of the class, student attendance was recorded without the instructor mentioning attendance. Just before the "baseline" period had ended, students were told that an attendance policy would be put in place to attempt to improve attendance. They were told they would be given an extra credit point for each day they attended class for (at that point) a potential increase of 27 points. After 14 days, students were told that the previous attendance policy had no change on attendance so the policy would be altered. Students would lose one point from their total for each class that was missed in the last 13 days in the term. Their results indicated no significant difference between these two policies.

Our Experiment

To examine the relative effectiveness of positive versus negative reinforcement techniques to encourage student attendance, the following experiment was designed. During the first semester, a student's attendance average was included as part of the student's grade. Thus, the student was "punished" for not attending class. In the second semester, the attendance policy was altered; students could use their attendance average as a substitution for their lowest unit examination score. In this case, the student was "rewarded" for showing up for class often. However, students who frequently missed class but performed well on exams were not penalized at all. In a third semester, no attendance policy was used but attendance was recorded each class period. Table 1 shows the breakdown of the students' grades for each semester. Note that the "stick" in the "punish" policy is equal to the "carrot" in the "reward" policy (15 percent of the student's final grade) [3].

Table 1. Breakdown of Students' Grades

"Punish" Policy		"Reward" Policy		No Attendance Policy	
3 unit exams	45%	4 unit exams	60%	4 unit exams	60%
Attendance	15%	Homework	15%	Homework	15%
Homework	15%	Final Exam	25%	Final Exam	25%
Final Exam	25%				
	100%		100%		100%

A Simple Model

Becker's time allocation (1965) and household production (1981) models provide the basic framework for our model. We start by assuming that students are utility maximizers with a utility function of

$$U=U(G, Z),$$

where G is the outcome of the course for the student (e.g. the grade earned or knowledge gained) and Z is an aggregate consumption good. Of course, G cannot be purchased in the marketplace and must be produced by the student using time along with other purchased inputs. In the production function,

$$G = g(x, t_{ic}, t_{oc}; E),$$

x represents purchased inputs (tuition, textbooks, etc.), t_{ic} represents time spent in class (class attendance), t_{oc} represents time spent studying outside of class, and E is a vector of environmental variables including ability, human capital, and social and physical climate. The student will then choose x, t_{ic}, t_{oc}, and Z to maximize his or her utility subject to income and time constraints.

The attendance policies discussed above will affect the student's decision by altering the marginal product of time spent in class (or alternatively the cost of missing class). Therefore, we expect that, compared to the semester with no attendance policy, students in either the class that rewarded attendance or the one that punished nonattendance will have higher attendance rates.

In addition, because the economic cost of missing class is the same under either attendance policy, we would expect the effects of each policy to be equal. However, the "reward" policy allows students to substitute time spent in class (t_{ic}) for time spent outside of class (t_{oc}), because students may drop their lowest unit exam grade and substitute their attendance average. Likewise, students may be able to substitute time outside of class for time in class when there is no attendance policy present. Thus, it is possible that the effects of these policies may vary across students who are more willing and able to make these substitutions [4].

Data

The data for the current study comes from several principles of economics courses taught at two midwestern institutions. The first is a medium-size public university with an enrollment of approximately 11,000 and the other is a relatively small private liberal arts college with an enrollment of around 1,300 students

. All of the sections examined in this study are taught by only one instructor at each of the two institutions. The courses taught were the second course in a two-course principles sequence [5].

At the beginning of each semester, students were given a survey that asked questions concerning gender, race, age, class standing, major, grade point average (GPA), and previous enrollment in other economics courses [6]. These data were then matched with the students' attendance averages at the end of each semester. Students were not told about the experiment for fear that such knowledge may alter their behavior.

Table 2 reports the sample means. The first column reports the means for the entire sample of students over the two semesters. The next three columns provide sample means by the type of attendance policy used.

For the entire sample, class attendance averaged over 90 percent. This number is much larger than that reported by most studies, but may in fact be due to the relatively small size of each section [7]. The average age of the students was 20, fewer than half were females, while the majority were white (84 percent). Almost half of the students (49 percent) were sophomores and a relatively small proportion of the students were freshmen or seniors. Two-thirds of the students plan on majoring in business, with another five percent interested in majoring in economics. Almost 70 percent of the students had previously taken the first principles course in the two-course sequence. Looking at the remaining three columns, we find that the attendance average across the two policies is very similar. In fact, a t-test indicates no significant difference between these values (p-value = 0.5386). Differences across the samples include the proportion of the students who were female (which varies from 34 to 58 percent), the proportion of students who were freshmen (which varies from two to 30 percent), and the proportion of our sample from the private college (which varies from 30 to 54 percent) [8].

OLS Results

The next step in the analysis is to see if we can determine how the presence of an attendance policy affects a student's attendance average. More specifically, we are interested in knowing if these two policies ("reward" and "punish") have similar effects on a student's attendance in our courses. Table 3 reports the results from an ordinary least-squares (OLS) regression with attendance average as the dependent variable. Independent variables included in the analysis are age, gender, race [9], class standing [10], GPA, whether the student is an economics or business major [11], whether the student is enrolled at the public or private institution, and the type of attendance policy used.

Table 2. Sample Means - By Attendance Policy (standard deviations in parentheses)

	Full Sample	"Punish"	"Reward"	No Attendance Policy
Attendance	90.16 (12.54)	90.61 (10.50)	91.76 (12.92)	88.63 (13.77)
Age	20.16 (2.64)	19.80 (1.39)	20.31 (1.97)	20.37 (3.68)
Female	0.44 (0.50)	0.34 (0.48)	0.58 (0.50)	0.44 (0.50)
Race:				
White	0.84 (0.37)	0.87 (0.34)	0.85 (0.36)	0.80 (0.40)
African-American	0.09 (0.29)	0.07 (0.26)	0.10 (0.30)	0.11 (0.31)
Hispanic	0.03 (0.16)	0.05 (0.22)	0.01 (0.11)	0.02 (0.13)
Asian	0.01 (0.10)	0.00 (0.00)	0.01 (0.11)	0.02 (0.13)
Other	0.03 (0.17)	0.01 (0.10)	0.03 (0.16)	0.05 (0.23)
Class:				
Freshman	0.15 (0.35)	0.02 (0.14)	0.09 (0.28)	0.30 (0.46)
Sophomore	0.49 (0.50)	0.58 (0.50)	0.54 (0.50)	0.39 (0.49)
Junior	0.27 (0.44)	0.30 (0.46)	0.30 (0.46)	0.22 (0.41)
Senior	0.08 (0.27)	0.09 (0.29)	0.05 (0.22)	0.08 (0.27)
Economics Major	0.05 (0.22)	0.04 (0.20)	0.04 (0.19)	0.07 (0.26)
Business Major	0.68 (0.47)	0.71 (0.46)	0.78 (0.42)	0.59 (0.49)
GPA:				
3.5-4.0	0.17 (0.38)	0.12 (0.33)	0.16 (0.37)	0.23 (0.42)
3.0-3.49	0.31 (0.46)	0.34 (0.48)	0.31 (0.47)	0.27 (0.45)
2.5-2.99	0.28 (0.45)	0.32 (0.47)	0.26 (0.44)	0.26 (0.44)
2.0-2.49	0.20 (0.40)	0.20 (0.40)	0.24 (0.43)	0.19 (0.39)
1.5-1.99	0.03 (0.18)	0.02 (0.14)	0.03 (0.16)	0.05 (0.23)
Other Econ Courses:				
Social Issues	0.15 (0.36)	0.18 (0.38)	0.19 (0.39)	0.10 (0.30)
1st Principles	0.69 (0.46)	0.75 (0.43)	0.61 (0.49)	0.70 (0.46)
Private School	0.41 (0.49)	0.30 (0.46)	0.38 (0.49)	0.54 (0.50)
"Punish"	0.34 (0.47)	----	----	----
"Reward"	0.28 (0.45)	----	----	----
N	288	97	80	111

Table 3. Regression Results - Full Sample

Variable	Coefficient (t-statistic)
Constant	85.29* (13.14)
Age	0.32 (1.06)
Female	2.91* (1.94)
Non-White	3.33** (1.75)
Upperclassman	-5.00* (-2.99)
Economics or Business Major	-0.55 (-0.34)
GPA:	
3.0-3.49	-0.36 (-0.17)
2.5-2.99	-4.25* (-1.94)
2.0-2.49	-6.47* (-2.73)
1.5-1.99	-18.44* (-4.45)
Private School	0.58 (0.40)
Type of Attendance Policy:	
"Reward"	3.13** (1.78)
"Punish"	2.99** (1.74)
R^2	.1613
N	288

* $\alpha<0.05$ ** $\alpha<0.10$.

As we can see in Table 3, the presence of an attendance policy increases attendance averages by about 3 percentage points. However, the type of policy used has no effect on outcome [12]. This is not surprising given the similar attendance averages across the two semesters when an attendance policy was in place and the results of Beaulieu and Sheffler (1988) discussed above.

Some of the other significant variables are of interest, however. Females and nonwhites have a significantly higher attendance average then do males and whites, while upperclassmen have a significantly lower attendance average than do underclassmen. This latter result may be the result of collegiate experience, where more experienced students may feel better able to gauge their need to attend class. Likewise, this result could indicate that upperclassmen face a higher opportunity cost of time because of their involvement in campus activities or because they are enrolled in more time-consuming courses [13].

The coefficients on the dummy variables for GPA are as expected. Relative to the students with a GPA greater than 3.5, students with a GPA between 2.5 and 2.99 have an attendance average that is more than four percentage points lower. Students with a GPA between 1.5 and 1.99 have an attendance average that is more than 18 points lower than those with a GPA above 3.5. In this case, GPA may reflect a student's prior level of academic effort including class attendance. Although not a perfect measure, including this variable in the analysis provides some way of controlling for individual student motivation.

The most disappointing coefficient is the insignificant coefficient on major. We hypothesized that students majoring in either business or economics would have some interest in the material presented in these courses and would therefore have higher attendance averages. Alas, this was not the case as the coefficient is negative and insignificant. This could be due to the fact that students are enrolled in the course only because their major requires them to. Conversely, students in majors other than economics or business may feel less familiar or comfortable with the material taught in economics courses and thus are more likely to attend class to ensure a better understanding.

DIFFERENCES ACROSS ATTENDANCE POLICIES

To examine whether the effects of the attendance policies varies across student characteristics, OLS estimation on attendance averages was performed separately for each policy (including no policy) [14]. The results are in Table 4.

Table 4. Regression Results - By Policy[a]

"Punish"	"Reward"	Variable	No Attendance Policy
116.71* (7.18)	76.10* (4.26)	Constant	79.02* (8.85)
-1.09 (-1.32)	1.20 (1.32)	Age	0.47 (1.18)
-0.98 (-0.48)	7.00* (2.31)	Female	2.53 (0.94)
3.01 (1.15)	3.18 (0.74)	Non-White	3.55 (1.06)
-1.26 (-0.57)	-7.28** (-1.89)	Upperclassman	-6.44* (-2.02)
1.68 (2.12)	-6.88** (-1.78)	Economics or Business Major	-0.56 (0.20)
		GPA:	
-0.56 (-0.19)	-4.52 (-1.01)	3.0-3.49	2.95 (0.80)
-7.64* (-2.56)	-4.89 (-1.02)	2.5-2.99	-0.74 (-0.20)
-7.55* (3.25)	-5.72 (-1.19)	2.0-2.49	-6.75 (-1.59)
-41.03* (6.27)	-20.34* (-2.05)	1.5-1.99	-11.27** (-1.80)
-0.98 (-0.49)	-1.33 (-0.43)	Private School	3.50 (1.33)
.4135	.2077	R^2	.1553
97	80	N	111
		* $\alpha<0.05$ ** $\alpha<0.10$	

[a]T-statistics are in parentheses.

Table 5. Sample Means - By Institution Type (standard deviations in parentheses)

	Full Sample	Public	Private
Attendance	90.16	90.43	89.78
	(12.54)	(13.44)	(11.18)
Age	20.16	20.17	20.15
	(2.64)	(3.11)	(1.77)
Female	0.44	0.39	0.52
	(0.50)	(0.49)	(0.50)
Race:			
White	0.84	0.85	0.82
	(0.37)	(0.36)	(0.39)
African-American	0.09	0.08	0.12
	(0.29)	(0.27)	(0.32)
Hispanic	0.03	0.03	0.03
	(0.16)	(0.17)	(0.02)
Asian	0.01	0.02	0.00
	(0.10)	(0.13)	(0.00)
Other	0.03	0.02	0.04
	(0.17)	(0.15)	(0.20)
Class:			
Freshman	0.15	0.12	0.18
	(0.35)	(0.33)	(0.38)
Sophomore	0.49	0.53	0.45
	(0.50)	(0.50)	(0.50)
Junior	0.27	0.28	0.25
	(0.44)	(0.45)	(0.44)
Senior	0.08	0.06	0.10
	(0.27)	(0.24)	(0.30)
Economics Major	0.05	0.04	0.07
	(0.22)	(0.20)	(0.25)
Business Major	0.68	0.70	0.66
	(0.47)	(0.46)	(0.48)
GPA:			
3.5-4.0	0.17	0.18	0.17
	(0.38)	(0.38)	(0.38)
3.0-3.49	0.31	0.33	0.28
	(0.46)	(0.47)	(0.45)
2.5-2.99	0.28	0.28	0.28
	(0.45)	(0.45)	(0.45)
2.0-2.49	0.20	0.20	0.21
	(0.40)	(0.40)	(0.41)
1.5-1.99	0.03	0.01	0.07
	(0.18)	(0.11)	(0.25)
Other Econ Courses:			
Social Issues	0.15	0.11	0.20
	(0.36)	(0.32)	(0.40)
	Full Sample	Public	Private
1st Principles	0.69	0.95	0.34
	(0.46)	(0.23)	(0.47)
Private School	0.41	----	----
	(0.49)		
"Punish"	0.34	0.40	0.24
	(0.47)	(0.49)	(0.43)
"Reward"	0.28	0.30	0.25
	(0.45)	(0.46)	(0.44)
N	288	169	119

In a similar fashion, the negative and significant coefficient for economics or business majors during the semester with the "reward" policy may mean that these students (because of prior knowledge or interest) may be more able to substitute time outside of class for time in class. If this is the case, we should also expect a significant negative coefficient for economics or business majors in the estimation for the semester when there was no attendance policy. As you can see in Table 4, the coefficient is negative but not significant.

DIFFERENCES ACROSS INSTITUTION TYPE

As mentioned above, this experiment was performed at a medium-size public university and a relatively small private liberal arts college. Because the students attending these two schools may differ in important characteristics, we have examined the effects of these attendance policies at these two institutions separately. Table 5 presents summary statistics for the sample as a whole as well as for each school type.

Surprisingly, there are few differences across these two institutions. The private liberal arts college has a higher proportion of female students and a lower proportion of Caucasian students. In addition, a much smaller percentage of students at the private school had taken the first Principles course in the sequence. However, more students at the private school had taken an introductory "Social Issues" economics course for non-majors.

Table 6 reports the OLS results for each institution type. There are notable differences in the gender and race coefficients. For example, females and nonwhites both have significantly higher attendance averages at the private college, but gender and race have no impact on attendance at the public university. In addition, the effects of lower grade point averages on attendance appear to be larger at the public university.

Table 6. Regression Results - By Institution Type[a]

Variable	Public	Private
Constant	81.55* (9.82)	98.82* (8.40)
Age	0.55 (1.50)	-0.45 (-0.76)
Female	0.96 (0.43)	5.48* (2.90)
Non-White	2.36 (0.83)	6.27* (2.57)
Upperclassman	-5.96* (-2.43)	-4.27** (2.28)
Economics or Business Major	-1.42 (-0.56)	0.49 (0.24)
GPA:		
3.0-3.49	0.61 (0.20)	-2.31 (-0.80)
2.5-2.99	-7.48* (-2.37)	0.34 (0.12)
2.0-2.49	-7.27* (-2.15)	-5.66** (-1.67)
1.5-1.99	-26.21* (-2.74)	-16.57* (-4.00)
Type of Attendance Policy:		
"Reward"	5.32* (2.01)	1.13 (0.62)
"Punish"	5.79* (2.35)	-0.56 (-0.25)
R^2	.1683	.2939
N	169	119
* α<0.05 ** α<0.10		

[a]T-statistics are in parentheses.

Of greater interest are the coefficients for the attendance policies. These coefficients are positive and significant for students at the public university, but not for students at the private college. It appears that students at the private college did not respond to the attendance policies. Although the size difference between sections at the public university and the private college is small (28.3 students versus 24.8 students), students at the private college may be more accustomed to smaller class sizes and thus believe that their attendance is more easily noticed by their professors.

An F-test was performed to examine whether or not pooling across these institution types is appropriate. Specifically, the null hypothesis that the two sets of regression coefficients in Table 6 are equal cannot be rejected at any conventional significance level. This is not surprising since the coefficient on "private" was insignificant in Table 3 [16].

CONCLUSIONS

The results from our analysis indicate that the presence of an attendance policy increases a student's attendance average. However, the type of policy used ("reward" versus "punish") does not matter as each policy simply raises the economic cost of missing class. Thus, students viewed the incentives in similar fashions and acted accordingly. Interestingly, students at the private liberal arts college did not respond to the attendance policies.

While attendance is not the most important measure of student outcome in a course, it is vital that educators understand how classroom policies can alter student behavior. More importantly, as economists, it is rewarding to see that our students respond in ways that economic theory predicts. Students do respond to incentives and it is opportunity costs that matter.

NOTES

[1] Of course, there is an opportunity cost in the form of extra credit points foregone.

[2] Van Blerkon (1992) also documents a drop in the attendance rate as the semester progresses. He suggests that this result may be due to a number of factors including impending deadlines for class assignments, a better sense of how necessary attendance is for good performance, or student discouragement if they are performing poorly.

[3] At the public university, the class times were constant across the three semesters. At the private college, class times varied slightly, but all sections met during late morning or early afternoon.

[4] It is likely that students who are more risk averse will opt to increase their attendance under the "reward" policy because exam performance is often uncertain, while class attendance is completely controlled by the student.

[5] At the public university, the second course of the sequence is the principles of microeconomics course. The first course in the sequence (principles of macroeconomics) is a prerequisite and most students take these courses in the order listed in the catalog. At the private institution, the second course in the sequence is also the principles of microeconomics course. In this case, the first course is not an enforced prerequisite for the second.

[6] Unfortunately, data concerning alternative uses of time (work, other courses, athletics, or family obligations) were not collected at the time of the survey. While these variables are important in the determination of attendance, attendance policies raise the *relative* cost of missing class regardless of these alternative uses of time. Because our focus is on the effects of these policies, the omission of this information is likely to be small.

[7] The average section size at the public university was 28.3 students, while the average section size at the private institution was 24.8 students.

[8] Differences across institution type are addressed below.

[9] Race has been divided into only two categories (white and nonwhite) because of the small sample sizes of Asians, Hispanics, and individuals who reported "other" as race.

[10]Because such a small portion of the sample are freshmen and seniors, we have combined freshmen with sophomores (underclassmen) and juniors and seniors (upperclassmen).

[11]Given the small number of economics majors, the two majors (business and economics) have been combined.

[12]This is confirmed by an F-test with the null hypothesis that the coefficients for "reward" and "punish" are equal. The F-statistic (1, 275) is equal to 0.01 with a p-value of 0.9372. Thus, we cannot reject the null hypothesis and conclude that the two coefficients are equal.

[13]This could also be caused by a sample selection problem. These are upperclassmen taking a course that is generally considered to be at the freshman- or sophomore-level.

[14]It is in this section of our analysis where we would like to have information on alternative uses of time. After all, the student's other time commitments will affect his or her ability to substitute time outside of class for time in class.

[15]The end result of this substitution (the effect on performance) will be examined in a future paper.

[16]The calculated F-statistic is 1.25 with (13, 262) degrees of freedom which is much lower than the critical value of 2.18 ($\alpha = 0.05$).

REFERENCES

Beaulieu, R.P. and D.E. Sheffler. 1985. Controlling absenteeism: reward versus punishment contingencies. *Journal of Instructional Psychology* 12: 72-79.

Becker, Gary S. 1965. A theory of the allocation of time. *Economic Journal* 75: 493-517.

Becker, Gary S. 1981. *A treatise on the family*. Cambridge, Massachusetts: Harvard University Press.

Hovell, Melbourne F., Randy 1. Williams, and George Semb. 1979. Analysis of undergraduates' attendance at class meetings with and without grade-related contingencies: a contrast effect. *The Journal of Educational Research* 73: 50-53.

Marburger, Daniel R. 2006. Does mandatory attendance improve student performance? *Journal of Economic Education* 37: 148-155.

McCutcheon, Lynn. 1988. Three experimental attempts to reduce absenteeism from college classes. *Community-Junior College Quarterly of Research and Practice* 12: 91-97.

Shimoff, Eliot and A. Charles Catania. 2001. "Effects of recording attendance on grades in introductory psychology." *Teaching of Psychology* 28, 192-195.

Van Blerkom, Malcolm L. 1992. Class attendance in undergraduate courses. *Journal of Psychology* 1265: 487-485.

Wilder, David A., William A. Flood, and Wibecke Stromsnes. 2001. The use of random extra credit quizzes to increase student attendance. *Journal of Instructional Psychology* 28: 117-120.

In: Expanding Teaching and Learning Horizons
Editors: F. G. Mixon, Jr. and R. J. Cebula
ISBN 978-1-60741-971-6

Chapter 8

HEY, SAILOR! WANT TO GET A HIGH SCHOOL DIPLOMA?*

Jennie W. Wenger

INTRODUCTION

The last thirty years have seen substantive education reform at the high school level. In particular, attention to the standards and curricula of public high schools increased sharply in the wake of the publication of *A Nation at Risk* (Gardner et al. 1983). This report sharply criticized graduation standards in public schools and argued that the decreasing performance of high school students would negatively affect America's world standing. Additionally, this report included a number of detailed recommendations to raise standards. For example, a specific recommendation for the curriculum including 4 years (or "Carnegie units") of English, 3 years of social studies, science, and mathematics; college bound students were advised to include 2 years of foreign language study as well [1]. During the same time period, states began enacting "exit exams"—standardized tests that students were required to pass, in addition to all coursework, before graduation. These two reforms provide the primary routes states have used to tighten graduation standards over the last 20 to 30 years. Concurrent with heightened graduation standards, the number of young adults earning General Educational Development (GED) certificates, rather than high school diplomas, increased sharply.

In the near future, more states plan to enact exit exams. Also, the most recent proposals under the No Child Left Behind (NCLB) Legislation suggest that the federal government is about to become more involved in secondary education, perhaps even setting preferred Carnegie Unit (CU) requirements to certify students from particular high schools for

* I am indebted to many of my colleagues for their assistance on this project. In particular, David Gregory formulated the Navy dataset, Diana Lien analyzed some of the data for an earlier version of this paper, and Aline Quester provided insightful comments. Dinah Sunday edited an earlier version of the paper while Pat Blackmore prepared the earlier version for dissemination. Thanks also to Kathy Christie of the Education Commission of the States for providing detailed notes on past high school graduation requirements in a cheerful, timely manner. Also, this paper benefitted from the comments of the participants at the Western Economic Association Meetings. Any errors are, of course, my own. The opinions reflected in this paper are also my own, rather than those of CNA or the Department of the Navy.

scholarships (Dillon 2006). In light of these changes, understanding the impact of increasing graduation standards on typical high school students is crucial. Despite considerable disagreement among studies to date, the literature does suggest that reforms are likely to affect different students in different ways.

In this research, we use a unique dataset including multiple measures of workplace performance on a very large number of students who did not attend college—the records of those who enlist in the Navy over a 10-year period. Using this dataset allows us to glean information about quality and performance that generally is not available on national surveys; additionally, our dataset includes some 450,000 people and thus provides a very large sample. We supplement these findings with information from the 2000 Census, as well as state-level measures, to measures the total effects of policies on all young adults. By comparing and contrasting the results from these datasets, we are able to comment upon the relative effects of graduation policies with particular attention to a group likely to be influenced most by these policies.

Our findings for the population as a whole indicate that education reforms have subtle but important effects on the probabilities that people will complete high school, attend college, and participate in the labor force. Effects on wages, however, are small. We find evidence of sorting effects in some cases—policies may help some students while harming others. Our state-level analysis indicates that graduation standards do affect the proportion of young people who earn a GED rather than a high school diploma. Finally, our findings for the Navy indicate that strengthening Carnegie unit requirements is likely to hinder, rather than help, job performance, while the increasing use of exit exams has some positive effects.

BACKGROUND

As shown in table 1, only 5 states had exit exams prior to the publication of *A Nation at Risk*. However, states have enacted these exams at a fairly steady rate; by 2008, 25 state, including 70% of all public school students, will include such exams as a graduation requirement [2].

Table 1. Exit exam requirements by state, current and planned

Year	States	Total with exit exam
By 1984	FL, GA, HI, NV, NJ, NC	6
By 1990	AL, LA, MD, MS, NM, NY, SC, TN, TX, VA	15 (HI abolished exam in 2000)
By 2004	AK, IN, MA, MN, OH	20
Planned by 2008	AZ, CA, ID, UT, WA	25
No exam	(All others)	25

Sources: Berliner and Amrein (2002), Alabama Department of Education (2003), Gayler et al. (2004), California Department of Education website, Center on Education Policy (2003), Jacob (2001), Hawaii Department of Education website.

The standard high school graduation exam is first administered in the tenth grade, and most states give students multiple opportunities to take the exam. Although the exit exams often require knowledge of material at or below the 10th grade level, there is some evidence that the difficulty of the tests tends to increase over time (Achieve Inc 2004, Center on Education Policy 2003). Despite the historically low difficulty level of exit exams, significant numbers of students do not pass (Center on Education Policy 2003). In addition, if exit exams influence the decision to drop out of high school, exit exams could be associated with an increase in the number of GED recipients. Of course, exit exams also could raise the quality of high school graduates.

The research on whether exit exams influence students' propensity to drop out has produced mixed results. Some studies find no association between exit exams and high school completion rates (i.e., Carnoy and Loeb 2002). Other researchers have found that dropout behavior *is* influenced by the presence of exit exams—in particular, that exit exams have negative effects, at least in the cases of low-achieving students and more difficult exit exams. For example, Jacob (2001) finds that low-achieving students in states with exit exams are 25 percent more likely to drop out than comparable students in states without exams. Comparing the difficulty of exams across states, Warren et al. (2004) find that the high school completion rates were 1.2 percent lower in states with "minimum competency" exams and 3.2 percent lower for states with "more difficult" exams when compared with states without exit exams. Dee (2003) finds a negative effect on high school completion for black men. At the same time, there are some indications that exit exams have positive effects on achievement and labor market outcomes of those who do complete high school [3].

As shown in figure 1, both the number and the type of Carnegie units earned by high school graduates have changed over time [4]. The increases have come largely within "academic" subjects (i.e., math as opposed to vocational education) [5]. Specifically, the average high school graduate today leaves school having taken 1 more math course (most likely a course requiring Algebra), one-half more English course, 1 more science course, and 1 more foreign language course than the typical graduate in 1980. [6]. The number of vocational courses fell slightly over the period; the total number of credits increased by about 4.5 (National Center for Education Statistics 2004). Such increased coursework should help to prepare students for exit exams and is likely to increase the AFQT score of the typical high school graduate. Although CU requirements have been the focus of less research than exit exams, most of the existing research suggests the requirements prove discouraging to some students while less research finds positive outcomes from increased requirements (see Lillard and DeCicca 2001, Dee 2003).

Despite the increase in CUs earned over time, most students in nearly all states are required to earn fewer units than was recommended by *A Nation at Risk*. But there are indications that, through No Child Left Behind, CU requirements will receive more attention in the near future (Dillon 2006).

The General Educational Development (GED) certificate has become an important credential for those who do not complete a traditional high school diploma. The GED program began during World War II as a route to certification for the many returning veterans who had not completed high school before enlistment; by passing the GED, these veterans could take advantage of the GI Bill and go directly to college. However, states soon began allowing non-veterans to take the test [7]. Over the last 20 years, there has been a substantial increase in the number and proportion of young people (age 19 or younger) who earn GED certificates rather than high school diplomas. For example in 1993, 157,000 such young people earned GEDs; by 2000, the number had increased by roughly 40 percent to more than 217,000 while the number of high school graduates increased by no more than 15 percent [8].

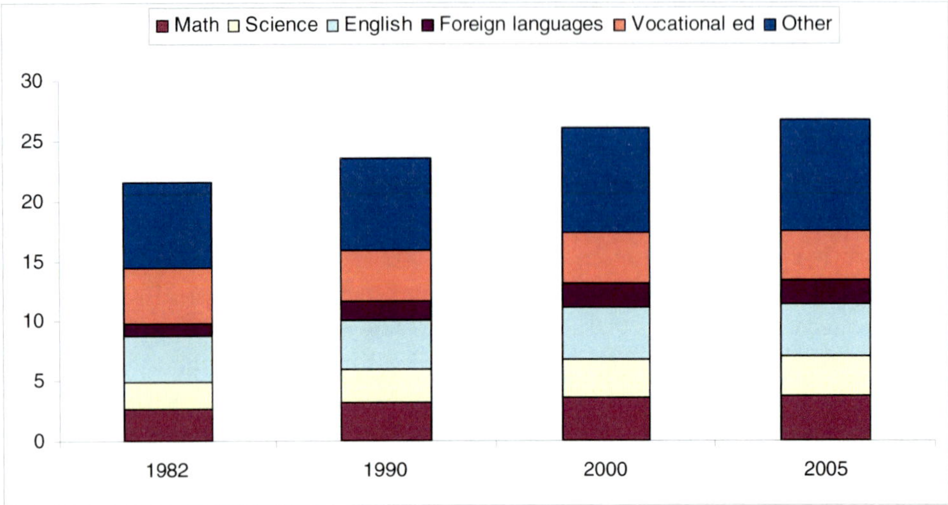

Figure 1. Carnegie units earned by graduation high school Seniors.

Although many people who receive GEDs consider themselves high school graduates, substantial research indicates that a GED is *not* the equivalent of a traditional high school diploma [9]. The definitive research remains that of Cameron and Heckman (1993), who found that GED recipients earned less overall, were less likely to be employed, earned less while employed, and had higher job turnover than high school graduates.

A number of studies indicate that GED-holders also have poorer outcomes than high school diploma graduates in postsecondary education. A Wisconsin study found that GED-holders have lower grades and a higher chance of dropping out of college/university than high school diploma graduates (Quinn and Haberman 1986). Cameron and Heckman (1993) found similar results for a national sample. These findings hold despite the fact that GED-holders seem to have cognitive abilities that are relatively close to high school graduates, especially the group of high school graduates who do not attend college (Boesel et al. 1998, Carneiro and Heckman 2004).

Moreover, this increase in GED holders is not readily apparent from glancing at statistics on U.S. educational attainment; it is the norm to track the number who completed high school through graduation *or an equivalent certificate* versus dropouts but not to distinguish between traditional high school diplomas and alternate credentials [10]. We plot the ratio of new, young GED-holders to every hundred new high school diploma graduates in figure 2. The large drop in GED recipiency between 2000 and 2001 stems from a re-design of the tests. This drop occurred across age groups.

Accepting the difference between outcomes of GED-holders and high school graduates, many researchers instead focus on a different question: Given that a student decides to leave school, does acquiring a GED help the person either to acquire more education or to attain higher earnings? To this question, the answer is a qualified "yes." Murnane, Willett and Boudet (1997), for example, find that dropouts who earn a GED are more likely to attend college, and to get training, than other dropouts. However, the probability that a GED-holder will attend college is relatively low. In a review of the literature, Tyler (2002) cites several other studies consistent with this finding and summarizes the research as finding that GED benefits (as measured by wage increases) accrue gradually over time rather than immediately, and that the largest wage gains go to those who have relatively weak cognitive skills.

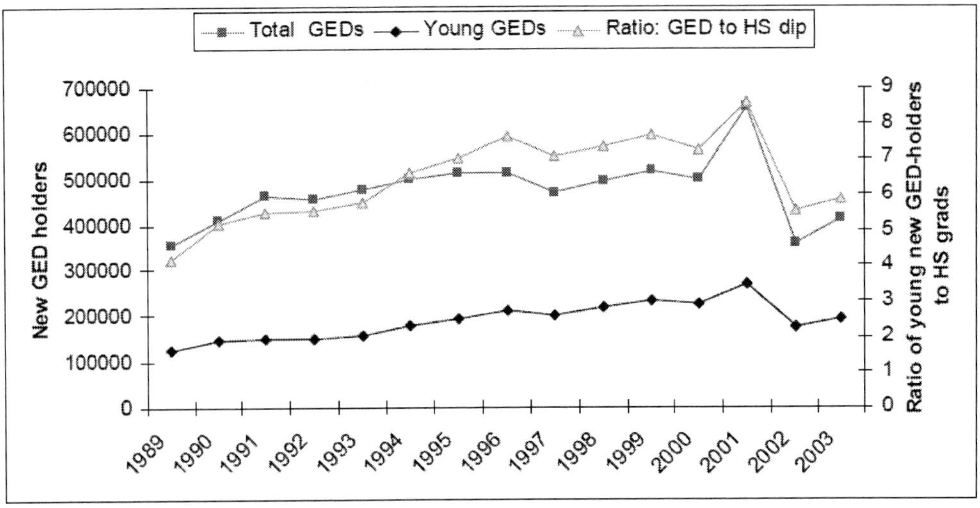

Figure 2. GED-holders and others.

However, researchers also note important differences, on average, between GED recipients and other dropouts. As noted by Tyler (2002) as well as Boesel et al. (1998), GED-holders are relatively advantaged; they have more years of schooling, higher standardized test scores, and more advantaged backgrounds than other dropouts. The findings of Cawley, Heckman and Vytlacil (2001) suggest that male GED-holders have cognitive abilities similar to those of high school graduates who do *not* attend college. In fact, these researchers find that the wage differences between male high school graduates and GED-holders are *not* related to cognitive ability but instead are related to different non-cognitive factors (behaviors). Similarly, Carneiro and Heckman (2001) note that male GED-holders actually have higher levels of such negative behaviors as fighting in school, as well as shoplifting and various other illegal actions, than other male dropouts; these authors suggest that the GED essentially selects those dropouts who possess relatively high cognitive skills but who also have relatively high levels of behavioral problems. Boesel et al. (1998) note that GED-holders, men in particular, seem to have problems of persistence—first in high school, but also in the military, postsecondary education, and the labor market.

Finally, research suggests that state-level policies concerning the GED program induce some students to drop out of high school (Tyler 2002, Chaplin 2002, Lillard 2004, Haney 2000). The size of the effect is uncertain, partly because over the last 10 to 15 years states (and American Council on Education, the governing body of the GED) changed GED policies while states simultaneously changed a number of other education policies. For example, Lillard and DeCicca (2001) note that required Carnegie units increased over the same period, and Tyler (2002) posits that the relatively large effects linked to state-level policies (such as small changes in the GED fee) found by Chaplin (2002) as well as Lillard and DeCicca

(2001) are consistent with omitted variable bias; the most likely cause is the difficulty of controlling for other state-level education policies.

The findings on military performance of GED-holders accord very well with those on civilian performance. Those who enlist in the Navy sign a contract for a specific term of service (most often 4 years). However, many who enlist do not complete their first term, instead leaving the Navy early for a variety of reasons. Some who leave the Service early do so for reasons beyond their control, such as physical injury or disability; others officially leave the enlisted Navy to enter Officer training programs. However, the vast majority who leave before the end of their initial term of service ("attrite") do so for reasons that can be broadly classified as "failure to adapt." Specific reasons include, for example, various types of misconduct, patterns of minor infractions, drug use, or other "discreditable incidents" as well as court martial or conviction in a civil court case [11].

There is strong evidence that education credentials are good predictors of attrition. Specifically, substantial evidence indicates that, across the four Services and over long time periods, those who enlist with GEDs (as well as those who enlist with other alternate credentials) are much less likely to complete their initial obligation than those who enlist with high school diplomas [12]. Attrition is very expensive for the Navy because new enlistees must be recruited and trained to replace those who leave without fulfilling their obligation. In an attempt to minimize attrition all credentials are classified using a tier system based mainly upon historical attrition rates.

As shown in table 2, a high school diploma is considered tier 1 while a GED is the most common credential in tier 2. The Navy (as well as the other Services) sharply limits the number who may enter with alternate credentials and place additional requirements on those who enlist with tier 2 or 3 credentials.

Those who enlist with an alternate credential generally must score a minimum of 50 on the Armed Forces Qualification Test (AFQT); this ensures that the average level of cognitive ability of dropouts and those holding GEDs in the military is actually higher than the average level of cognitive ability of high school diploma graduates (as measured by the AFQT) [13]. Despite this potential mitigating factor, attrition of those holding GEDs remains substantially higher than attrition of those holding high school diplomas. Such attrition for "failure to adapt" may be viewed as a measure of the negative behaviors evidenced in civilian GED-holders.

To summarize the research on graduation standards, exit exams have been shown to have both positive and negative outcomes. Carnegie unit standards, which seem to have the potential to better prepare students for work and further education, also evidence some negative outcomes. Some researchers, although not all, have found that both policies can "push" students out of school. More research exists about the GED; in general, it seems that high school dropouts gain from earning the credential although there is substantial evidence that lowering GED passing standards has the effect of "pulling" some students out of high school. While GED-holders have similar achievement to high school graduates who do not attend college, there is evidence that GED-holders differ in terms of non-cognitive factors (i.e., behavior). The evidence from the performance of GED-holders in the military accords with this.

The evidence of negative outcomes, from CU standards in particular, suggests that standards are not implemented in a straightforward manner. It is fairly clear that increased graduation standards are likely to raise the cost of graduation to the "marginal" student—the student who has a good, but not assured, chance of completing all coursework and passing a graduation exam. However, it is also likely that graduation standards increase the achievement level of such "marginal" students. In fact, it is possible that graduation standards will increase the average achievement level of both graduates and non-graduates. Consider the enactment of an exit exam, testing material at the 10th grade level (and thus, more rigorous than many).

Table 2. Navy classification of education credentials

Credential	Tier
High school diploma	1
Adult education certificate	1
1 semester of college (no high school diploma)	1
GED	2
Other credential: Correspondence diploma, occupational-vocational certificate	2
No credential ("dropout")	3

Some students who would otherwise complete high school are likely to fail the exam, and thus not to graduate. Other students are likely to work harder than otherwise, barely pass the test, and therefore graduate. The graduates, then, will have higher levels of achievement (and be fewer in number) than without the exam. The non-graduates will also have higher average levels of achievement, and be larger in number. In this example, it is clear that the effects of reforms should be largest on the marginal student. As argued by Betts and Costrell (2001), increased standards will have little effect on the highest and lowest achievers, affecting primarily those in the middle.

Research on graduation standards focuses on high school completion and standardized test gains; there is little evidence of how these reforms affect students in the labor market. Because many students enter college before working full-time, and many others "churn" through several employers in their first few years in the labor market, it can be difficult to tie reforms to specific outcomes. However, Dee (2003) uses Census data to explore the impacts of education reforms (specifically, of exit exams and CU requirements), and finds more nuanced results by looking at high school graduation rates, college attendance rates, and earnings.

We use a very similar technique with data from the 2000 (as opposed to the 1990) Census. But we also utilize a second unique dataset, which allows us to observe on-the-job performance of a large number of youth who do not attend college. Specifically, we use tracking files to follow those who enlist in either the US Navy before attending college. Using this dataset allows us to glean information about job performance that is missing from national surveys (such as the Current Population Series), and to look at a far larger sample of youth than is available in other datasets (such as the National Longitudinal Survey of Youth, High School and Beyond, the National Education Longitudinal Study of 1988). Moreover, we argue that the Navy dataset includes the "marginal" student; there are both high school graduates and non-graduates in our sample but Navy enlistees include neither the college-bound nor those with the lowest levels of achievement.

Data and Methodology

We utilize three data sources. As a first step, we use Census data to look at how changes in public education policies affect *all* young adults [14]. We focus our attention on the increased use of exit exams and Carnegie unit (CU) requirements, as well as on GED policies. Using Census data, we examine how the likelihood that each person will complete high school, attend college, and work (or search for work) differs depending upon graduation requirements. We also ask whether otherwise similar people earn more or less based upon the education policies in effect during their schooling. (See appendix A for more information on matching individuals to public education policies in place during their schooling).

The Census data are useful because they allow us to measure the impact of education reforms on the entire population. However, Census data contain no details about job performance beyond measures such as labor force participation and total earnings; additionally, the Census data do not allow us to differentiate between high school graduates and GED-holders. Therefore, we supplement our analysis with state-level data to determine how graduation requirements affect the number of young GED-holders in each state.

Finally, we utilize Navy data to examine how job performance varies based upon these same graduation requirements. Our Navy data allow us to track detailed measures of achievement and job performance. We link Navy enlistees to policies that were in place when they attended high school and test the theory that education policies affect the job performance of these recruits. Because of the likely sorting effects of these policies, we examine graduates and non-graduates separately.

It is common to use wages as a measure of productivity or job performance. While those in the Navy who perform better are likely to be promoted somewhat faster, early career wages provide only a very weak signal of recruits' relative quality. This is because wages are based upon paygrade and time in the Navy; for example, all who are E-3s in their second year of service receive identical base pay [15]. Other pays differ, but often do not depend upon job performance; for example, those with dependents and those stationed in more expensive areas receive higher housing allowances. However, using Navy data avoids several problems common in civilian data; first, while many young people in the civilian sector work part-time and spend periods unemployed, those in the Navy do not experience unemployment [16]. Second, the Navy data include a number of potential quality/job performance measures. For example, the data include a standardized test score (the AFQT score) on all enlistees; also, records include waivers required, and the reasons behind such waivers. Finally, records include a final measure of job performance: attrition, as well as the reason for attrition.

To model our outcomes of interest, we use the Census data and the Navy data in somewhat similar manners. First, we use our Census data to estimate the probability of completing high school (or earning a GED or other credential that the person views as equivalent) [17]. We also look at the probability of attending college. Finally, we consider how education reforms affect the probabilities of these events, as well as the likelihood of working (or looking for work), and average weekly earnings [18]

For each out come of interest, we estimate a logit model: [19]

$$\Pr(Y_{ist} = 1) = F(\beta X_{ist} + \pi G_{st} + \psi E_{st} + \phi C_{st} + \varpi STATE_{st} + \upsilon_{st} + \eta_t)$$

where:

Y = individual-level outcome (i.e., high school completion)
X = individual-level characteristics, such as gender
G = state-level GED policies
E = dummy variable that signifies whether a state, in any given year, had an exit exam
C = a measure of Carnegie units required for graduation by each state in each year
STATE = a vector of state-level characteristics likely to influence educational attainment, such as per-pupil expenditures at public elementary and secondary schools or the unemployment rate.

We match people to state-level education policies based upon the policies in effect when the people were 17 years of age. Except where noted, all of our models include state fixed effects to account for time invariant state-specific characteristics. In addition, we include year fixed effects to account for non-state-specific changes over time.

We define our CU requirements as follow: the state is considered to have a "basic" CU requirement it if requires at least 3 CUs of English, 2 of Social Studies, and 1 each of Math and Science; this is the standard suggested and tested by Dee (2003). The state is considered to have a "strict" CU requirement if it requires at least 4 CUs of English, and 3 of Math, Science, and Social Studies; this is the standard recommended in *A Nation at Risk*. See appendix A for details on the sources of our state-level policy measures and other state-level variables.

RESULTS

As shown in table 3, our Census sample includes information on over 1.3 million young adults, which weights to represent nearly 28 million people. Nearly 87 percent have completed high school; over 58 percent have attended college and about 70 percent are in the labor force. Over 40 percent were required to pass an exit exam; the vast majority faced a basic CU requirement, but only about 10 percent faced a strict CU requirement [20].

Of greater interest are the coefficients for the attendance policies. These coefficients are positive and significant for students at the public university, but not for students at the private college. It appears that students at the private college did not respond to the attendance policies. Although the size difference between sections at the public university and the private college is small (28.3 students versus 24.8 students), students at the private college may be more accustomed to smaller class sizes and thus believe that their attendance is more easily noticed by their professors.

An F-test was performed to examine whether or not pooling across these institution types is appropriate. Specifically, the null hypothesis that the two sets of regression coefficients in Table 6 are equal cannot be rejected at any conventional significance level. This is not surprising since the coefficient on "private" was insignificant in Table 3 [16].

Table 3. Descriptive Statistics, Census Sample and Navy Sample

Variable	Mean	Std dev	Min	Max
CENSUS DATA [21]				
Age	23.9	2.63	20	28
Male	0.50	0.50	0	1
White	0.76	0.43	0	1
Black	0.15	0.35	0	1
Asian/PI	0.015	0.12	0	1
American Indian	0.011	0.11	0	1
Other	0.066	0.25	0	1
Hispanic	0.094	0.29	0	1
Completed HS	0.865	0.34	0	1
Attended college	0.582	0.49	0	1
In labor force	0.709	0.45	0	1
Weekly earnings [22]	$530.75	$1,100.01	$0.09	$369,453
Moved since birth	0.31	0.46	0	1
State has exit exam	0.42	0.49	0	1
State has basic CU requirement	0.85	0.36	0	1
State has strict CU requirement	0.11	0.31	0	1
Number of observations	1,305,668 weighted to 27,704,732			
NAVY DATA [23]				
High school graduate (HSDG)	0.89	0.31	0	1
GED-holder	0.034	0.18	0	1
Any NHSDG	0.11	0.31	0	1
Male	0.83	0.38	0	1
Age	18.8	1.1	17	21
AFQT score	59.2	18.4	31	99
Any waiver	0.24	.43	0	1
Serious waiver	0.089	0.29	0	1
12-month attrition	0.20	.40	0	1
24-month attrition	0.28	.45	0	1
36-month attrition	0.35	.48	0	1
12-month attrition, HSDGs	0.12	0.18	0	1
12-month attrition, NHSDGs	0.31	0.46	0	1
Number of observations	470,071			

Table 3 also shows some descriptive statistics on our Navy sample of nearly 500,000 enlistees. Navy enlistees are slightly more likely that the population to have completed high school. The sample is predominantly male; average AFQT score is 59, somewhat over the average for the youth population. Because of our later focus on AFQT scores, we include more detailed descriptive statistics of the score distributions, both for high school diploma graduates (HSDGs) and for non-graduates (NHSDGs), see figure 3. As discussed above, those who enlist with a credential classified as tier 2 or 3 are required to have an AFQT score of 50 or better. Those who enlist with a high school diploma, or an alternate credential considered equivalent, are required to have scores of 30 or better. Thus, on average NHSDGs actually have higher AFQT scores than high school graduates.

Table 4 includes the results of our fixed-effects regressions of the Census sample modeling educational attainment [24]. Many of the results are not surprising; in particular, gender and ethnicity predict educational attainment. State-level characteristics also have some influence, but the coefficients (and the marginal effects) tend to be quite small.

Table 4. Logistic regressions—High school completion, college attendance; Census sample[1]

	High school completion		College attendance	
	Coefficient	Std error	Coefficient	Std error
INDIVIDUAL-LEVEL CHARACTERISTICS				
Male	-.342*	.00114	-.398*	.00079
Black	-.866*	.00146	-.741*	.00116
Asian	.648*	.00699	.834*	.00404
Native American	-.929*	.00448	-.853*	.00383
Other	-.287*	.00243	-.223 *	.00193
Hispanic	-.916*	.00215	-.696 *	.00171
STATE-LEVEL CHARACTERISTICS				
K-12 $ per pupil	.000044*	.000003	0.000028*	0.000002
Youth pop, aged 15 to 19, in 1000's	.000354*	.0000215	-.000277*	.000016
Unemployment rate	.0179*	.00105	-.00065	.00077
Average weekly wage	.000062*	.000017	.000099*	.000012
EDUCATION REFORM REQUIREMENTS				
High Carnegie units	-.220*	.0191	-.132*	.0117
Strict Carnegie units	-.0705*	.00632	.00954+	.00489
Exit exam	-.0459*	.00505	.0426*	.0034
GED SPECIFIC REQUIREMENTS				
GED centers per 1k youth	0.240*	0.018	.327*	.0109
Min age 17	-.0135^	.00525	-.0096^	.0037
Min age 18	.00324	.00384	-.0042	.0027
Min age 18.5	.163*	.0122	.0785*	.0077
Min age 19	.0240+	.0115	.0427*	.0087
Min age 21	.151*	.0143	.0818*	.0103
Average GED score required	-.00541^	.00194	.0055*	.0012
May meet avg or min score req	.0155*	.00479	-.0020	.0037
Number of Observations	1,305,117		1,305,107	
Pseudo R-squared	.0476		.0392	

[1] The regressions also controlled for year and state fixed effects. Omitted categories include female, white, non-Hispanic, no high Carnegie units or strict Carnegie unit requirement, no exit exam, GED minimum age requirement of 16, and must meet GED score requirements on all tests. College attendance is conditional upon high school graduation or earning an alternate credential. Standard errors clustered on state of birth. Levels of significance: + 5-percent or better; ^ 1-percent or better; *.1-percent or better.

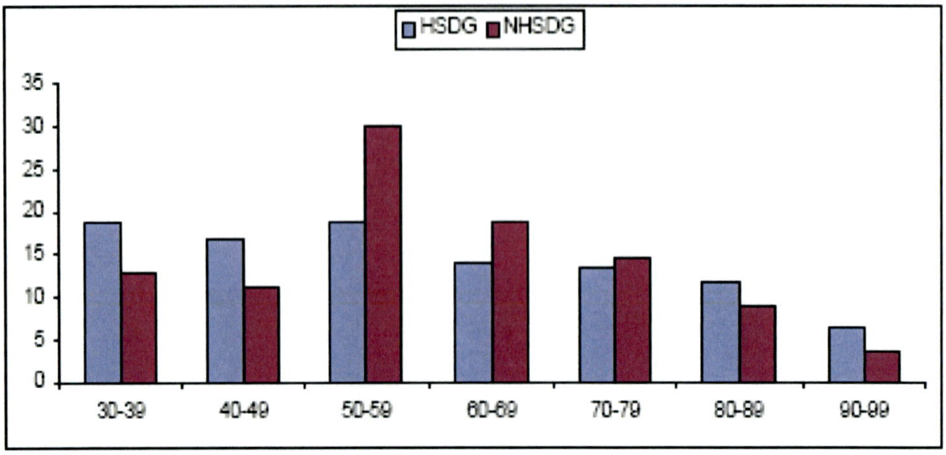

Figure 3. Distribution of AFQT scores for enlistees with and without high school diplomas.

Some of the GED requirements are important; in particular, states with more testing centers have higher educational attainment although this may not be causal. Higher minimum GED ages are associated with higher educational attainment. The other education reforms are important as well—states with basic CU requirements have lower educational attainment. Strict CU requirements and exit exams have more nuanced effects—both are associated with lower levels of high school completion *and* higher levels of college attendance. These policies, then, seem to have a sorting effect—helping students who complete high school, but also discouraging some from completion.

The marginal effects are substantial at the high school level; living in a state with an exit exam decreases the probability that a person will complete high school by about .5 percentage points (from 86.9 percent to 86.4 percent). This is equivalent to increasing the probability of dropping out by 4 percent (from 13.1 percent to 13.6 percent). The effect of having a basic CU requirement decreases the graduation probability from 88.7 percent to 86.4 percent while a strict CU requirement decreases the probability less, to 88.0 percent. Again, these effects substantively raise the probability of dropping out. Finally, the effects of GED policies are smaller; for example, raising the minimum age from 16 to 19 increases the probability of completing school from 86.6 percent to 86.8 percent. Recall that the Census does not differentiate between HSDGs and GED-holders; this last effect suggests that low GED ages may draw students out of school, and that some of these students (but not all) actually complete the credential. This is consistent with the findings of Chaplin (2002).

Because of the potential sorting effects of these education policies, we model our labor force outcomes separately for those who complete high school versus those who do not. We model both the probability of working (or looking for work), and the weekly wage of those employed. As shown in table 5, for both HSDGs and NHSDGs, exit exams increase the probability of being in the labor force; the marginal effect is larger for graduates. Basic CU requirements have a negative coefficient for both, although the effect achieves statistical significance only for HSDGs. In the case of both groups, increased GED minimum age requirements generally are associated with higher labor force participation rates. The effect of exit exams is sizable; for both high school graduates and non-graduate, those coming from a state with an exit exam have about a 1 percentage point higher change of being in the labor force than a similar person from another state. As the base probability is about 71 percent, this translates to a three percent difference in the likelihood of being *out* of the labor force.

Table 5. Regressions—Labor Force participation; Census sample[1]

	NHSDGs		HSDGs	
	Coefficient	Std error	Coefficient	Std error
INDIVIDUAL-LEVEL CHARACTERISTICS				
Male	.130*	.00105	.543*	.00161
Black	-.858*	.00146	-.774*	.00213
Asian	-.421*	.00386	-.565*	.00883
Native American	-.793*	.00480	-.696*	.00660
Other	-.169*	.00249	-.117*	.00379
Hispanic	-.396*	.00219	-.291*	.00335
In school	-.397*	.00115	-.523*	.00259
STATE-LEVEL CHARACTERISTICS				
K-12 $ per pupil	.000111*	.0000028	.0000554*	.0000043
Youth pop, aged 15 to 19, in 1000's	.00141*	.0000202	.000408*	.0000315
Unemployment rate	.0169*	.00103	.00353+	.00158
Average weekly wages	.0000121	.0000153	.000087*	.0000236
Average tuition, state college	-.0000153*	.0000025	.0000322*	.0000038
EDUCATION REFORM REQUIREMENTS				
High Carnegie units	-.107	.0157	-.151*	.0238
Strict Carnegie units	.0109	.00608	-.0126	.00908
Exit exam	.0378*	.00480	.0586*	.00690
GED SPECIFIC REFORMS				
GED centers per 1k youth	-.326*	.0132	-.393*	.0227
Min age 17	.0665*	.0049	.0601*	.00733
Min age 18	.0500*	.00348	.0206*	.00535
Min age 18.5	.112*	.0106	-.131*	.0165
Min age 19	.0544*	.0110	.181*	.0165
Min age 21	-.0469*	.0133	-0.534*	.0200
Avg GED score required	-.00306	.00173	-.00534+	.00261
Meet avg or min score req	-.00066	.00463	.0424*	.00709
Number of Observations (weighted)	19,864,984		7,839,748	
Pseudo R-squared	.0499		.0389	

[1] The regressions also controlled for year and state fixed effects. Omitted categories include female, white, non-Hispanic, no high Carnegie units or strict Carnegie unit requirement, no exit exam, GED minimum age requirement of 16, and must meet GED score requirements on all tests. Standard errors were clustered on state. LFPR equation is logistic; weekly wage equation is OLS. Levels of significance: + 5-percent or better; ^ 1-percent or better; *.1-percent or better.

We also model weekly wages (separately for HSDGs and NHSDGs). These results, available upon request, indicate that neither exit exams nor CU requirements affect wages of HSDGs. However, in the case of NHSDGs, coming from a state with basic CU requirements is associated with a slightly higher wage (less than 5 percent); strict CU requirements are associated with smaller increases.

In general, then, our Census results indicate that the effects of some state-level policies are fairly straightforward, while the effects of others are more nuanced. First, the effects of basic CU requirements generally are negative (with the exception of raising wages of NHSDGs). Basic CU requirements seem to decrease educational attainment, as well as work effort. The effects of the GED minimum age also are fairly consistent. Raising the GED minimum age is associated with generally higher educational attainment and work effort levels. This indicates that lower age requirements draw students out of high school; presumably some of these students complete GEDs but others do not [25]. The effects of exit exams and strict CU requirements, however, are less straightforward; these two policies seem to have sorting effects. Both are associated with lower levels of high school completion, but higher levels of college attainment among those who complete high school. Exit exams raise work effort of graduates and non-graduates; strict CU requirements raise wages slightly for NHSDGs.

In many cases, our results agree with those of Dee (2003), who performed a similar analysis using data from the 1990 Census. For example, like Dee we find a negative effect of CU requirements on high school completion although our effect is somewhat larger than his. While Dee finds positive effects of both CU requirements and exams on employment (but not wages), we find CU requirements affect wages of NHSDGs while exit exams increase work effort for everyone. Differences between our results and those of Dee may stem from today's more difficult exit exams, or from our inclusion of GED variables in our regressions. It is worth noting that in a separate analysis, Dee finds that CU requirements actually *decrease* some individual students' level of effort. This provides a potential explanation for the negative effects of CU requirements.

Additionally, we estimate a simple state-level model to measure the relationship between state-level GED policies and the number of young people in the state who earn a GED (recall that the Census data do not include sufficient information for us to differentiate between GED-holders and high school graduates). In any single year, the proportion of young people (aged 16 to 25) who earn a GED is quite small (on the order of 1 percent). However, we believe the ratio of young new GED-holders (aged 19 or less) to new high school diploma graduates provides a more accurate measure of the extent to which young people opt for GEDs. Across states, this ratio averages roughly 8 (for every 100 high school diplomas issued, 8 GEDs are issued) but varies substantially. In some states, the ratio is less than 2; in others, it is close to 20. (This is the ratio plotted in figure 2, above.)

Our state-level regression models the proportion with GEDs as a function of the state-level characteristics, education reforms, and GED specific reforms included in tables 4 and 5. Figure 2, above, indicates how this ratio has increased over time; our regression results indicate that this trend remains even when holding constant other factors. Additionally, more young people earn GEDs in state with basic CU requirements. Our results indicate that, in a state with a basic CU requirement, the ratio of GEDs to diplomas is about 8.3; it is roughly 6.7 in states without basic CU requirements. The coefficient on exit exams is positive, but statistically insignificant (results available upon request). Next, we turn to our Navy data. As shown in table 3, some 11 percent of the roughly 470,000 Navy enlistees in our dataset held some form of alternate credential. (See appendix A for more details on the formation of our Navy dataset).

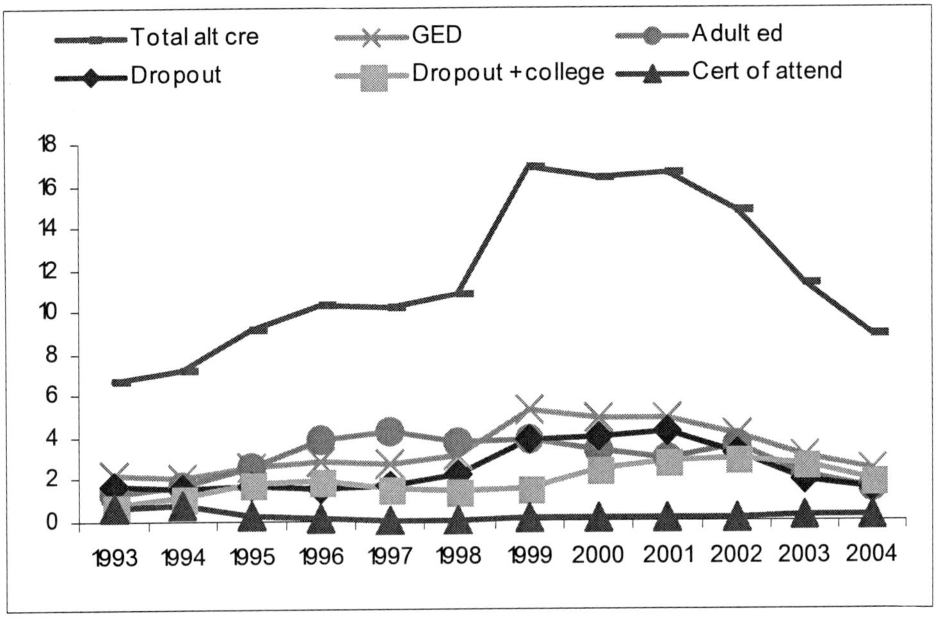

Figure 4. Alternate credential holders in the Navy.

As shown in figure 4, the proportion of people entering the Navy with GEDs, as well as with other alternate credentials, increased somewhat over the sample period (despite the general decrease in the total number of accessions). In particular, the proportion with GEDs trended upwards sharply around 1999. However, the total proportion with alternate credentials has fallen in more recent years. This suggests that the sharp growth in alternate credential holders is a product of the difficult recruiting years of the late 1990s, and thus of the strong civilian economy during this period. We note as well that the growth in accessions holding adult education certificates or college credits (but no high school diplomas) increased markedly; these two credentials are considered tier1 for recruiting purposes (recall table 2).

Our descriptive statistics suggest it will be important to control for time-varying effects in our analysis of Navy enlistees. We do so by using the same fixed-effects strategy that we employed on the Census data, above. Our initial Navy outcome measure is AFQT scores; because of the sorting effects that some education policies evidence on the civilian population, we model the scores separately for those with high school diplomas versus those with alternate credentials.

As shown in table 6, our regression results indicate that among Navy accessions, men have higher AFQT scores than women and (non-Hispanic) whites generally score higher than others. Those who are older at enlistment have lower scores, perhaps because they have been out of school (and away from test-taking situations) for longer periods. This effect, however, is larger for HSDGs than for non-graduates. State variables have small effects.

Table 6. Regressions—AFQT Score, by high school diploma status, Navy sample[1]

	AFQT score, HSDGs		AFQT score, NHSDGs	
	Coefficient	Std error	Coefficient	Std error
INDIVIDUAL-LEVEL CHARACTERISTICS				
Male	1.91*	.086	1.08*	.287
Black	-13.96*	.091	-9.32*	.253
Other	-4.00*	.144	-.940*	.322
Hispanic	-7.76*	.117	-3.85*	.265
Married	1.77*	.224	.626	.398
18 at accession	-.978*	.150	.640	.368
19 at accession	-3.68*	.154	-.975^	.367
20 at accession	-2.04*	.165	-1.48*	.384
21 at accession	-.638*	.188	-1.58*	.416
(Any) waiver				
STATE-LEVEL CHARACTERISTICS				
K-12 $ per pupil	.00056*	.00017	.000518	.000436
Tuition, state college	.00028	.000182	-.00079	.00046
Average weekly wages	.0023^	.00092	-.00094	.0025
Unemployment rate	.155	.092	.222	.238
EDUCATION REFORM REQUIREMENTS				
High Carnegie units	-.108	.633	-.692	1.74
Strict Carnegie units	-1.27*	.333	-2.67*	.833
Exit exam	1.53*	.308	.591	1.02
GED SPECIFIC REFORMS				
GED centers per 1k youth	-.843	1.05	-1.58	2.41
Min age 17	.737^	.333	.360	.797
Min age 18	.131	.228	-.0645	.549
Min age 18.5	-.779	.748	-3.97+	1.91
Min age 19	-.522	.682	-4.84*	1.48
Min age 21	1.20	.783	-1.09	1.78
Avg GED score required	-.409	.110	.229	.249
Meet avg or min score req	.218	.246	.866	.592
Number of Observations	294,401		34,076	
Adjusted R-squared	0.1049		0.0843	

[1] The regressions also controlled for year and state fixed effects. Omitted categories include female, white, non-Hispanic, no high Carnegie units or strict Carnegie unit requirement, no exit exam, GED minimum age requirement of 16, and must meet GED score requirements on all tests. Standard errors were clustered on state. Levels of significance: + 5-percent or better; ^ 1-percent or better; *.1-percent or better.

Table 7. Logistic regressions—12-month attrition rates, Navy sample[1]

	HSDGs		NHSDGs	
	Coefficient	Std error	Coefficient	Std error
INDIVIDUAL-LEVEL CHARACTERISTICS				
Male	-.157*	.0122	-.0924+	.0404
Black	-.188*	.0132	-.299*	.0363
Hispanic	-.272*	.0178	-.259*	.0386
Other	-.325*	.0222	-.131*	.0460
Married	-.148*	.0322	-.252*	.0585
18 at accession	-.0272	.0222	-.108+	.0502
19 at accession	.170*	.0227	-.196*	.0503
20 at accession	.215*	.0241	-.294*	.0529
21 at accession	.237*	.0269	-.328*	.0578
(Any) waiver	.260*	.0107	.138*	.0242
STATE-LEVEL CHARACTERISTICS				
K-12 $ per pupil	-.000004	.000025	.0000457	.0000613
Unemployment rate	-.0155	.0134	.0668+	.0334
Average weekly wages	.000110	.00013	.000320	.000347
Average tuition, state college	.000018	.000026	.0000459	.0000651
EDUCATION REFORM REQUIREMENTS				
High Carnegie units	-.0862	.0956	-.466	.245
Strict Carnegie units	.0512	.0490	.0201	.115
Exit exam	-.0721	.0414	-.0307	.138
GED SPECIFIC REFORMS				
GED centers per 1k youth	.755	.144	.338	.326
Min age 17	-.0251	.0451	-.0889	.109
Min age 18	-.0244	.0311	-.131	.0741
Min age 18.5	.201	.107	-.175	.264
Min age 19	.119	.094	-.133	.202
Min age 21	.171	.113	-.156	.251
Avg GED score required	-.00101	.0162	.0337	.0359
Meet avg or min score req	-.0912**	.0349	-.0700	.0809
Number of Observations	294,401		34,076	
Pseudo R-squared	0.0122		0.0159	

[1] The regressions also controlled for year and state fixed effects. Omitted categories include female, white, non-Hispanic, no high Carnegie units or strict Carnegie unit requirement, no exit exam, GED minimum age requirement of 16, and must meet GED score requirements on all tests. Standard errors clustered on home state. Levels of significance: + 5-percent or better; ^ 1-percent or better; *.1-percent or better.

We find that education policies predict AFQT scores. In particular, non-graduates from state with higher minimum GED ages have lower scores; this is consistent with high minimum ages encouraging the marginal student to complete high school. Also, HSDGs from states with exit exams have higher scores (by about 1.5 points); there is no effect on non-graduates. CU requirements also have substantial effects. Recruits from states with strict CU requirements have lower AFQT scores than similar recruits from other states; this is true both for HSDGs and NHSDGs. The effect for NHSDGs is substantive, nearly 3 points.

Next, we examine a common measure of recruit success—attrition. Historically, those with alternate credentials have "attrited" (left the Navy before completing their obligation) at far higher rates than high school diploma graduates. However, our civilian results suggest that education policies influence individual outcomes; specifically, some students who would otherwise have graduated will not do so when a state enacts an exit exam or a CU requirement. If such "marginal" students enlist, they may complete a GED or have some other alternate credential. Past research on GED-holders suggests that many with a GED may perform poorly for non-cognitive reasons. Thus, by discouraging graduation, these educational policies could actually decrease the level of attrition among NHSDGs. In a parallel manner, such policies could improve the average performance of NHSDGs in the job market. These policies also have the potential to decrease attrition among HSDGs, if the "marginal" high school student is less likely to succeed in the Navy than others. However, our analysis of the Census data along with our regressions explaining AFQT scores of enlistees suggest that some reforms may actually lower the overall quality of education. In that case, the effect on attrition is unclear.

As shown in table 7, graduation policies have no effect on the attrition of enlistees with high school diplomas. In fact, the state-level variables as a group do little to explain attrition. In the case of NHSDGs, the coefficients on graduation requirements do not achieve significance. The coefficient on basic CU requirements indicates that NHSDGs from states with basic CU requirements have substantially lower attrition than others, but the coefficient achieves significance at only the 6-percent level. Thus, the overall effects of graduation requirements on attrition rates appear to be minimal.

CONCLUSION

Based on these findings, it is fair to say that several of the graduation policies we consider have both positive and negative impacts, in the civilian world and among Navy accessions. Graduation exams are an important education policy because they are widely used today and their use will continue to increase in the near future. These exams seem to have a sorting effect-- while their presence increases the probability that some people will leave school, they also increase the probability that a high school graduate will attend college, and they increase the probability that a person will work for pay or search for work (as opposed to leaving the labor force). Thus, exit exams seem to hurt students who have a high probability of dropping out of high school, but also have some positive effects. In general, our results are consistent with those of Jacob (2001) and Dee (2003), among others. Navy accessions who graduate from high school in states with exit exams have higher AFQT scores than accessions from states without exams; the scores of non-graduates do not depend upon exit exams. This, too, suggests a sorting effect from these exams. Thus, the effects of exit exams are likely to be largely positive—but weighing the decrease in high school completion rates against gains in learning among graduates is difficult.

Carnegie-unit requirements also seem to have both negative and positive effects, but basic CU requirements lower both educational attainment and labor force participation. Strict CU requirements (which require more coursework than the basic CU requirements) discourage some from completing school, but those who do graduate under these requirements are more likely to attend college. Among Navy accessions, those from states with strict CU requirements have lower AFQT scores; the effect is larger for non-graduates than for graduates. While the effects of basic CU requirements are consistently negative in the Census data, our AFQT result suggest that the marginal student may actually be harmed by strict CU requirements. Indeed, our results are broadly consistent with the finding of Dee (2003) that CU requirements actually serve to *lower* student effort. Clearly, understanding the full effects of CU requirements will require additional analysis of how courses change in light of new requirements as well as how students select courses. Additionally, to the extent that states loosen GED requirements as they tighten graduation requirements, the negative effects of the graduation requirements are likely to be exacerbated.

Our results have implications for the broader labor market. At the very least, our results suggest that increasing graduation standards will *not* uniformly increase the performance of young workers. The majority of states have or are in the process of enacting exit exams and CU requirements are likely to continue to change in the near future. *A Nation at Risk* was published over 20 years ago; high school graduates today complete more courses than their counterparts 2 decades ago but still, few complete the recommended coursework. Currently proposed legislation is likely to bring increased attention to states' CU requirements; in light of this, a much better understanding of how CU requirements affect students is necessary.

Unlike most businesses, the Navy has the ability to substitute recruits from one state for those in another so, for example, the Navy can potentially alleviate negative effects of graduation requirements by recruiting more enlistees from states with improving outcomes and fewer from states with worsening outcomes. Therefore, our results may be best viewed as a lower bound on the effects likely to be experienced by employers in the face of education reform.

NOTES

[1] The common measure of credit for coursework is the Carnegie unit (CU). One unit represents completion of one year's worth of coursework, typically consisting of 250 minutes per week over the course of a 180-day school year (see Lillard and DeCicca 2001).

[2] Author's calculation from National Center for Education Statistics (2004).

[3] See Dee (2003), Carnoy and Loeb (2002), as well as Bishop and Mane (2001).

[4] Figure 1 traces the number of units actually earned—not those required for graduation. This increase is a reflection of increased requirements. Source: National Center for Education Statistics, various years. In our empirical analysis, we classify states based upon specific requirements.

[5] Vocational credits include those in general vocational courses as well as those in business, marketing, health, and technical courses.

[6] Within subjects, the shift has also been toward more difficult courses; for example, the number of courses requiring Algebra increased from 1.74 to 2.25 over the period, while the number requiring no Algebra fell from 0.90 to 0.61 (National Center for Education Statistics 2004).

[7] See Boesel et al (1998) and Tyler (2002) for thorough treatments of the background of the GED.

[8] Author's calculations from GED Testing Service, various years; National Center for Education Statistics, 2004.

[9] The GED Testing Service, the group that develops, oversees, and collects information on the GED tests, encourages this viewpoint. See, for example, GED Testing Service (2001: 3-4).

[10]Both the Current Population Survey (CPS) and the Census collect information in this manner. See Chaplin (2002) for a discussion of changes in educational attainment over time, with a particular emphasis on the increase in those holding GEDs. Alternate credentials include, but are not limited to, credentials awarded for completing the GED, a correspondence school program, a vocational/occupational program, or an adult education program.

[11]Our attrition numbers include only those who attrited for "failure to adapt."

[12]See Garcia et al 2004; Wenger and Hodari 2004; Laurence, Ramsberger, and Arabian 1996; Cooke and Quester 1998; Laurence 1984.

[13]AFQT scores are computed by combining the scores on the following subtests of the Armed Services Vocational Aptitude Battery (ASVAB): (1) Arithmetic Reasoning, (2) Word Knowledge, (3) Paragraph Comprehension, and (4) Mathematics Knowledge. The scores are normed to the youth population; 50 is the average score. AFQT scores are predictive of job performance in the military (see, e.g., Scribner et al. 1986; Fernandez 1992).

[14]We use the 5% Public Use Microdata Sample (PUMS) files—see http://www.census.gov/Press-Release/www/2003/PUMS5.html for more details about the sample.

[15]An E-3 in the Navy is referred to as a "Seaman;" the parallel rank in the Army is "Private First Class" while an E-3 in the Marine Corps is referred to as "Lance Corporal."

[16]During the drawdown of the 1990s, some Sailors were offered separation bonuses but no Sailors in our dataset were separated from the Navy.

[17]Census categories to choose from when indicating education level include: 10th grade, 11th grade, 12th grade but no diploma, high school graduate.

[18]We follow the methodology of Dee(2003) closely for much of this section, but we utilize the 2000 Census rather than the 1990 Census and we include measures of GED policies.

[19]To model weekly wages, we use instead a simple log-linear specification. To model state-level outcomes, we use a model of the form: (New young GED-holders/new HSDGs) = f(state-level variables).

[20]Exit exams and CU requirements affect only *public* schools. Fewer than 10 percent of students graduate from private schools (National Center for Education Statistics 2004). It is impossible to exclude private school students from either the Census or the Navy data; their presence is likely to lessen the effect of graduation policies and thus bias our results downward.

[21]Our sample includes 1,305,668 observations, weighted to represent 27,704,732 people.

[22]Some individuals reported implausibly high or low earnings. When we excluded those whose hourly earnings placed them in the top or bottom 1% of our sample, our results were unchanged; without those in the top or bottom 1%, minimum reported weekly earnings was $.153 while the maximum was $8371.

[23]We use the CNA Corporation's Personalized Recruiting for Immediate and Delayed Entry Enlisted Street-to-Fleet database; we supplemented this data with information from CNA's Enlisted Master Files. These files represent up-to-date and accurate information on all enlisted Navy personnel. We select all non-prior-service accessions who entered the Navy between October 1992 and September 2004 (FY90-FY04) and who were no more than 21 years of age at accession. We also delete those who entered with a (2- or 4-year) college degree; this final deletion decreased the sample by less than 1%. We have a total of 470,071 observations.

[24]All of the results in this section were virtually unchanged when we excluded Nebraska, the state with absolutely no CU requirements. We defined two alternate Census samples using slightly different rules to assign people to a home state. Also, we defined a more restrictive dataset excluding those with a disability, those in the military, and those who do not speak English well. When we examine the regressions using our alternate samples, we find that, in general, the results do not differ from the preferred specification in a substantive manner. Because our Navy sample is predominantly male, any differences between the two samples could be due to different effects of graduation requirements on men versus women. However, when we estimate our Census models separately by gender, we find no systematic differences. See appendix A for more discussion of our alternate samples.

[25]States with lower-quality schools tend to have easier requirements for passing the GED; in our specification without state-level fixed effects, states with more centers per 1,000 youth and/or lower passing scores had *lower* high school completion. While we would predict that high school completion will increase as states add centers and lower passing criteria, these variables are correlated with overall state education quality.

APPENDIX A. DETAILS ON DATA SOURCES AS WELL AS SAMPLE AND VARIABLE DEFINITIONS

Census Data

The Census is a cross-sectional dataset; it includes observations on all people at a specific point in time. We want to see how state-level education policies affect various outcomes for young adults. To do this, we merge data from the 2000 Census with state-level policy data (further discussion of our state-level data on education policies follows). Because we are concerned with students who have recently completed high school, we select only those age 20 to 28 as of April of 2000. We do not include younger students because to do so would likely conflate two of our outcome measures: high school completion and postsecondary enrollment. By 20 years of age, most students have completed high school and the majority of those who will enroll in postsecondary institutions have done so.

One key aspect of our research is the linking of individual Census outcomes to state-level education policy variables. To do so, we must determine where each person in our dataset was educated. The Census does not provide this exact information, but it does indicate where each person was born, lives now, and lived 5 years earlier. Our primary dataset includes all who were born in 1 of the 50 states, or the District of Columbia, and who lived in the United States both at the time of the 2000 Census and 5 years before. (We delete those who lived in foreign countries, as well as those who lived in U.S. territories, in 1995 because the state-level education policy variables are likely to be unreflective of their educational experience.) We also test a more restrictive dataset, while excludes all people who reported having a disability, those who reported speaking a foreign language *and* reported not speaking English "very well," and those who were on active duty in the military at the time of the Census. Our logic is that these factors are likely to influence educational attainment, labor force participation, and/or wages.

We use information on where people live and where they lived in the past to assign state-level education variables to each person. In our primary dataset, we assign education variables (such as per-pupil spending and exit exam policies) based on the state where the person was *born*. In selecting this methodology, we follow Dee (2003), who argues that although this method may produce biased results, the results are biased downward (true effects are likely to be attenuated by any mismatches), which means that the estimates provide a lower bound of the true effects. We also experiment with two other datasets using slightly different matching methodologies. First, we assign state education variables based on the state in which the person lived 5 years earlier. Second, we test a more detailed methodology in which we:

- Assign those who currently live in their birth states to that state,
- Assign to state B all who were born in state A but now live in state B and resided in state B 5 years earlier,
- Delete "frequent movers"—those who were born in state A, lived in state B 5 years earlier, and now reside in state C.

In general, these alternative samples provide results quite similar to those we find with our primary dataset. We report results from these alternate datasets in the footnotes in the Results section.

Navy Data

We delete observations on people who have home states of record outside the 50 United States and the District of Columbia (e.g., we delete all who listed Puerto Rico as their home state). We also delete observations with no home state listed. We delete observations with other key variables missing: specifically, those missing information on sex, age, or AFQT score. We delete observations in which the person was 22 years of age or older at accession (many of these people are likely to have moved between high school and enlistment, so their home state may not be the state in which they were educated; also, many have substantial postsecondary education and work experience).

We also delete those who accessed with a (2- or 4-year) college degree, as well as those who were homeschooled through the end of high school and those who accessed after completing the National Guard Youth Challenge (ChalleNGe) program along with a GED. These exclusions decrease the sample size by 4,850 observations, or less than 1 percent. We exclude those who earned college degrees because their schooling experience is less reflective of state school policies, and many have moved (most were over 21 years of age anyway). We exclude homeschoolers and ChalleNGe graduates because they were part of a 5-year pilot program from FY99 through FY04; during this period, these credentials were considered tier 1 for enlistment purposes; this, along with problems certifying the authenticity of homeschoolers, is likely to have artificially increased the number in these categories.

During the time period included in our sample, the Navy drew down total endstrength; accessions ranged between 53k and 31k per year, trending downwards over the sample period. Because of these changes in overall "mission" we focus on ratios, rather than numbers, of alternate-credential-holders.

We matched individuals to state-level data indicating education policy the year each person was 17, with one exception: in the case of those who entered the Navy at age 17, we match to the (likely) last year in high school—the previous year. The vast majority of these people are high school graduates; it is likely that they skipped a grade at some point and therefore completed high school early.

When measuring attrition, we consider those who left the enlisted ranks to become Officers as having fulfilled their obligation. Additionally, we do not consider those who retire due to disability or die while enlisted as having attrited. The number who are disabled or die is very small and most deaths do not occur in the line of duty.

State-Level Data

Exit exams: See table 1 for sources

Carnegie-unit data: Sources are reports published periodically by the Education Commission of the States, as well as the National Center for Education Statistics.

GED data: For each state during each year, the GED data include indicators of the number of GED credentials awarded, the number awarded to those 19 or younger, the number of GED testing centers, the minimum age requirement, and the scores required for passing the test. This information is detailed in yearly publications produced by the General Education Development (GED) Testing Service.

Other (State-Level) Data and Sources

Per-pupil expenditures, based on average daily attendance. Source: Digest of Education Statistics, various years.

Size of the youth population—an estimate of the number age 15-19, inclusive, for each year. Source: Series ST-99-8, Population Estimates for the U.S., Regions, Divisions, and States for 5-year Age Groups and Sex. http://www.census.gov/popest/archives/ 1990s/ST-99-08.txt, and similar. Accessed 30 March 2005.

State unemployment rate. Source: Bureau of Labor Statistics, calculated from data collected through the Current Population Survey (CPS), using Local Area Unemployment Statistics (LAUS).

Average weekly wage of young male workers, defined as those age 19-24, using the March Current Population Survey (CPS) files for 1993-2002 (retrospective earnings data for 1992-2001). We excluded those who were in school or out of the labor force, as well as those who had $0 in earnings during the previous year. Finally, we excluded those earning in the top and bottom 1 percent (those making less than ~$1.20 per hour or more than ~$49 per hour).

We inflated all monetary figures to 2004 dollars using the CPI. Specifically, we use the CPI-U-RS (Consumer Price Index Research Series; for details, see http://www.bls.gov/. cpi/cpiurstx.htm, accessed 30 March 2005).

REFERENCES

Achieve, Inc. 2004. The Expectations Gap: A 50-State Review of High School Graduation Requirements, (Washington, DC).

Alabama Department of Education, Great Expectations: A Guide to Alabama's High School Graduation Exam. Montgomery, AL: revised October 2003;

Berliner, David and Audrey Amrein, An Analysis of Some Unintended and Negative Consequences of High-Stakes Testing, December 2002;

Betts, Julian and Robert Costrell. 2001. "Incentives and Equity under Standards Based Reform" *Brookings Papers on Education Policy,* ed. Diane Ravitch, (Washington, DC: The Brookings Institution), 9-74.

Bishop, John H. and Ferran Mane. 2001. "The Impacts of Minimum Competency Exam Graduation Requirements on High School Graduation, College Attendance, and Early Labor Market Success" In G. Orfield and M. L. Kornhaber (eds.), Raising Standards or Raising Barriers? Inequality and High-Stakes Testing in Public Education. (New York: The Century Foundation Press).

Boesel, David, Nabeel Alsalam, and Thomas Smith. 1998. "Educational and Labor Market Performance of GED Recipients," (Washington, DC: Office of Educational Research and Improvement, U.S. Department of Education, National Library of Education Research Synthesis)

California Department of Education website, http://www.cde.ca.gov/ta/tg/hs/overview.asp, accessed April 8, 2005.

Cameron, Stephen and James Heckman. 1993. "The Nonequivalence of High School Equivalents," Journal of Labor Economics 11(1): 1-47.

Carneiro, Pedro and James Heckman. 2004. "Human Capital Policy." In James Heckman and Alan Krueger (Benjamin M. Friedman, ed.), Inequality in America: What Role for Human Capital Policies? (Cambridge, MA: MIT Press).

Carnoy, Martin and Susanna Loeb. 2002. "Does External Accountability Affect Student Outcomes? A Cross-State Analysis," Educational Evaluation and Policy Analysis 24(4): 305-331.

Cawley, J., J. Heckman, and E. Vytlacil. 2001. "Three Observations on Wages and Measured Cognitive Ability," Labour Economics 8(4): 419-42.

Center on Education Policy. 2003. "State High School Exit Exams: Put to the Test," (Washington, DC).

Chaplin, Duncan. 2002. "Tassels on the Cheap: The GED and the Falling Graduation Rate," Education Next: 24-29.

Cooke, Timothy W. and Aline O. Quester. Jun 1998. Who Stays and Who Leaves? Identifying Successful Navy Recruits, (CNA Research Memorandum 88-75).

Dee, Thomas. 2003. "The 'First Wave' of Accountability" In Paul E. Peterson and Martin R. West (eds), No Child Left Behind? The Politics and Practice of Accountability. (Washington, DC: Brookings Press).

Dillon, Sam. "College Aid Plan Widens U.S. Role in High Schools" *New York Times* 22 January 2006, late ed.: Page 1, column 1.

Education Commission of the States, "Clearinghouse Notes—High School Graduation Requirements" November 1996, July 1990, and November 1984.

Fernandez, Judith C. 1992. "Soldier Quality and Job Performance in Team Tasks," Social Science Quarterly, (73): 253-65.

Garcia, Federico E.et al. July 2004. Evaluation of the Pilot Program for Home School and ChalleNGe Program Recruits, (CNA Research Memorandum D0004598.A4).

Gardner, D.P. et al. 1983. A Nation at Risk: The Imperative for Reform, (Washington, DC: National Commission for Excellence in Education).

Gayler, Keith, Naomi Chudowsky, Madlene Hamilton, Nancy Kober, and Margery Yeager, State High School Exit Exams: A Maturing Reform. Center on Education Policy Washington, DC: August 2004.

General Education Development Testing Service. 2001. Who Took the GED Tests? 2000 Statistical Report, (Washington, DC: American Council on Education).

General Education Development Testing Service. 1995. Who Took the GED Tests? 1994 Statistical Report, (Washington, DC: American Council on Education).

Hawaii Department of Education website, http:// arch.k12.hi.us/info/faq/ student.html,accessed April 8,2005

Jacob, Brian. 2001. "Getting Tough? The Impact of High School Graduation Exams," Educational Evaluation and Policy Analysis 23(2): 99-121.

Laurence, Janice H. 1984. Education Standards for Military Enlistment and the Search for Successful Recruits, Feb 1984 (Human Resources Research Organization Final Report 84-4, FR-PRD-84-4).

Laurence, Janice H., Peter F. Ramsberger, and Jane Arabian. Sep 1996. Education Credential Tier Evaluation, (Human Resources Research Organization Final Report 96-19, FR0EADD-96-19).

Lillard, Dean R. and Phillip P. DeCicca. 2001. "Higher Standards, More Dropouts? Evidence Within and Across Time," Economics of Education Review 20: 459-73.

Murnane, Richard, John Willett, and Kathryn Boudett. 1997. "Does a GED Lead to More Training, Post-Secondary Education, and Military Service for School Dropouts?" Industrial and Labor Relations Review 51(1): 100-116.

National Center for Education Statistics. 2004, and various other years. Digest of Education Statistics 2003, (Washington, DC: U.S. Department of Education).

Quinn, L. and M. Haberman. "Are GED Certificate Holders Ready for Postsecondary Education?" 1986. Metropolitan Education 1, 2: 72-82 (Cited in Boesel, Alsalam, and Smith).

Scribner, Barry L., D. Alton Smith, Robert H. Baldwin, and Robert Phillips, "Are Smart Tankers Better? AFQT and Military Productivity," 1986. Armed Forces and Society, (12): 193-206.

Tyler, John. "The Economic Benefits of the GED: Lessons From Recent Research," 2002 (Brown University and NBER, working paper).

Warren, John Robert, Krista N. Jenkins, and Rachel B. Kulick. "High School Exit Examinations and State-Level Completion and GED Rates, 1975 Through 2002," 2006. Educational Evaluation and Policy Analysis, 28(2): 131-52.

Wenger, Jennie W. and Apriel K. Hodari. Predictors of Attrition: Attitudes, Behaviors and Educational Characteristics, Jul 2004 (CNA Research Memorandum D0010146.A2).

PART II. TEACHING AND CONTENT

In: Expanding Teaching and Learning Horizons
Editors: F. G. Mixon, Jr. and R. J. Cebula
ISBN 978-1-60741-971-6

Chapter 9

Teaching Political Economy: On the Economics Significance of the Public's Job Approval Rating of the President

Richard J. Cebula and Heather Smith

Introduction

Political science, public policy, and economics arguably can be classified as the most basic components of what is referred to as "political economy." Typically, students, especially graduate students, from each of these disciplines are taught in such a fashion as to concentrate narrowly and intensely on the study of their own particular field and the techniques thereof. However practical this pedagogy may prove to be in the short run (with most such students seeking jobs and needing finely honed skills to perform their jobs or to publish, especially in academia) this mode of teaching may be myopic and a disservice to the students because they are not made sufficiently aware of the extreme interrelationships and ties that exist among their disciplines. Students from each of these three disciplines could well benefit from an increased appreciation of the myriad interfaces that exist among these seemingly disparate fields of interest. Indeed, society might well benefit should students among these disciplines look more closely at the other disciplines so as to work better together to serve society.

This study seeks to demonstrate concretely the interdisciplinary nature of political economy so as to engender a greater understanding of and appreciation of the scope of economics and its myriad linkages to and interrelationships with other fields of study. In this study, the emphasis will be on the linkages between economics and economic behavior on the one hand and political phenomena which are most directly (easily) classified under the rubric of political science on the other hand. The public's job approval rating of the President, which is a comparatively transparent reflection of the assessment of the President by the U.S. population, is to serve as the medium through which the analysis is undertaken.

The public's job approval rating of the President, which has been reported on a monthly and annual basis for more than a half century, is a frequently discussed topic in the media. Newspaper and magazine stories on the public's job approval rating of the President appear monthly and oftentimes are discussed in a variety of ways for days at a time. Political pundits on television and on the radio ("talk-radio") speculate as to the implications for the President's approval rating for his/her (hereafter, simply "his") political agenda and for actions undertaken or being planned as President. Generally, for example, it typically is speculated by writers and political pundits that consistently low Presidential job approval ratings reduce the President's ability to influence Congress and to form alliances with Congress. In turn, the latter phenomenon implies a reduced likelihood of the President's achieving his legislative and/or Constitutional goals and/or obtaining funding for or continued funding for his other projects and commitments, including potentially the pursuit of military and/or national defense objectives. Moreover, the political party to which the President belongs may also be affected in other ways as a consequence of his having consistently low job approval ratings. For example, contributions to the coffers for re-election campaigns for candidates of the same political party as the President may well be reduced if the public's approval rating of his job performance is low. Naturally, consistently high public job approval ratings of the President could well have the opposite effects, i.e., serve to empower the President and his pursuing his political agenda.

The present study seeks to demonstrate that the public's job approval rating of the President may have much less obvious but nevertheless very powerful other *economic* ramifications. In particular, this study shows that the political economy of the Presidency may have serious implications for the Internal Revenue Service (IRS) in terms of its tax collections. More specifically, it is shown in this study that if the public's job approval rating of the President is low, the public is more inclined to engage in federal personal income tax evasion. The latter of course results in reduced federal tax collections, which tend to increase the size of the federal budget deficit. Conversely, it follows that a higher job approval rating for the President will reduce the public's inclination to engage in income tax evasion.

Studies of income tax evasion behavior tend fall into three broad categories. First, there are the principally theoretical models of tax evasion behavior, such as Falkinger (1988), Allingham and Sandmo (1972), Klepper, Nagin, and Spurr (1991), Das-Gupta (1994), Pestieau, Possen, and Slutsky (1994), and Caballe and Panades (1997). Second, there are a number of studies that either (a) use questionnaires or (b) undertake experiments, such as Spicer and Lundstedt (1976), Friedland (1982), Spicer and Thomas (1982), Benjamini and Maital (1985), Alm, Jackson, and McGee (1992), Baldry (1987), De Juan (1989), Thurman (1991), and Alm, McClelland, and Schulze (1999). Third, are those studies that use what is referred to as "official data," e.g., Tanzi (1982), Clotfelter (1983), Pommerehne and Weck-Hannemann (1989), Erard and Feinstein (1994), Feige (1994), Cebula (2004), and Feinstein (1999).

This study seeks to add to the political economy literature (as well as to the literature on income tax evasion) by investigating whether the degree of aggregate federal personal income tax evasion is influenced by the public's job approval rating of the President. In particular, this study attempts to provide insight as to whether the degree of personal income tax evasion rises (declines) when the public's approval rating of the President declines (increases). The model is presented in the following Section. The subsequent section provides the formal empirical analysis, whereas the final section provides concluding observations.

THE FRAMEWORK

In this study, the *relative* probability that the *representative* economic agent will *not* report his/her taxable income to the IRS is treated as being positively (directly) related to the expected gross benefits to the agent of not reporting income, eb, and as being negatively (inversely) related to the expected gross costs to the agent of not reporting income, ec. Thus, the ratio of the probability of not reporting income to the IRS, pnr, to the probability of reporting income to the IRS, (1-pnr), is described for the representative economic agent by:

$$pnr/(1-pnr) = f(eb, ec),\ f_{eb} > 0,\ f_{ec} < 0 \qquad (1)$$

Since the values for pnr will vary across the many diverse members of the economy, pnr may be viewed as an average of these various probabilities. Expressing probabilities in *relative* terms such as shown in equation (1) possesses the virtue that it thereby reflects the form of the data, i.e., data where (as described in the following section) the aggregate degree of federal personal income tax evasion (DTE) is expressed in relative terms.

The gross benefits from *not* reporting income to the IRS are expected to be directly related to the federal personal income tax rate (Cagan, 1958; Bawley, 1982; Tanzi, 1982; Clotfelter, 1983; Pyle, 1989; Feige, 1994). To reflect the federal personal income tax rate, most previous studies using official data for the U.S. have adopted either of two alternative measures: an average effective federal personal income tax rate (AEPT) or the maximum marginal federal personal income tax rate (MAXT). In this study, the AEPT measure of the income tax rate is adopted because, as argued in Feige (1994), this tax rate is likely to be a more representative measure of the personal income rate for a larger portion of the taxpaying public than MAXT would be. Accordingly, it is hypothesized, *ceteris paribus*, that:

$$eb = g(AEPT),\ g_{AEPT} > 0 \qquad (2)$$

Next, this study endeavors to allow for the potential impact of legal tax avoidance on illegal tax evasion in the U.S. To do this, we test the hypothesis proffered by Cebula (2004, p. 419) that "...the higher the tax-free interest rate yield on high grade municipal bonds (TF) relative to the taxable interest rate yield on..." high quality bonds or notes such as ten year U.S. Treasury notes (TEN), "...the greater the incentive to engage in legal tax avoidance and the lower the incentive to engage in tax evasion." Thus, the greater the TF/TEN ratio, the lower the DTE, *ceteris paribus*. Hence, (2) is now rewritten as:

$$eb = h(AEPT, TF/TEN),\ h_{AEPT} > 0,\ h_{TF/TEN} < 0 \qquad (3)$$

As an age control variable, we include the percentage of the population that is age 65 and older (AGE65+). In this age cohort, the *official* labor force participation rate for both males and females falls sharply at age 65. Given that the elderly to a large extent depend upon Social Security and Medicare for their economic survival, however, it may well be that many persons in this category may work "off the books," i.e., are paid in cash and hence do not report their earnings to the IRS. Indeed, given their age and circumstances (need), employers (especially unscrupulous ones) in many cases may be willing to hire the elderly *only if they do agree to work off the books*. Thus, it is plausible that the higher the percent of the population that is age 65 and older, the smaller the percentage of the population whose income is reported to the IRS. Thus, it is hypothesized that the greater the value of AGE65+, the greater may be the DTE. Hence, equation (3) becomes:

$$eb= i(AEPT, TF/TEN, AGE65+), i_{AEPT} > 0, i_{TF/TEN} < 0, i_{AGE65+} > 0 \quad (4)$$

The Tax Reform Act of 1986 (TRA) may have been perceived by the general public as an honest effort to reform, improve, simplify and increase the fairness of the Internal Revenue Code. As Musgrave observes (1987, p. 59), "The Tax Reform Act of 1986 is the most sweeping reform since the early 1940s..." Musgrave (1987, p. 59) further observes that prior to the TRA, a slow erosion of the income tax base had been occurring. Musgrave (1987, p. 57) was dismayed by the widening of tax loopholes and the emergence of high income tax shelters that had "...gained momentum in recent years and undermined the public's faith in the income tax. " Musgrave (1987, p. 59) also expresses concern that the "...compounding of the investment tax credit and accelerated depreciation diluted and distorted the base of the corporate income tax." Musgrave (1987, p. 59) asserted that the TRA "...reversed these trends, a major accomplishment that all reformers will welcome." Based on Musgrave's (1987) arguments, it is expected in the present study that taxpayers would favorably regard the TRA and be less resentful of the Internal Revenue Code than before, at least initially. Thus, it is hypothesized here that reduced taxpayer resentment of the federal tax system would, at least at the time the TRA was enacted, result in a reduced degree of tax evasion. Consequently, it is hypothesized here that for the year the TRA enacted, the DTE was reduced. Equation (4) is now replaced by:

$$eb= j (AEPT, TF/TEN, Age65+, TRA), j_{AEPT} > 0, j_{TF/TEN} < 0, j_{AGE65+} > 0, j_{TRA} < 0 \quad (5)$$

Next, there is the central issue of the public's job approval rating of the President (APPROV), which is the primary focus of this study in teaching political economy. The higher the public's approval rating of the President, the greater the degree to which there is satisfaction with the President's job performance and the less dissatisfaction the public manifests with the President's actions and policies. The latter can be interpreted as, at least to some degree, implying less resentment towards his various spending and/or tax policies (and perhaps even his record of budget deficits). Conversely, the lower the public's approval rating of the President, the lower the degree to which there is satisfaction with the President's job performance and the greater the degree to which the public is dissatisfied with the President's actions and policies. In turn, it can be reasonably argued that the latter can be interpreted, to at least some extent, as implying greater resentment towards his various spending and/or tax policies (as well perhaps as his budget deficit record). Stated somewhat differently, the lower the level of APPROV, the greater the subjective benefits from personal income tax evasion, whereas the higher the APPROV the lower the subjective benefits of personal income tax evasion. Based on this symmetrical argument, it is hypothesized that the greater the public's approval rating of the President, the lower the DTE, so that (6) becomes:

$$eb= k (AEPT, TF/TEN, AGE65+, TRA, APPROV), k_{AEPT} > 0, k_{TF/TEN} < 0, k_{AGE65+} > 0, k_{APPROV} < 0 \quad (6)$$

The expected gross costs of not reporting income to the IRS are hypothesized to be an increasing function of the risks thereof (Alm, Jackson, and McKee, 1992; Pestieau, Possen, and Slutsky, 1994; Erard and Feinstein, 1994; Caballe and Panades, 1997). In this study, to the representative economic agent, the expected penalty from not reporting or from underreporting taxable income to the IRS, is enhanced by an increase in AUDIT, the percentage of filed federal personal income tax returns that is formally audited by IRS examiners/personnel. Indeed, the experience of an IRS tax audit would imply non-pecuniary ("psychic") costs as well as pecuniary costs (including outlays for legal or other representation, along with the value of one's own time) above and beyond any potential added taxes, penalties, and interest assessed by the IRS. In addition to AUDIT, it is hypothesized that the expected risks associated with tax evasion rise with the magnitude of the IRS imposed penalties (PENALTY) should one's tax evasion activities be detected by the IRS. To reflect this penalty, this study adopts the average interest rate charged by the IRS in each year on detected unreported income. Thus, we have:

$$ec = j(AUDIT, PENALTY),\ j_{AUDIT} > 0,\ j_{PENALTY} > 0 \tag{7}$$

Substituting from (6) and (7) into (1) yields:

$$pnr/(1\text{-}pnr) = b(AEPT, TF/TEN, AGE65+, TRA, APPROV, AUDIT, PENALTY),$$

$$b_{AEPT} > 0, b_{TFTEN} < 0, b_{AGE65+} > 0, b_{TRA} < 0, b_{APPROV} < 0, b_{AUDIT} < 0, b_{PENALTY} < 0 \tag{8}$$

Let AGI represent the *actual total value of the aggregate federal adjusted gross income* in the economy, i.e., AGI=UAGI+RAGI, where UAGI is the dollar size of the *unreported aggregate federal adjusted gross income* in the economy, and RAGI is the dollar size of the *reported aggregate federal adjusted gross income* in the economy. It reasonably follows that:

$$UAGI = (pnr)*AGI \quad \text{and} \tag{9}$$

$$RAGI = (1\text{-}pnr)*AGI \tag{10}$$

It then follows logically that:

$$UAGI/RAGI = (pnr)*AGI/(1\text{-}pnr)*AGI = (pnr)/(1\text{-}pnr) \tag{11}$$

From (8) and (11), we obtain, by substitution for pnr/(1-pnr):

$$UAGI/RAGI = b(AEPT, TF/TEN, AGE65+, TRA, APPROV, AUDIT, PENALTY),$$

$$b_{AEPT} > 0,\ b_{TF/TEN} < 0,\ b_{AGE65+} > 0,\ b_{TRA} < 0,\ b_{APPROV} < 0,\ b_{AUDIT} < 0,\ b_{PENALTY} < 0 \tag{12}$$

Empirical Results

To statistically test our political-economy hypothesis regarding the effect of the public's job approval rating of the President on income tax evasion, this study adopts regression analysis. In particular, it adopts the technique known as Ordinary Least Squares, or simply OLS. Based on the framework provided in (12) above, the following equation is to be estimated using OLS:

$$(UAGI/RAGI)_t = a_0 + a_1\ AEPT_{t-1} + a_2\ (TF/TEN)_{t-1} + a_3\ (AGE65+)_{t-1} + {}_4\ TRA_t + a_5\ APPROV_{t-1} + a_6\ AUDIT_{t-1} + a_7\ PENALTY_{t-1} + u \quad (13)$$

where:

$(UAGI/RAGI)_t$ = the ratio of the aggregate *unreported* federal adjusted gross income in year t to the aggregate *reported* federal adjusted gross income in year t, expressed as a percent;

a_0 = constant;

$AEPT_{t-1}$ = the average effective federal personal income tax rate in year t-1, expressed as a percent;

$(TF/TEN)_{t-1}$ = the ratio for year t-1 of the average annual tax-free interest rate yield on high grade municipal bonds to the average annual taxable interest rate yield on ten-year U.S. Treasury notes, as a percent;

$(AGE65+)_{t-1}$ = the percentage of the population in year t-1 that was age 65 years or older;

TRA_t= a binary (dummy) variable for the year 1986, when the TRA reform Act of 1986 was enacted: TRA_t=1 for the year 1986 and TRA_t =0 otherwise;

$APPROV_{t-1}$ = the Presidential approval rating in year in year t-1: values for $APPROV_{t-1}$ lie between 0 and 100;

$AUDIT_{t-1}$ = the percentage of filed federal personal income tax returns in year t-1 that was subjected to a formal IRS audit involving IRS examiners;

$PENALTY_{t-1}$ = the percentage interest rate used by the IRS in year t-1 to assess penalties on detected unreported income; and

u = stochastic error term.

The study period for this study runs from 1960 through 1997, reflecting availability of the tax evasion and the audit data. The data are annual. The data for variables AEPT, AUDIT, and PENALTY were obtained from the IRS (1960-1997) and the IRS (2003). The TRA variable is a dummy variable. A dummy variable is a binary (0,1) variable used in this case to reflect the year 1986, the year during which the Tax Reform Act of 1986 was first implemented. The data for the variables TF/TEN and AGE65+ were obtained from the Council of Economic Advisors (2008, Tables B-73 and B-34). The data for political-economy variable APPROV were obtained from the website: http://www.geocities.com /americanpresidencynet/approval.html. The series adopted to measure the variable UAGI/RAGI were obtained from Feige (1989; 1996; 1997), extended back through 1960. Based on the General Currency Ratio (GCR) model, Feige has estimated the ratio of aggregate *unreported* adjusted gross income to aggregate *reported* adjusted gross income, using an IRS estimate for this ratio in 1973 of 14.84%. Over the study period, mean of the UAGI/RAGI series was 20.28, with a standard deviation of 5.68.

The P-P (Phillips-Perron) unit root test indicates that the variables UAGI/RAGI, AUDIT, AGE65+, and AEPT are stationary in only in first differences; alternatively stated, the data for these variables were found to exhibit a strong time trend. The variables TF/TEN, APPROV, and PENALTY are stationary in levels, implying that the data for these variables did not exhibit a strong time trend. Accordingly, in the estimations, the variables UAGI/RAGI, AUDIT, AGE65+, and AEPT are expressed in first differences, whereas the remaining variables are not thusly adjusted.

The OLS estimation of equation (13), adopting the Newey-West heteroskedasticity correction, is given by:

$$\underset{}{z(UAGI/RAGI)_t} = 8.07 + \underset{(+2.05)}{0.1155\, zAEPT_{t-1}} - \underset{(-1.27)}{4.19\, (TF/TEN)_{t-1}} + \underset{(+2.75)}{13.36\, z(AGE65+)_{t-1}}$$

$$- \underset{(-5.63)}{2.446\, TRA} - \underset{(-2.09)}{0.054\, APPROV_{t-1}} - \underset{(-2.43)}{3.93\, zAUDIT_{t-1}} - \underset{(-4.23)}{0.352\, PENALTY_{t-1}}$$

$$R^2 = 0.44,\ adjR^2 = 0.30,\ F= 3.05, DW = 2.03,\ Rho = -\ 0.01 \qquad (14)$$

where terms in parentheses are t-values and z is the first-differences operator.

In equation (14), the estimated coefficients on all seven of the explanatory variables exhibit the hypothesized signs, with three of the seven being statistically significant at beyond the five percent level and three others being significant at the one percent level. The coefficient of determination is 0.44, so that the model explains roughly three-sevenths of the variation in the dependent variable. The F-statistic is significant at far beyond the one percent level. There is no concern regarding autocorrelation.

The estimated coefficient on the AEPT variable is positive and statistically significant at the five percent level. Thus, the higher the average effective federal personal income tax rate, the greater the degree of income tax evasion by households. The coefficient on the TF/TEN variable, while negative, is not significant. However, the coefficient on the AGE65+ variable is positive and statistically significant at the one percent level, as hypothesized. Next, the estimated coefficient on the tax reform (TRA) variable is negative, as expected (Musgrave, 1987), and statistically significant at the one percent level. The estimated coefficients on the AUDIT and PENALTY variables are negative and statistically significant at the 2.5 and one percent levels, respectively, affirming the conventional wisdom that the prospect of risk and penalties in the forms of higher audit rates and higher interest rate assessments on detected unreported income act to discourage income tax evasion.

Finally, the estimated coefficient on the Presidential approval variable (APPROV) is negative, as hypothesized, and statistically significant at the five percent level. This result provides support for the hypothesis that a lower (higher) public approval rating of the President acts to increase (decrease) the aggregate degree of federal personal income tax evasion. Going further, it logically follows that a lower public job approval rating of the President would lead to reduced tax collections and increased budget deficits, with the latter then likely leading to higher interest rates (in a non-Ricardian equivalence world).

Furthermore, this finding also clearly demonstrates that what might appear at first glance to be a fundamentally political/political science phenomenon/issue, is in fact also an economic phenomenon/issue. Alternatively stated, this finding demonstrates clearly that both political science factors and economic conditions can be closely related and fall jointly under the rubric of what is referred to as political economy. Students in the political science and economics disciplines (and, arguably, the public policy discipline) should be made more acutely cognizant of these interrelationships among their disciplines so that they can more effectively practice their skills and training and perhaps even better interact with one another.

CONCLUSION

This study in political economy uses the well-known dataset on the public's job approval rating of the President and the well-known dataset developed by Feige (1989, 1994, 1996, 1997) on income tax evasion to provide insights into the nature of political economy. In particular, this study investigates the political-economy hypothesis that the higher the public approval rating of the President, the lower the aggregate degree of federal personal income taxation. The study period runs from 1960 through 1997. The study finds empirical support for this hypothesis. As observed in the preceding section of this study, this finding is a clear demonstration of the complex nuances that exist in the real world setting that constitutes "political economy," nuances with which students of economics, public policy, and political science should be made acutely aware.

REFERENCES

Allingham, M.G., and Sandmo, A. (1972). "Income Tax Evasion". *Journal of Public Economics*, 1 (3), 1972, 323-338.

Alm, J., Jackson, B., and McKee, M. (1992). "Institutional Uncertainty and Taxpayer Compliance". *American Economic Review*, 82 (4), 1018-1026.

Alm, J., McClelland, G.H. and Schulze, W.D. (1999). "Changing the Social Norm of Tax Compliance by Voting". *Kyklos*, 52 (1), 141-171.

Bawley, D. (1982). *The Subterranean Economy*. New York, McGraw-Hill.

Caballe, J. and J. Panades, J. (1997). "Tax Evasion and Economic Growth". *Public Finance/Finances Publiques*, 52 (2), 318-340.

Cagan, P. (1958). "The Demand for Currency Relative to the Total Money Supply". *Journal of Political Economy*, 66 (2), 1958, 303-328.

Carson, C. (1984). "The Underground Economy: An Introduction". *Survey of Current Business*, 64 (1), 24-35.

Cebula, R. J. (2004). "Income Tax Evasion Revisited: The Impact of Interest Rate Yields on Tax-Free Municipal Bonds". *Southern Economic Journal*, 71 (2), 418-423.

Clotfelter, C.T. (1983). "Tax Evasion and Tax Rates: An Analysis of Individual Returns". *Review of Economics and Statistics*, 65 (2), 363-373.

Council of Economic Advisors. (2008). *Economic Report of the President, 2008*. Washington, D.C., U.S. Government Printing Office.

Erard, B., and Feinstein, J.S. (1994). "The Role of Moral Sentiments and Audit Perceptions in Tax Compliance," *Public Finance/Finances Publiques*, 49 (1), 70-89.

Feige, E. L. (1989). *The Underground Economies: Tax Evasion and Information Distortion.* Cambridge, Cambridge University Press.

Feige, E.L. (1994). "The Underground Economy and the Currency Enigma". *Public Finance/Finances Publiques*, 49 (1), 119-136.

Feige, E.L. (1996). "Overseas Holdings of U.S. Currency and the Underground Economy". in Pozo, S., editor, *Exploring the Underground Economy*. Kalamazoo, MI, W.E. Upjohn Institute for Employment Research, 215-235.

Feige, E.L. (1997). "Revised Estimates of the Size of the U.S. Underground Economy: Implications of U.S. Currency Held Abroad," in Lippert, O. and Walker, M. editors. *The Underground Economy: Global Evidence of Its Size and Impact.* Vancouver, Canada, Fraser Institute, 146-165.

http://www.geocities.com/americanpresidencynet/approval.html

Internal Revenue Service. (1957-1997). *Annual Report of the Commissioner and Chief Counsel of the Internal Revenue Service*, Washington, D.C., U.S. Government Printing Office.

Internal Revenue Service. (2003). *Statistics of Income*. Washington, D.C., U.S. Government Printing Office.

Musgrave, R.A. (1987). "Short of Euphoria". *Journal Economic Perspectives*, 1 (1), 1987, pp. 59-71.

Pestieau, P., Possen, U., and Slutsky, S. (1994). "Optimal Differential Taxes and Penalties". *Public Finance/Finances Publiques*, 49 (1), 15-27.

Pozo, S. (1996). Editor. *Exploring the Underground Economy*, Kalamazoo, MI, Upjohn.

Pyle, D. (1989). *Tax Evasion and the Black Economy*, New York, St. Martin's Press.

Tanzi, V., (1982). *The Underground Economy in the United States and Abroad*, Lexington, MA, Lexington Books.

In: Expanding Teaching and Learning Horizons
Editors: F. G. Mixon, Jr. and R. J. Cebula
ISBN 978-1-60741-971-6

Chapter 10

RECENT FILM SCENES FOR TEACHING INTRODUCTORY ECONOMICS

G. Dirk Mateer

INTRODUCTION

Much has been written of late about the use of movies in teaching economics. Sexton (2006) compiled a list of 47 films that relate to economics. Mateer (2005) created a supplement for the principles market that contains 20 streaming videos. Becker (2004) and Dixit (2005) describe how films can be used to stimulate discussion in introductory classes and Leet and Houser (2003) explored the use of full-length films to teach introductory economics.

The focus of this paper is to augment the list of films available to economists by providing instructors with a set of recent film scenes that has not been previously discussed in the literature. These additional films add to the developing database of useful films for instruction.

In addition, there are a number of lists that have been created for specific fields. Shor (2004) has compiled a comprehensive list of films that highlight game theoretic applications like the prisoner's dilemma, strategic behavior, and bargaining. Mulder (2002) catalogs how current labor issues are treated in the movies. Ribstein (2004) and Formaini (2001) explore how capitalism is portrayed in film.

More broadly, teaching with film is an extension of the work done by Becker (2004) and Becker and Watts (1998, 2001, 2003, 2006) who examined the way that economics was taught at the college level and found that the discipline had been slow to adopt innovative approaches to teaching. Similarly, Hoyt (2003) discussed the need to make economic education more fulfilling. Utilizing movie clips is one notable example of a non-traditional approach to economic education. Other non-traditional examples include: Watts' (2003) inspection of economics in literature, and Tinari and Khandke's (2000) use of popular songs, dating back to the 1930s, to help teach economics.

SUGGESTIONS FOR TEACHING WITH FILM CLIPS

In my introductory classes film scenes are interspersed throughout the material and provide stimulating fodder for learning. Each class typically includes at least one film scene. A short capsule of the film scenes that are recommended is included in Table I.

Table I. Film Scenes

Introductory Material:				
Film	Year	Basic Message	Economic Concepts	DVD location
Bourne Identity	2002	Trade can be beneficial to both parties.	Consumer and producer surplus, gains from trade	Chapter 8, 25:40 to 27:00
Charlie and the Chocolate Factory	2005	Roald Dahl's well-known classic is filled with economics.	Supply and demand, substitution effects, scarcity	Chapter 5, 14:45 to 19:35
The Count of Monte Cristo	2002	The scene makes a very powerful point about the nature of economics and expenditures.	Adam Smith, What is economics?	Chapter 12, 47:11 to 47:26
Dirty Pretty Things	2002	The movie is about illegal kidney harvesting. There are serious ethical dimensions here as well as the exploitation of the poor.	Property rights, gains from trade	Chapter 10, 49:00 to 51:01
A Knight's Tale	2001	Three peasants wrestle with how to spend 15 silver coins that they have won in a jousting tournament.	Production possibilities curve, capital goods, consumer goods	Chapter 1, 5:38 to 14:23
The Merchant of Venice	2004	Shakespeare's tale of greed and love.	Opportunity cost, time preference, risk	Chapter 5, 18:27 to 23:48
Old School	2003	A bread maker is re-gifted twice. An excellent introduction to Joel Waldfogel's *AER* article, "The Deadweight Loss of Christmas."	Consumer surplus, producer surplus, gains from trade, preferences	Chapter 3, 12:40 to 13:29; Chapter 11, 48:20 to 49:01
Swordfish	2001	A rogue federal agent believes that the best way to fight terrorism is to respond to each act of terror with a response that is greater in magnitude than the original act.	Incentives, trade-offs	Chapter 20, 1:06:39 to 1:08:37
The Terminal	2004	Luggage carts provide an unusual source of income for man stuck in an airport.	Incentives, comparative advantage, opportunity cost	Chapter 10, 29:41 to 32: 08

Microeconomics:				
Film	Year	Basic Message	Economic Concepts	DVD location
Anchorman: The Legend of Ron Burgundy	2004	Discrimination in the broadcasting business in the 1970s.	Causes of discrimination, occupational crowding, marginal revenue product	Chapter 5, 13:46 to 17:13
Blow	2001	A West Coast cocaine dealer decides to market his product on the East Coast because he can sell it there at a higher price.	Supply and demand, partnerships, entrepreneurship, economics of crime.	Chapter 4, 14:15 to 16:00
How to Lose a Guy in 10 Days	2003	A spoof of the diamond industry and the "a diamond is forever" campaign made famous by DeBeers.	Elasticity of demand, luxury goods, market power, cartels, specialization.	Chapter 2, 6:06 to 7:11; Chapter 4 13:43 to 16:02
Million Dollar Baby	2004	Academy award winner for best picture. A successful boxer buys a small house for her impoverished mother and family and meets with surprising resistance.	Public assistance programs, incentives, trade-offs	Chapter 21, 1:12:34 to 1:14:22
Murder by Numbers	2002	A great example of the prisoner's dilemma.	Game theory, dominant strategies, cooperative games	Chapter 21, 1:27:10 to 1:29:11
Rent	2006	This Broadway musical, adapted for film, explores poverty.	Rent Controls, urban economics, property rights, incentives, substitution effect.	Chapter 2, 4:35 to 13:42
Swept Away	2002	Desperate and hungry, a spoiled rich woman tries to buy a fish to no avail.	Elasticity of demand	Chapter 12, 39:42 to 41:12
Wimbledon	2004	When a British tennis player, whose career is on the wane, surprisingly makes the quarterfinals at Wimbledon his agent reappears and approaches him with new financial opportunities.	Labor demand and supply	Chapter 6, 32:30 to 34:00
Pay It Forward	2000	The parallels between the clip and Keynes' multiplier allow the instructor to develop the theoretical and practical dimensions of fiscal policy.	The multiplier, fiscal policy, actual deposit expansion multiplier	Chapter 10, 32:57 to 34:20
Seabiscuit	2003	A narrative by historian David McCullough helps explain the forces at work during the Great Depression.	The Great Depression, business cycles, unemployment, stock market	Chapter 3, 12:50 to 15:21

Table 1. (Continued)

Macroeconomics				
Film	Year	Basic Message	Economic Concepts	DVD location
Groundhog Day	1993	A weatherman is caught in a time warp where he relives the same day until he gets it right.	Rational expectations, adaptive expectations, learning by doing	Chapter 15, 41:00 to 42:09; Chapter 24, 1:23:02 to 1:24:37
The Full Monty	1997	Six unemployed men decide that they can make a small fortune by putting on a striptease show.	Discouraged workers, structural unemployment, cyclical unemployment	Chapter 4, 9:57 to 12:14
International Economics:				
Film	Year	Basic Message	Economic Concepts	DVD location
A Day Without a Mexican	2004	Imagine California without any Hispanics and you have the premise of this offbeat film.	Labor markets, trade barriers, immigration.	Chapter 4, 27:45 to 29:32; Chapter 8, 51:28 to 51:56
Eurotrip	2004	Four high school graduates travel to Europe and end up in an impoverished country where the U.S. dollar has enormous purchasing power.	Exchange rates, purchasing power parity	Chapter 13, 57:32 to 1:00:01
Life and Debt	2001	This documentary focuses on the Jamaican economy.	International trade, free trade agreements, poverty, comparative advantage, IMF, WTO	Chapters 7, 23:14 to 24:41; Chapter 10, 36:38 to 45:06
Topics Not Usually Covered in Introductory Economics:				
Film	Year	Basic Message	Economic Concepts	DVD location
Coyote Ugly	2000	An example of a successful auction with an unusual ending.	Auctioning mechanisms	Chapter 11, 36:27 to 39:59
Harold and Kumar Go To White Castle	2004	Jaywalking is not a good idea when the fine is $220.	Rational self-interest, economics of crime, externalities	Chapter 11, 51:46 to 54:22
John Q	2002	John Q is a luckless blue-collar worker with insufficient insurance to cover his son's emergency heart transplant.	Moral hazard, health economics	Chapter 5, 19:15 to 26:05

My suggestion is that instructors start with a few scenes that they are familiar with and build up. In part, I make this suggestion, because with any approach there are diminishing returns and some nontrivial costs in ramping up from zero. Each of the suggested scenes gets to the point in an amusing, dramatic, or thought-provoking way. Some of the scenes make points in humorous ways (especially *Anchorman; Harold and Kumar; Old School*). For example, in *Harold and Kumar Go to White Castle*, Harold and Kumar debate whether to cross a deserted street at 2:30 in the morning. When Harold pauses and looks both ways Kumar encourages him to cross even though the "do not walk" sign is flashing. Suddenly a cop appears out of nowhere to ticket Harold for jaywalking and an outrageous discussion about the calculus of crime and discrimination ensues. Both topics offer significant appeal to students.

Many of the film scenes are thought-provoking (see *The Bourne Identity; The Count of Monte Cristo; A Day Without a Mexican; Dirty Pretty Things; John Q; Life and Debt; Million Dollar Baby*). In *Million Dollar Baby*, when a female boxer purchases a small house for her mother she meets surprising resistance. Her mother turns down her offer in order to maintain her eligibility for welfare. This is a powerful way of motivating a discussion of public assistance. A third type of scene comes from *Coyote Ugly*, where one of the Coyotes decides to auction off a night with her boyfriend to the highest bidder, but she mistakenly ends the auction when the bidding reaches her reservation price. This is not the way to run an auction, but that is part of the beauty of the scene. Uncovering good economics is often more fun when Hollywood gets it wrong! *Coyote Ugly* gives the instructor a chance to discuss how value is determined, examine bidding strategies, and develop of richer understanding of various types of auctioning mechanisms. The common thread in all of the film scenes is that they convey a simple message in a persuasive or amusing way.

SETTING THE SCENE

When a film scene is introduced the instructor should provide a short synopsis of the film, alert the audience to watch for certain elements, and to take notes as appropriate. Afterwards, the instructor can relate the scene to the course material and ask for student input.

I have found that it is important to fully integrate the film scenes into the course. This can be achieved in a variety of ways. The most straightforward approach is to use the film scenes to amplify and reinforce core concepts. This is accomplished by utilizing film scenes as case studies in your lecture. Another mechanism that I use is to include one film scene on each exam. At beginning of each midterm I have students watch a short scene and write a paragraph response that identifies the economic content. In addition, I have students write a one-page paper on a film scene not discussed in class. This cements the discovery process by providing a platform for students to apply the concepts that they learn [1].

Finally, I use a supplement (Mateer, 2005) to assign streaming film clips as homework. The use of films as case studies, on exams, as short writing assignments, and also as homework makes the film scenes an integral part of the course.

The Scenes

The film scenes are organized into the topic areas typically covered in a one-year principles sequence. For each scene, the year the film was released is noted, followed by a brief description, the economic concepts that are covered, and the chapter location and starting and ending time on the DVD.

Introductory topics (9 clips) are well suited to this approach. In addition, since microeconomics deals with the "small picture," it is not surprising that the list includes many scenes that deal primarily with microeconomic concepts (8 clips). However, given the complexity of many macroeconomic topics (4 clips) and international issues (3 clips) it is much harder to find film clips that provide an adequate treatment of those areas.

Most of the film scenes mentioned here can be shown with little advance preparation or knowledge of the entire film. However, some of the scenes come from movies with complicated plot lines or themes. Here my suggestion is that the instructor view (or at least review the plot) of the entire film.

FAQs

(1) *Is this legal?* The use of short film scenes falls under the fair use exemption in the Federal Copyright Act. More broadly, the display of copyrighted materials during face-to-face teaching permits the instructor to show entire feature length films under most circumstances [2]

(2) *Will students be offended?* Instructors must be careful to screen each of the scenes before use. While most of the scenes listed here would pass the strictest of tests, some of the clips contain offensive language, prostitution, and recreational drug use. I begin the showing of each film by reminding students that we are watching the scene to ferret out the economics and that they should focus on this element and not the extraneous material.

(3) *How can I acquire the film clips?* Instructors who have a departmental or personal research budget could purchase the film. Most of the DVDs cost anywhere from $10-$20. This is the most economical route if the film scene is reused each semester. With rare exception, these films are also available at your local DVD rental store. Finally, a membership in an online rental company (e.g. Netflix or Blockbuster) allows the instructor to set up a queue that will send the DVDs directly to a campus address in a predetermined order. This requires a monthly membership.

(4) *What are some drawbacks that I need to avoid?*

   i. Instructors should be clear in providing the necessary links between real-world events and the fictional scenes viewed the in movies.

   ii. It takes time to integrate film clips into a course. Care should be taken to make sure that the value added warrants the use of scarce class time.

   iii. Stay focused on the message you want to bring out in the scene.

(5) *What are some ways to focus attention?* I use the subtitles feature. This is especially useful in bringing out what is being said. I also turn the lights off to avoid glare on the screen.

CONCLUSION

Viewing film scenes in class has many advantages. First, it stimulates discussion through focused-viewing. This allows everyone in attendance to experience the film and critically analyze the scene, something that would not be possible if the film was assigned for viewing outside of class. Second, this provides a superior alternative to the lecture-discussion format. Third, if you teach in a technology classroom with a large screen and a sound system the experience can rival going to see a film in the theatre. Moreover, the learning experience is one that works well with all students, regardless of their quantitative background or interest level in economics.

NOTES

[1] As an instructor, I have been actively soliciting input for the last five years and students have suggested most of the film scenes described here. I view the emphasis on recent films as a plus since many films slowly become dated over time.

[2] Section 110.1, in the Federal Copyright Act, Public Law 94-553, Title 17.

REFERENCES

Becker, W. E., and Watts, M. 1998. Teaching economics to undergraduates: *Alternatives to chalk and talk.* Cheltenham: Edward Elgar.

Becker, W. E., and Watts, M. 2001. Teaching methods in U.S. undergraduate courses. Journal of Economic Education 32 (Summer): 269-280.

Becker, W. E., and Watts, M. and Becker, S. (eds.) 2006. Teaching *Economics: More Alternatives to Chalk and Talk.* Edward Elgar.

Becker, W. E. 2003. How to make economics the sexy social science. *Southern Economic Journal* 70 (Summer): 195-198.

Becker, W. E. 2004. Good-bye old, hello new in teaching economics. *Australasian Journal of Economics Education* 1 (March): 5-17.

Dixit, A. (2005). Restoring fun to game theory. Journal of Economic Education 36 (Summer): 205-218.

Formaini, R. 2001. Free markets on film: Hollywood and capitalism. *Journal of Private Enterprise* 16 (Spring): 122-129.

Hoyt, Gail 2003. How to make economics the fulfilling social science. *Southern Economics Journal* 70 (1): 216-218.

Internet Movie Database. (http://www.imdb.com/)

Kish-Goodling, D. M. 1998. Using The Merchant of Venice in teaching monetary economics. *Journal of Economic Education* 29 (Fall): 330-339.

Leet, D. and Houser, S. 2003. Economics goes to Hollywood: Using classic films to create an undergraduate economics course. *Journal of Economic Education* 34 (Fall): 326-332.

Mateer, G. D. 2005. *Economics in the Movies.* South-Western, Thomson.

Mulder, C. 2002. Current Labor Issues in Film. (http://fandm.edu/departments/tdf/FilmPages/Courses/Other-02/syllabus-2002.htm)

Ribstein, L. 2004. Busfilm. (http://busmovie.typepad.com/busfilm/)

Tinari, F. D., and Khandke, K. 2000. From rhythm and blues to Broadway: Using music to teach economics. *Journal of Economic Education* 31 (Summer): 253-270.

Sexton, R. 2006. Using short movie and television clips in the economics principles class. *Journal of Economic Education*. 37 (Fall): 406-417.

Shor, M. 2004. Resources for learning and teaching strategy for business and life. (http://www.gametheory.net)

Watts, M. (ed.) 2003. *The Literary Book of Economics*, Wilmington, Delaware, ISI Books.

In: Expanding Teaching and Learning Horizons
Editors: F. G. Mixon, Jr. and R. J. Cebula
ISBN 978-1-60741-971-6

Chapter 11

AN ARMCHAIR VIEW OF ESCALATORS AND MOVING WALKWAYS

Roger W. Garrison

INTRODUCTION

There is much pedagogical value in applying the economist's standard analytical tools to issues about which students already have a common-sense understanding. By demonstrating this point repeatedly, Steven Landsburg has become the profession's pre-eminent *Armchair Economist* (Landsburg, 1993). "Why Popcorn Costs More at the Movies" (pp. 157-167) may not be a critical issue in its own right, but addressing it with just the right kernel of economic truth can be an effective way of teaching analytical skills.

Almost a decade after manning his armchair, Landsburg (2002) dealt with a pair of downright frivolous questions: Why don't people walk up escalators? And why don't people stand still on stairs? Landsburg's answer, which he attributes to Mark Bils, involves taking escalators and stairs to be instances of inferior and superior machines. Just as workers should spend less time with an inferior machine, people should spend less time on stairs. Well, all right, standing still on stairs clearly violates that maxim. While Bils and Landsburg get points here for matching answer to question in terms of the degree of frivolity, they forgo the opportunity to showcase the economic way of thinking by applying standard indifference-curve analysis.

RESTING AND MOVING

The relevant decision, undoubtedly made subconsciously by the typical stair climber or escalator rider, involves a tradeoff between resting and moving towards their ultimate destination. This tradeoff is perfectly analogous to the one that underlies much of labor economics, namely the tradeoff between leisure and income (McConnell *et al.*, 2006, pp. 15-22). For a given period of time, enjoying leisure and earning income can be achieved in various proportions, and under favorable conditions, people can choose the optimal mix. For a given increment of time spent on stairs or escalators, resting and moving are the two relevant alternatives. And while resting can be interpreted as not moving at all, moving slowly entails a degree of resting—analogous to labor theory's "on-the-job leisure."

So, we let the two gerunds (resting and moving) label the vertical axis and the horizontal axis, respectively, of the indifference-curve map in Figure 1. That extreme form of resting, i.e., standing still, defines the vertical intercept of a budget constraint, which we take to be linear. (A significant budget-constraint non-linearity in the case of moving walkways will be considered later.) The horizontal intercept corresponds to zero rest and has our stair climber racing at maximum speed. We take this budget constraint to be applicable only to ascending the stairs; the constraint applicable to descending would have a horizontal intercept lying further to the right. Most people can race down the stairs faster than they can race up them [1]. In either application and except in extreme circumstances, the actual tradeoff will be struck somewhere between standing still and racing as fast as possible.

Straightforwardly, the indifference-curve map shows our ascender's preferences when faced with a choice between resting more and moving faster. A tangency between the budget constraint and an indifference curve occurs at Point 1, which identifies the optimal combination of resting and moving on the stairway. If the stairway is replaced by an escalator, our budget constraint must be replaced as well. The new constraint has the same slope as the old one but is shifted to the right to take into account the speed of the escalator. Having the same slope implies that walking up an escalator and walking up stairs at a given speed are equally unrestful activities. If walking up an escalator is judged to be more unrestful (because of the higher steps and less suitable rise-to-run ratio) then the budget constraint for the escalator would be a little steeper than the one for the stairs.

Important for our application is the fact that the new budget constraint is truncated at the standing-still level of rest. The constraint does not extend upward from that point toward the vertical axis. This is only to say that you cannot improve on the restfulness associated with standing still by walking or running backwards on the escalator. Thus, the point that represents standing still and moving at escalator speed is a potential corner solution. The preference map shows that this corner, Point 2, is in fact the optimal choice for our typical rider.

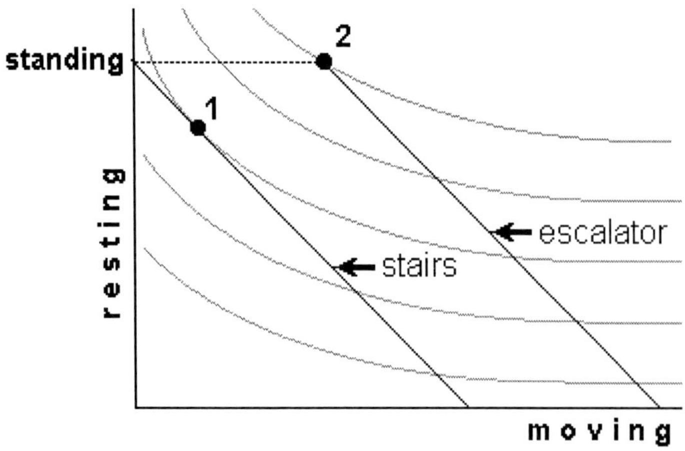

Figure 1.

We see from Figure 1 that our stair-climber-*cum*-escalator-rider deals with the gain offered by an escalator in conventional ways. The gain is taken partly in the form of more rest and partly in the form of more speed. The corner solution implies that some riders would actually go further in trading speed for rest at the margin if that were technologically possible. But given their actual options, they are constrained to move at escalator speed while just standing still. Would people be better off with escalators that allowed for tangency solutions? The general shape of the indifference curves suggests that achieving a tangency would require escalators to move more slowly. Figure 2 shows the case where the escalator moves at the optimal stair-climbing speed established in Figure 1. With the potential corner solution directly above Point 1, the typical rider would not adopt that corner as a solution. To stand still on this slow-moving escalator would mean taking the whole gain in the form of more resting (a possible—but probably not a typical—choice). Most everyone would walk up—with some, presumably, ascending faster than others. Note, however, that the tangency solution entails a degree of utility that is less than that associated with the corner solution in Figure 1. Riders are better off with a corner solution on a faster-moving escalator.

Providing answers to the original inquiry (Why don't people walk up escalators?) leads us to a related question that has a more satisfying answer: On what basis do escalator manufactures set the speed of their escalators? It would seem that they set the speed at a level that puts most riders at a corner solution.[2] With most riders standing still, the problem of congestion is minimized. Further, the dominance of the corner solution justifies an escalator design that best accommodates standers. (The slow-moving escalator of Figure 2 should have a step height and rise-to-run ratio of a conventional stairway. That design would best accommodate the climbers).

Even with the faster-moving escalator of Figure 1, some people will climb. Their preferences imply a tangency solution (with steeper indifference curves than the ones in Figures 1 and 2). Some may even climb as rapidly as they would climb stairs. These people are simply taking all of the gain provided by the escalator in the form of speed and none of the gain in the form of rest [3].

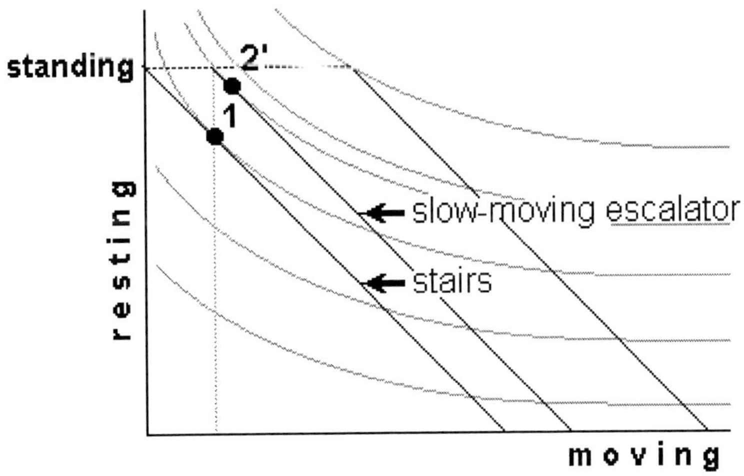

Figure 2.

It may well be the case that an escalator speed set so high that literally no one would walk or run up it is, at the same time, set so high that virtually no one would get on it. Further, we see in the following section that it is no contradiction of economic theory for some people in some circumstances to walk or run faster up an escalator than they would walk or run on stairs.

TRAIN STATIONS, AIRPORTS, CONVENTION HOTELS, AND SHOPPING MALLS

Figure 3 is identical to Figure 1 in terms of the shape and location of the budget constraints, but it differs from the earlier figure in terms of the preference map. Given the particular indifference curves of Figure 3, we get a tangency solution in which the rider actually leverages the gain provided by the escalator. As implied by a movement from Point 1 to Point 2, he runs up the escalator, though with stairs he would only have walked up. We can easily imagine the circumstances in which these preferences are understandable. Suppose it is very much worth while to get to the next floor quickly but failing that, it doesn't much matter whether you get there a little later or even later still. Train stations and airports provide circumstances where these indifference curves might apply.

The escalator may give the traveler just the leverage he or she needs to catch an on-time plane. But absent the escalator, all hope is lost. The stair-climber walks up the stairs at a normal pace on the chance that the train/plane is late or to check the time table for the next departure. (Undoubtedly, some of these travelers might have run up the stairs. Still, the case in which a traveler would walk up the stairs but run up the escalator is conceivable and even plausible.) The behavior motivated by the preference map in Figure 3 is probably common in train stations and airports but rare to non-existent in convention hotels. The conventioneers are not overly concerned about missing the first few minutes of some session on the application of indifference-curve analysis.

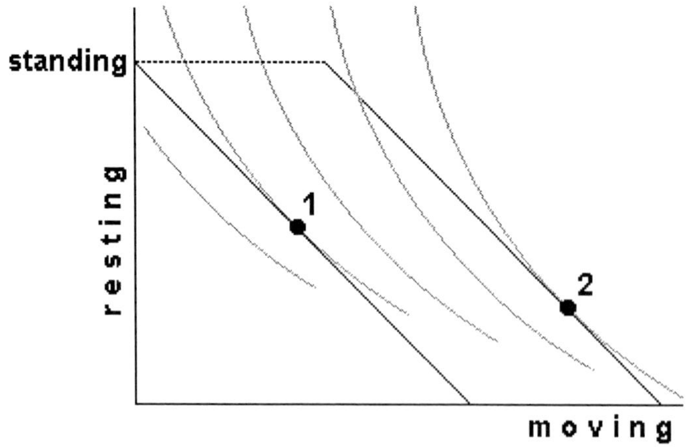

Figure 3.

Shopping malls are usually like convention hotels but are sometimes like train stations and airports. On the day after Christmas or on other special sales days, it is critical to get to the merchandise ahead of the crowd; but failing that, it will do just to see what's left over after the mad scramble. Shoppers whose preferences are more conventional (i.e., similar to the ones shown in Figure 1) might want to be put on notice that there are other shoppers among them whose preference maps are similar to the one shown in Figure 3. Possibly, mall managers would find it worthwhile to create an iconic symbol that captures the pattern of indifference curves of Figure 3 and post it near the mall entrance on sales days. The notice could serve a function similar to a posting at the beach that warns of a riptide.

MOVING WALKWAYS

An indifference-curve treatment of moving walkways would seem to be similar in all respects to our treatment of escalators. But there are critical differences. The budget constraint has a much shallower slope and possibly is non-linear at strolling speeds, virtually precluding the kind of dominant corner solution that characterizes our analysis of escalators. Figure 4 adopts the same indifference-curve map used in Figure 1. But the budget constraint has a slope that is considerably less than in Figure 1: On a level playing field, people can trade rest for speed on much more favorable terms.

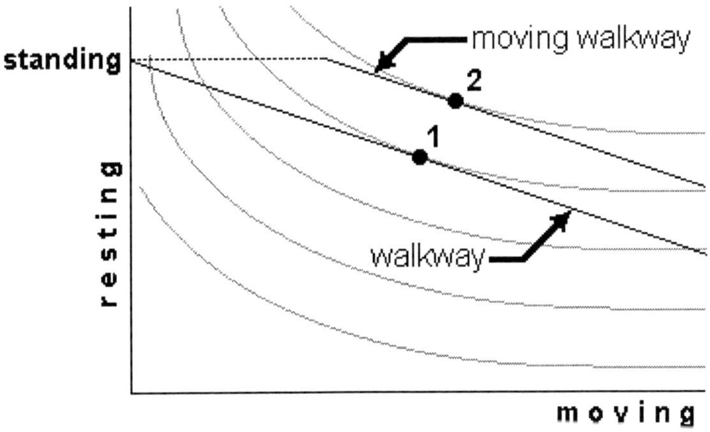

Figure 4.

The shallow slope alone makes it unlikely that a corner solution will dominate. In Figure 4, our typical rider takes advantage of a moving walkway by locating at Point 2, which constitutes a tangency solution. It is without contradiction, then, that many people (including the author) stand on an escalator but walk on a moving walkway. Making a corner solution even less likely is the fact that for many, strolling may seem more restful than standing. If strolling is preferred to walking *even on grounds of restfulness*, then the budget constraint itself rises from its standing-still level and then slopes downward at speeds beyond the stroll. As is clear in Figure 5, this kind of non-linearity precludes a corner solution.

Of course, some people do stand on moving walkways. Standing may even be typical for riders who have luggage or are otherwise encumbered. Others stroll for added restfulness or to avoid boredom. Still others walk, taking only part of the gain provided by the moving walkway in the form of rest, or they walk fast, leveraging the gain. Without a corner solution to fix a dominant mode of usage, measures need to be taken to deal with the variety of modes. Typically, moving walkways are wider than escalators, and riders are reminded by conspicuous signs or by a taped voice to stand on the right or walk on the left. Though less common, this same convention can be prescribed for escalator riders.

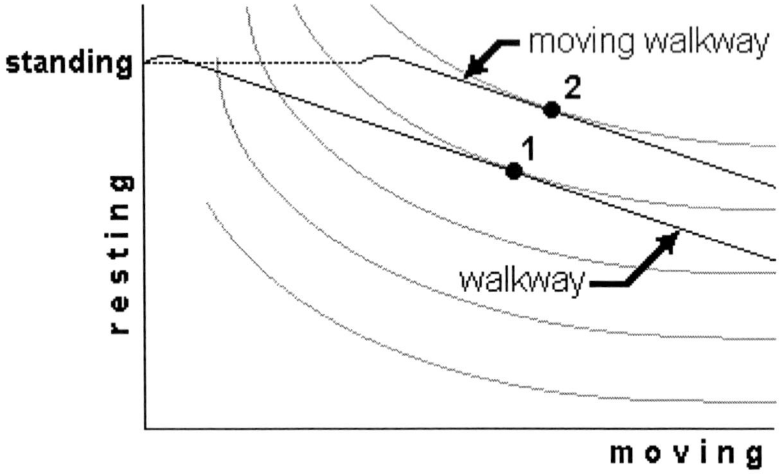

Figure 5.

Summary

Using indifference-curve analysis to show why people stand still on escalators but walk on moving walkways helps establish the near-universal applicability of neoclassical microeconomic theory. Working with contrasting preference maps (such as those in Figures 1 and 3) to deal with an issue where the student's own intuition is fully in play may help the student to read indifference curves in less intuitive cases. And challenging the students to apply basic economic tools to similarly frivolous issues can result in fun and even learning. The only downside to exposing students to this armchair view of escalators and moving walkways is that they may never again be able to pass through an airport without thinking of indifference-curve analysis.

Notes

[1] One of my colleagues whose armchair is much newer than my own claims that she can go up the stairs (taking three steps at a time) faster than she can go down (having to use every step).

[2] Actually polling the manufacturers of escalators on this question, of course, would violate the spirit of armchair theorizing. In any case, we can claim they *behave as if* they have a corner solution in mind.

[3] According to Landsburg (2002), the Bils-Landsburg argument "proves...that even if you choose to walk on the escalator, you should *always* walk even faster on the stairs" (*emphasis added*). The "always," it turns out, makes their statement too strong.

REFERENCES

Landsburg, S. E. (2002). Everyday Economics: Why do you walk up staircases but not up escalators? *Slate* (http://slate.msm.com), August 28.

Landsburg, S. E. (1993). *The Armchair Economist: Economics and Everyday Life*. New York: The Free Press.

McConnell, C. R., S. L. Brue, and D. A. Macpherson (2006). *Contemporary Labor Economics*, Boston: McGraw-Hill Irwin.

In: Expanding Teaching and Learning Horizons
Editors: F. G. Mixon, Jr. and R. J. Cebula

ISBN 978-1-60741-971-6

Chapter 12

TEACHING TARIFFS USING WELFARE ECONOMICS: TO THINK "IN AN ECONOMICS WAY" VIA E-LEARNING

David R. Lange and Carel M. Ligeon

INTRODUCTION

Research on e-Learning includes a significant focus on cognition, a basic component to thinking 'in an Economics Way'. In a study of five Social Sciences Citation Index (SSCI) e-Learning journals from 2001 to 2005, Shih, Feng and Tsai (2008) found that almost half (43.2%, 444 of 1027 articles) were related to the field of cognition. The intent of this paper is to demonstrate an e-Learning graphical representation of Tariffs using Welfare Economics as an example of cognitive learning – to think 'in an Economics Way'.

When using e-Learning it is very important to explain an economic theory in a logical and systematic approach. The absence of a classroom environment makes it harder for students to ask questions when the steps to the economic theory or concept are not clear. Simkins and Maier (2004) note, e-Learning could also be utilized as a pre-classroom exercise, identified as a 'Just-in-Time' teaching technique. Students work an e-learning assignment and forward questions shortly before class. The Professor then adapts the lecture or presentation as a response to the questions and directly addresses any conceptual understanding problems. This may also be described as a 'hybrid' course in which the class meets in the classroom some portion of the time, maybe every other normally scheduled meeting, and uses e-learning outside of the classroom. The logical and systematic approach combined with animation benefits e-learning students more because the students can visualize the steps that lead to an economic theory or concept, understanding each step before they move to the next one.

Ping (2003) noted "economics is a way of thinking about problems, not a set of answers ready to be taken off the shelf". The effective framework for Ping's (2003) notion of students thinking 'in an economics way' is the cognitive theory of learning first offered by Bloom (1956). Referring to Figure 1: To Think 'In an Economics Way', Bloom's (1956) Cognitive Learning Taxonomy is listed in the first row, from the left to right in increasing levels -

Knowledge, Comprehension, Application, Analysis, Evaluation, and Synthesis. Anderson and Krathwohl (2001) provided a revised taxonomy, with two dimensions, the Cognitive Process and Knowledge. The Cognitive Process, similar to the Bloom's base Taxonomy, included Remember, Understand, Apply, Analyze, Evaluate and Create. Additional descriptive terms are included below the respective levels of the Cognitive Process. The Knowledge dimension is divided into Factual (Terminology), Conceptual (Principles, Models), Procedural (Methods, Algorithms) and Meta-Cognitive (Awareness). According to Ping (2003), the goal of economics education is "to provide students with an adequate knowledge and understanding of the tools of economic analysis and of the situations and problems to which these tools are applied". Ping (2003) identifies assessment levels of testing which include all of the above Cognitive Processes, along with 'organization and presentation'. For example, Economics exams may include definitions as in terminology, to concepts, to problems, to evaluations of economic scenarios.

Economic pedagogy relies heavily on graphical representations and graphical analyses of economic theories, models and concepts in both the classroom and textbooks, Shiu and Sin (2006), Mankiw (2007); Appleyard, Field and Cobb (2008); and Pugel (2007). Shiu and Sin (2006) suggest these graphical representations and analyses [middle-out] connect abstract concepts and theories [top-down] with the empirical world specific knowledge [bottom-up]. Thus, graphical representations and graphical analyses [middle-out] may be viewed within in the framework of Figure 1 as part of cognitive science to understand learning and thinking, Shiu and Sin (2006). Accordingly, graphical representations and graphical analyses [middle-out] serve as a 'bridge', Bloom's (1956) Application and Analysis, between and to Bloom's (1956) Knowledge and Comprehension [bottom-up] and Evaluation and Synthesis [top-down] learning and thinking. Graphical applications and analysis are most beneficial when the economic theories are complex or the interactions of economic factors are complicated. Graphing the causal process, sequence of steps, is a common pedagogical approach in economics, Shiu and Sin (2006).

A similar theme may be identified as 'Cognitive Scaffolding' via information and communication technologies (ICT) in economics education, Ping (2003). The very nature of economics requires both deductive and inductive thinking to avoid having students see economics as a large number of concepts that must be memorized for exams. Thus "learning and teaching activities must scaffold deductive and inductive thinking processes" Ping (2003). Overall, information and communication technologies offer economics teachers many more pedagogical opportunities for effective learning and have students 'to think in an economics way'; including, visualization and animation, cognitive scaffolding, immediate feedback, a relevance to real life, and dialogic dimensions of learning, Ping (2003). Most importantly, research studies have found that information and communication technologies support the cognitive processes leading to effective economic analysis, the [middle-out] bridge from above.

In summary, to think 'in an economics way' is a cognitive process of learning, from fundamental definitions to abstract concepts and complex theories. Graphical representations and analyses are a bridging pedagogic approach providing the structural scaffolding necessary for deductive and inductive reasoning. Fortunately, research supports the success of e-Learning, information and communication technologies, as a successful cognitive pedagogical approach.

Cognitive Learning Taxonomy Bloom (1956)	*Knowledge*	*Comprehension*	*Application*	*Analysis*	*Evaluation*	*Synthesis*
	Anderson & Krathwohl (2001) Two Dimensions					
Cognitive *Process* *Knowledge*	Remember	Understand	Apply	Analyze	Evaluate	Create
Factual Terminology	Recognize Recall	Interpret Explain	Calculate Solve	Distinguish Relate	Critique Test	Hypothesize Devise
Conceptual Principles Models						
Procedural Methods Algorithms	Bottom-up	Shiu & Sin (2006) Middle-out		Middle-out		Top-down
Meta-Cognitive Awareness			Ping (2003)	+ Organization & Presentation		

Figure 1. To Think 'In an Economics Way'.

TARIFFS AND WELFARE ANALYSIS EXAMPLE

In this example, it is assumed that students are already familiar with and understand demand and supply curves, as well as the concepts of consumer and producer surplus. The example starts with a supply and demand curve for a product X in country A. As shown in Figure 2, the equilibrium price is $66 and the equilibrium quantity is 33 units before international trade. In Figure 3, consumer and producer surplus are introduced in the supply and demand schedule. In both Figures 2 and 3, previous knowledge and understanding of the supply and demand schedule and the consumer surplus and producer surplus are reviewed. The example continues by assuming that country A is opening up for international trade, and will buy some portion of product X in the world market. The analytical aspect of learning starts with the introduction of the world price of $44 for product X in the basic supply and demand schedule (see figure 4). At the price of $44, the domestic demand for product X is 55 units, but the domestic producers are only producing 11 units of product X, which requires country A to import 44 units of product X.

In figure 5, the new consumer and producer surplus for international trade are introduced in the model. Learning is further improved by comparing the consumer and producer surplus without international trade with the consumer and producer surplus with international trade as is done in figure 6. This comparison is helpful because students can see that with international trade the consumer surplus is larger than without international trade, indicating that consumers are better off with international trade. The opposite is true for the domestic producer. The domestic producers are worse off with international trade than without international trade. This is indicated by the smaller producer surplus in the international trade model.

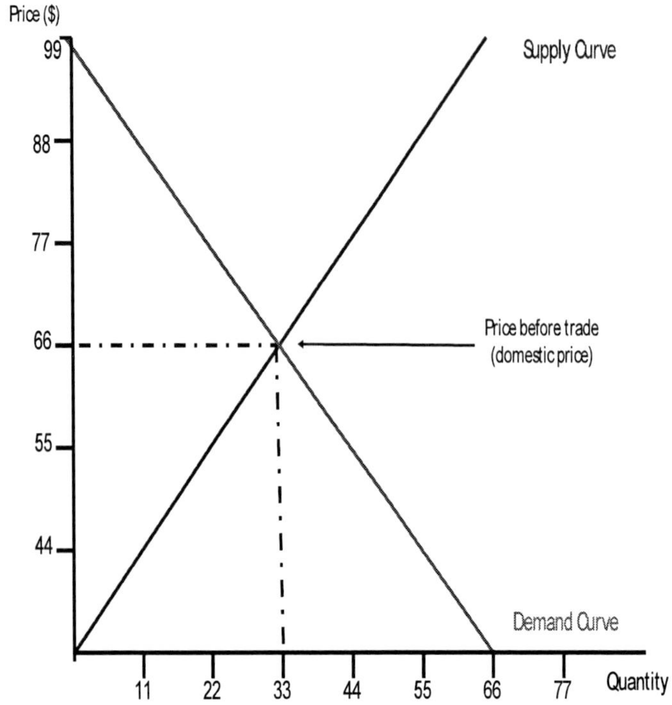

Figure 2. Demand and Supply curve without international trade.

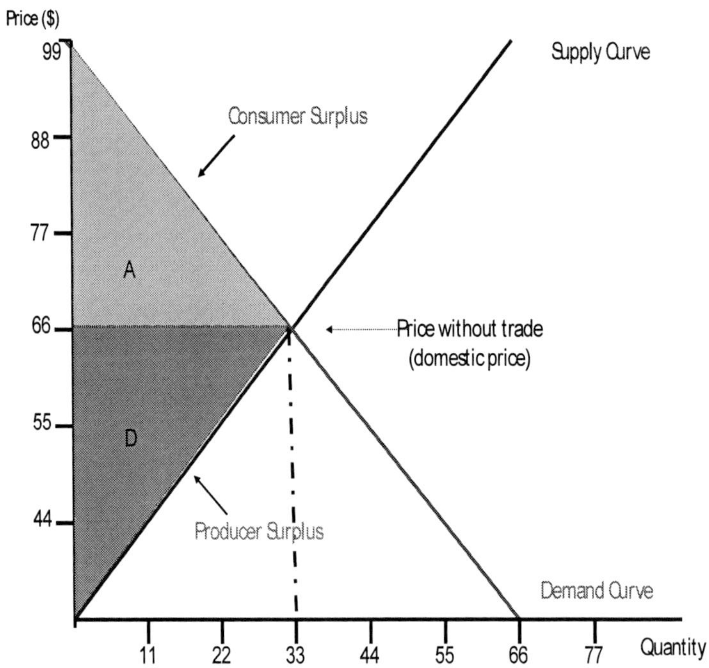

Figure 3. Consumer and producer surplus without international trade.

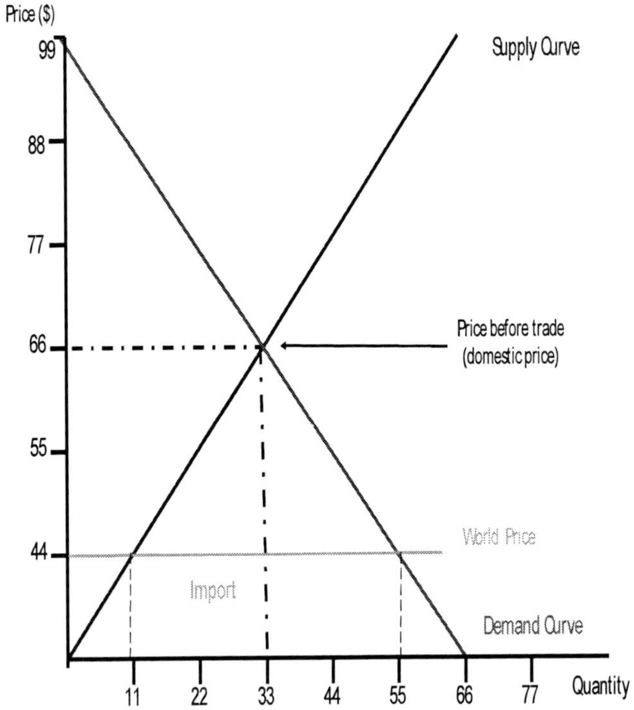

Figure 4. Demand and Supply curve with international trade.

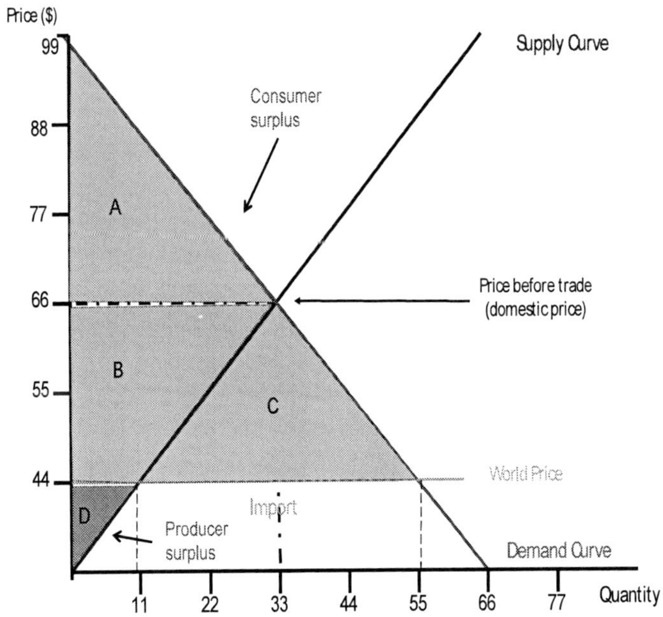

Figure 5. Consumer and producer surplus with international trade.

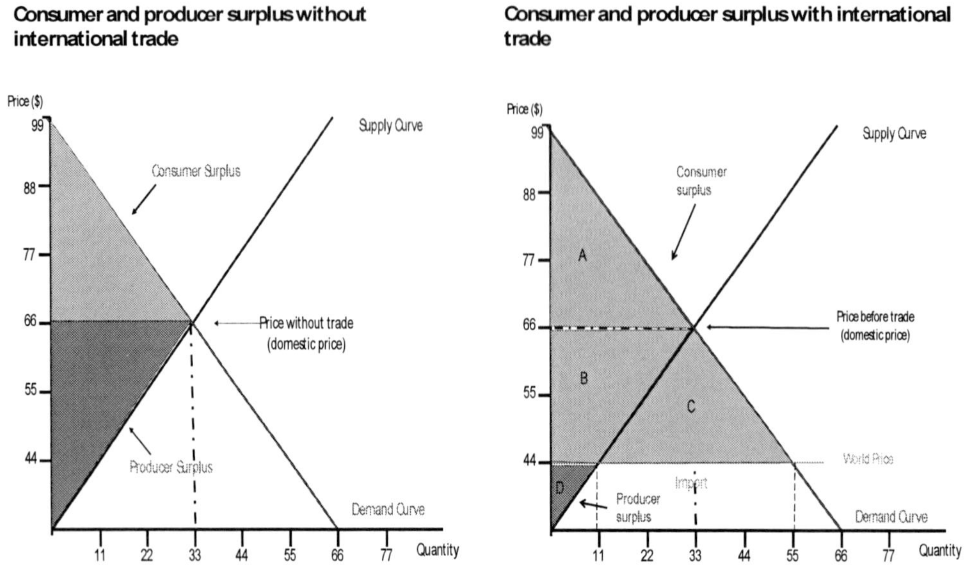

Figure 6. Comparison of consumer and producer surplus without international trade and with international trade.

In the next step of this example, a tariff of $11 is introduced in the model, which is depicted in figure 7. The tariff of $11 is added to the world price, which causes the domestic price for product X, to increase to $55. With the domestic price at $55, the domestic demand for that product is now 44 units, while the domestic producers are now producing 22 units of product X. Country A will now import 22 units of product X. The tariff causes the consumer surplus to decrease. This decline in the consumer surplus is caused by the higher price that the consumer needs to pay for product X. The higher price drives many consumers to the point that they cannot afford product X anymore. The consumers are therefore worse off with a tariff. The domestic producers are benefitting from the tariff because they receiving a higher price for product X domestically produced. The higher price domestic producers are receiving for their produced product X and the fact that more domestic producers start to produce product X causes the producer surplus to increase. The changes in consumer and producer surplus are giving in figure 8. The government revenue that the government receives and the deadweight loss areas are also giving in figure 8. The dead weight loss areas representing the economic inefficiencies that a tariff creates for the society.

To improve students understanding further of how international trade and how a tariff work, a comparison is made in Figure 9, that shows the differences between consumer and producer surplus without international trade, with international trade and with international trade and an imposed tariff. This comparison shows consumer surplus is larger with international trade, and therefore consumers are better off with free trade. The producer surplus is much smaller with international trade indicating that the domestic producers are worse off with international trade. When introducing a tariff, consumer surplus get smaller, but this still larger than the case where there is no international trade. This indicates that consumers are worse off with a tariff compared to the case of free international trade, but they are still better off than when there is no international trade. The producer surplus increases with a tariff indicating that domestic producers are better off with a tariff than with free international trade.

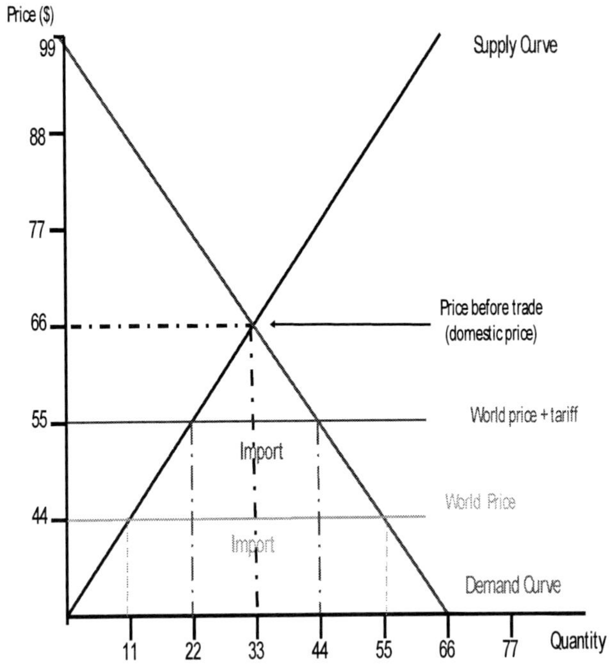

Figure 7. International trade and tariff.

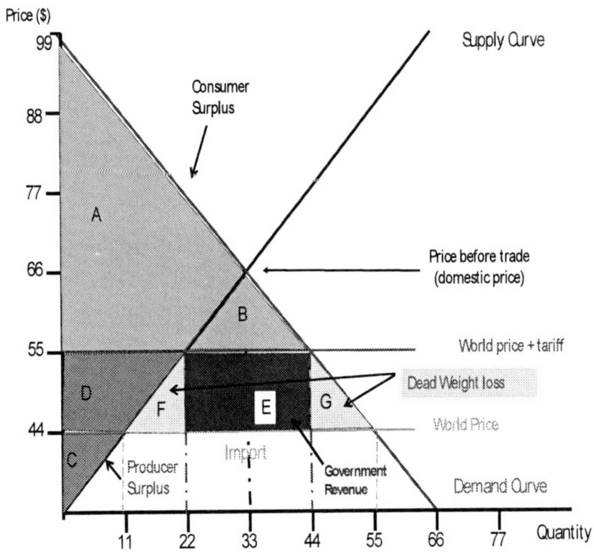

Figure 8. Consumer and producer surplus, government revenue and dead weight loss for the case of international trade and a tariff.

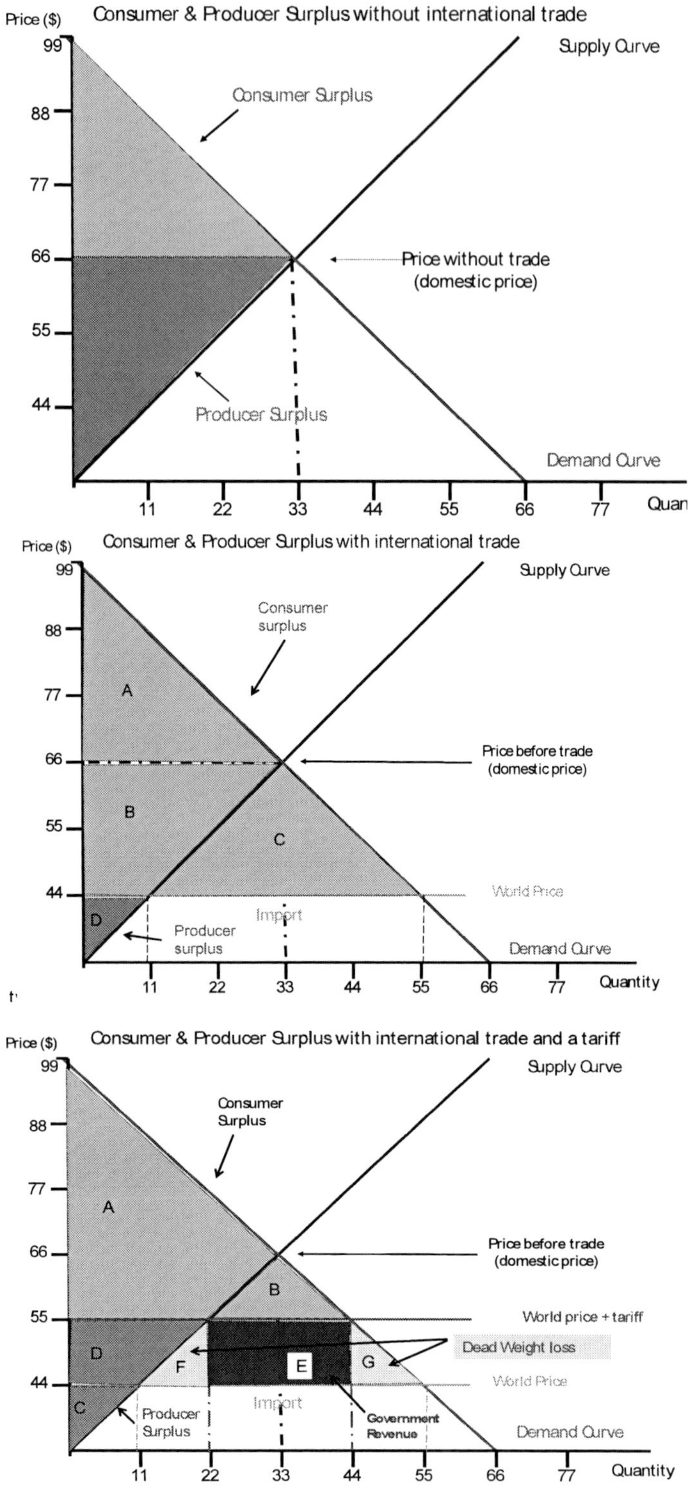

Figure 9. A comparison of the changes in consumer and producer surplus in a case without international trade, in a case with international trade and in a case with international trade and a tariff.

CONCLUSION

This paper demonstrates an e-Learning example of Tariffs using Welfare Economics. The step by step presentation represents a logical and systematic approach to support the cognitive learning and thinking process in the absence of feedback provided in a classroom environment. The implicit framework for thinking 'in an Economics way' is Bloom's (1956) Cognitive Learning Taxonomy. Bloom's (1956) Application and Analyses levels are identified as the cognitive scaffolding for inductive and deductive reasoning, Ping (2003), and as the Middle-out graphical representations and analyses pedagogy recommended by Shiu and Sin (2006).

REFERENCES

Anderson, L.W. and Krathwohl, D.R - Editors, (2001). *A Taxonomy for Learning, Teaching, and Assessing – A Revision of Bloom's Taxonomy of Educational Objectives*. New York, Longman Press.

Appleyard, D.R., Field, A.J. and Cobb, S.L. (2008). *International Economics 6th edition*. New York, McGraw-Hill/Irwin.

Bloom, B.S. (1956). Taxonomy *of Educational Objectives: The Classification of Educational Goals*. New York, David McKay Inc.

Lim C.P. (2003) "Information and Communication Technologies (ICT) Addressing the Challenges of Economics Education: To Be or Not To Be?" *International Review of Economics Education*, 2 (1), 25-54.

Mankiw N.G. (2007). *Principles of Economics 4th edition*. Ohio, Thomson South-Western.

Pugel, T.A. (2007). International Economics 13th edition. New York, McGraw-Hill/Irwin.

Shih, M., Feng, J. and Tsai, C.C. (2008). "Research and trends in the field of e-learning from 2001 to 2005: A content analysis of cognitive studies in selected journals". *Computers and Education*. 51, 955–967.

Shiu, L.P. and Sin, C.Y. (2006). "Top-down, Middle-out, and Bottom-up Processes: A Cognitive Perspective of Teaching and Learning Economics". *International Review of Economics Education*. 5 (1), 60-72.

Simkins, S. and Maier, M. (2004). "Using Just-in-Time Teaching Techniques in the Principles of Economics Course". *Social Science Computer Review*. 22, 444-456.

In: Expanding Teaching and Learning Horizons
Editors: F. G. Mixon, Jr. and R. J. Cebula

ISBN 978-1-60741-971-6

Chapter 13

USING *THE SIMS* TO TEACH MENGERIAN ECONOMICS*

Scott A. Kjar

INTRODUCTION

The Sims is a very popular computer game by Electronic Arts [1]. In the game, a "Sim" is a simulated person, a character created by the human player who is sitting at a computer. Players create virtual characters and houses, and then manipulate them by requiring that they perform particular actions within the constraints of their world. In short, the game is a "virtual dollhouse." [2]

The Sims is an intimate game, rather than an expansive one. Players do not conquer entire worlds, battle monsters, or even face opponents. Rather, *The Sims* is, as Alfred Marshall would say, about "mankind in the ordinary business of life (Marshall, 1938: 1)." The characters in the game interact with their environments, ranging from houseplants to home electronics, from bathtubs to basketballs; likewise, they take actions from dancing to fixing their leaky bathtubs, from sleeping to eating.

Players make decisions for their characters by choosing among a variety of options along a variety of margins. Given that time is scarce, players must allocate their characters' resources to fulfilling their needs through such things as working, taking care of normal bodily functions, or engaging in social interactions. Players can have their characters get jobs, chat with other characters, watch television, play basketball, read the newspaper, and otherwise participate in daily activities. When the players don't give explicit instructions to the characters, the characters have built-in default activities. For example, a tired Sim will go to bed unless told otherwise, and a hungry Sim will eat food unless the player gives a contrary instruction.

Interestingly, the creators of the game built a lot of economic concepts into the game. Players face scarcity, preferences, opportunity costs, inter-temporal trade-offs, decreasing

* I thank my student Kyle Price for first pointing out several of the microeconomic implications in the game *The Sims*. A slightly earlier version of this paper was presented at the Association of Private Enterprise Educators conference, Las Vegas, 2006.

marginal utility, specialization and the division of labor, and many other fundamental economic concepts [3]. This chapter will explore some of these economic concepts, and will particularly focus on the similarities between the game and the writings of Carl Menger.

The Sims and their Needs

The characters have 8 basic needs: hunger, comfort, hygiene, bladder, energy, fun, social, and room. Fulfilling these needs is the essence of the game. Sims whose needs are fulfilled are happy Sims, while those whose needs are not met are unhappy. The overall level of happiness, in turn, has further implications in the game, including on the ability to meet those very same needs [4].

For example, a Sim who has not eaten in several hours will be hungry, and so the hunger need will be seriously unfulfilled [5]. By contrast, a Sim who has just eaten will find that the hunger need is substantially, or even completely, fulfilled. However, needs do not stay fulfilled for long; moments after completing lunch, a Sim will start to experience a slight reduction of the extent to which the hunger need has been fulfilled. All needs are continuously moving toward being unfullfilled, and it takes regular and purposeful activity to meet them. In this respect, the characters are much like actual humans; from the moment we stop eating, hunger begins to build again, even though it will take a while for that hunger to become an important and immediate motivating factor in our daily lives.

If Sims meet some of their needs regularly (e.g., hunger and bladder), but do not meet other needs regularly (e.g., social and fun), they find themselves facing increasing difficulty. Their abilities to acquire new skills deteriorates, and even their abilities to fulfill other needs begins to decline. In extreme cases, if the Sims do not meet their needs, they can even die. All of this is consistent with Menger, who wrote:

> Needs arise from our drives and the drives are embedded in our nature. An imperfect satisfaction of our needs leads to the stunting of our nature. Failure to satisfy them brings about our destruction. But to satisfy our needs is to live and prosper. Thus the attempt to provide for the satisfaction of our needs is synonymous with the attempt to provide for our lives and well-being. It is the most important of all human endeavors, since it is the prerequisite and foundation of all others (Menger, 1994: 77).

Using Goods to Meet Needs

In general, characters fulfill their needs by using or consuming goods. A hungry Sim might eat lunch, a Sim with a heavy bladder will use a toilet, and a Sim who is low on energy could go to bed. This is because of the characteristics possessed by these different goods. Each good in the game has the ability to meet some need, based upon the collection of characteristics that it possesses.

Again, Menger covered this ground, particularly when he laid out the four pre-requisites necessary for a thing to be a good (Menger 1994: 52). First, humans have needs. It is important to recognize that Menger is *not* saying that humans *need the thing* in question. Rather, these needs are somewhat more abstract, and in his second edition, Menger identified needs as falling into three categories: physiological, altruistical, and egotistical. The needs in *The Sims* fit Menger's concept of needs quite well, since needs in *The Sims* are all physiological or psychological; that is, Sims don't merely need *things*, they *use* things to meet their needs.

Second, the thing in question has characteristics or attributes capable of satisfying the need. This need-satisfying ability is at the heart of the Mengerian system. Characteristics that are unable to satisfy human needs have no value, while those capable of satisfying needs are valued according to the needs that they can satisfy. The goods available to *The Sims* explicitly have such characteristics.

Third, humans are aware of the need-satisfying abilities of the thing. While it is possible, even likely, that there are many things with characteristics capable of satisfying human needs, they are of no value until humans because aware of such abilities. Again, it is not the characteristics that are important, it is their need-satisfying ability. In *The Sims*, players can explicitly explore these characteristics in order to know the extent to which they possess need-satisfying characteristics.

Finally, humans must possess the thing in the appropriate marginal unit that is capable of satisfying the need. The appropriate marginal unit may vary from situation to situation, or from need to need. In the case of *The Sims*, the unit is generally one of the particular thing, whether it is a bed, chess board, shower, or piano. Thus, when Sims use things to fulfill their needs, they are following Menger's analysis perfectly.

Human Relationships and Needs

In *The Sims*, physical products are not the only things necessary to fulfill needs; human relationships also are necessary. As mentioned above, one of the needs that the Sims feel is a social need. Sims like to have friends, and they like to spend time with their friends. Sims who have no friends are unhappy, and resist all efforts at self-improvement.

Again, Menger discussed human relationships as goods, pointing out that they may fulfill needs.

> Of special interest are the goods that have been treated by some writers in our discipline as a special class of goods called "relationships." In this category are firms, goodwill, monopolies, copyrights, patents, trade licenses, authors' rights, and also, according to some writers, family connections, friendship, love, religious and scientific fellowships, etc. (Menger, 1994: 54).

Sims can make friends with their neighbors, and interacting with their friends helps to fulfill their social needs. These friendships can even blossom into love, which further serves to meet this need. And when Sims do not see their friends for long periods of time, the friendships deteriorate, or even cease to exist. Such losses reduce the Sims' abilities to fulfill this need, so an on-going effort to maintain friendships is required.

Multiple Goods and Multiple Needs

There is generally more than one way to meet a particular need. A hungry Sim can have a meal, or consume a snack. The meal is more fulfilling, but takes longer to prepare and comes with a higher money price. Consuming the meal will more thoroughly meet the hunger need, but it will also use up scarce time and limited funds which could be allocated to meeting other needs. Thus, while the snack will less completely meet the hunger need, it might be preferred over the meal in order to free up the time and money to meet some other, more pressing, need.

Also, a particular good may possess various characteristics or attributes which make it capable of meeting more than one need. Taking a bath substantially fulfills the need for hygiene, but also partially fulfills the need for comfort. Sitting in an easy chair can provide energy, comfort, and room satisfactions. Dancing with another character is beneficial for both social and fun requirements.

Further, a particular type of good may come in more than one model. A basic refrigerator can help to fulfill the hunger need, but a better refrigerator can fulfill more of the need. A simple bathtub provides some hygiene and comfort fulfillment, but a larger bathtub provides more fulfillment in both areas. A small bed leads to some rejuvenation of energy and comfort, but a larger bed offers such rejuvenation to a greater extent. Not surprisingly, though, these better models have higher price tags. Since money is earned by working, and working takes time, and time is scarce, it is not always possible to acquire these better products.

By the same token, different goods can be used to meet the same need. A basketball hoop can serve to partially meet the fun need, but a virtual reality headset will more fully meet that need. Sleeping on the couch partially meets energy and comfort needs, while sleeping in a bed more fully meets them. And sleeping on the floor, while possible, provides very little energy and no comfort whatsoever.

Again, Menger seems to have fully anticipated *The Sims*. In discussing the value that goods have, and how that value may be derived from more than one source, he wrote:

> Usually not a single good but a *quantity* of goods stands opposite not a single concrete need but a *complex* of such needs. Sometimes a larger and sometimes a smaller number of satisfactions, of very different degrees of importance, depends on our command of a given quantity of goods, and each one of the goods has the ability to produce these satisfactions differing so greatly in importance (Menger, 1994: 129, emphasis in original).

Time and the Fulfillment of Needs

Because time is scarce, it is not possible for characters to have all of their needs filled at any given time. Thus, players must determine their own preferences for meeting the needs of their characters, and must allocate resources, including time, to fulfill the highest-ranked preferences. Once the highest-ranked preferences are met, the player goes on to allocate resources to fulfilling lower-ranked preferences.

In this, we see that opportunity costs are a crucial part of the game. Characters in *The Sims* are always paying opportunity costs. Being ready for work in the morning means not sleeping as late, spending longer in the shower means less time to read for pleasure, and cleaning the house takes time from acquiring new skills.

JOBS AND SKILLS (OR MEANS AND ENDS)

The Sims is substantially about the use of means to achieve ends. At the most basic level, the ends are the fulfillment of the various needs. The means are the interactions or consumptions of goods in and around the house. However, the acquisition of such goods is then an end which requires another set of means, namely, the acquisition of money.

In order to have money to purchase goods, Sims get jobs. When they start out, the Sims can select from entry-level positions in each of ten different career tracks: business (mailroom), entertainment (waiter/waitress), law enforcement (security guard), life of crime (pickpocket), medicine (medical technician), military (recruit), politics (campaign worker), pro athlete (team mascot), science (test subject), and x-treme (daredevil).

These entry-level positions offer low pay and generally require long hours. Thus, Sims generally look for advancement as soon as possible. In order to advance, they must acquire the skills required for the next higher rung of their selected career. Each career requires a little bit different set of skills. The skills themselves are merely categories or types of skills, and are as follows: cooking, mechanical, charisma, body, logic, and creativity.

A character in the military career path, for example, will want to acquire body skills immediately, since strong bodies are important in moving ahead in the military in the game. As the recruit moves up the ranks, charisma becomes important, since the Sim will be expected to lead others. By contrast, a medical technician will want to acquire a skill in repair, to keep equipment humming; a subsequent advancement might call for logic, in order to eventually diagnose and treat patients.

In order to acquire skills, Sims will, once again, interact with the goods in their environments. Body skills, for example, can be earned by pumping iron, or by swimming. Creativity can be developed by painting, or by playing the piano. Cooking skills are enhanced by reading from cookbooks. In each case, the player must direct the character first to save money, second to acquire these goods, and third to utilize them in order to build the appropriate skills needs for advancement. Thus, forward-looking behavior is rewarded, and its failure is punished.

In short, Sims use means to achieve ends, and those ends are means to achieve further ends, which in turn are means to even more fundamental ends. Sims use time and market goods to acquire skills, then use those skills to get better jobs (and more money), and use the increased financial resource to acquire better stuff, which more fully fulfills the Sims' needs.

DEATH, MOURNING, AND IMAGINARY GOODS

As Menger makes clear, not all "goods" can really satisfy needs. People may believe that a particular good possesses characteristics that have a needs-satisfying capability, but it need not be so. There are three possible ways in which this error may occur: 1) the good does not actually possess the characteristics that satisfy the need; 2) the good possesses the characteristics, but the characteristics do not actually meet the need; or 3) there is not actually a need. When any of these occur, Menger says, the good is really an "imaginary good" (Menger, 1994: 53-54).

Death is a catastrophe that can happen to a Sim within the confines of the game. To take one example, a character with no cooking skills who is trying to fix dinner could well start the stove on fire, and be killed in a fire than engulfs the house. Following the death, the Sim's loved ones will want to mourn their loss. Some amount of mourning is necessary to keep the deceased from returning as a ghost and haunting the other Sims—Sims being haunted will suffer a loss of comfort, lack of sleep, and various other problems.

The Sims naturally want to mourn. Built into their programming is the belief, mistaken, as it turns out, that mourning will satisfy several of their needs. When a Sim suffers the loss of a loved one, the automatic portion of the Sim's life, the part that functions regardless of whether the player gives direction, will desire to mourn constantly. In the process, the Sim gives up eating, sleeping, self-improvement activities, fun activities, and so on.

> Some interactions advertise falsely. They lure the autonomous Sim by promising fulfillment of a real need, but they don't actually raise that motive score. A good example is the phone. When it rings, the interaction "Answer" advertises 50 points each of Fun, Comfort, and Social. The act alone fulfills none directly.
>
> Another example is the somber interaction "Mourn." . . . The Mourn interaction advertises powerfully for 24 hours after a Sim death. It lures with false advertising, however, offering a 50 point increase for each of 5 needs, but satisfying none (Barba, 2000: 46).

Beyond the minimal amount of mourning necessary to keep the dead from haunting the living, mourning serves no purpose within the game. Yet, the living Sims have a strong desire to mourn that only lessens with the passing of time. That makes it a classic example of Menger's imaginary goods. (Whether mourning in real life is actually a Mengerian imaginary good is outside the scope of this point.)

CONCLUSION

Students who eschew studying to play computer games might find that playing *The Sims* allows them to do both simultaneously. By playing, they are exposed to many key concepts, including scarcity, preferences, opportunity costs, inter-temporal trade-offs, decreasing marginal utility, and specialization and the division of labor.

We can see that *The Sims* has a lot of economics in it, and that much of the economics involved is Mengerian in nature. While scarcity, opportunity cost, and preference rankings are reasonably common in economics, the Mengerian pre-requisites, human relationships as goods, the use of multiple goods to meet multiple needs, and the idea of imaginary goods are primarily Mengerian in nature. Thus, while Menger is gone, and we may mourn him (if only to keep him from haunting us), his work lives on, and is accessible to a new generation of students in *The Sims*.

NOTES

[1] "Electronic Arts (the maker) stated that The Sims has sold twice as fast as SimCity 3000, which was the top grossing game of 1999." David Laprad, "The Adrenaline Vault: New Sims Downloads Available" (February 10, 2000), www.avault.com/news/displaynews.asp?story=2102000-134326; "According to PC Data, The Sims was the top grossing game in North America for the first 6 months of 2000. . . . The Sims has been translated into 13 languages and has sold more than 18 million copies worldwide." Iron Thumbs, "The Sims is Number 1," (July 28, 2000) www.gamepro.com; "Almost a quarter of the game's registrants are women." Electronic Arts President John Riccitello, quoted by Iron Thumbs, "Over 1 Million Copies of The Sims has Shipped," (April 13, 2000) www.gamepro.com.

[2] Background information about *The Sims* comes from the game's help files, and from the game's manual, *The Sims: The People Simulator from the Creator of Sim City* (Redwood City, Calf.: Electronic Arts, 2000).

[3] Included in the "Suggested Reading" section of *The Sims* is David D. Friedman, *Hidden Order: The Economics of Everyday Life* (New York: HarperCollins, 1997). Thus, the designers were apparently cognizant of the economic implications of their game, and, it may be inferred, included some of these implications intentionally. However, Friedman is no Mengerian, and his book does not discuss Menger's pre-requisites, so it seems unlikely that the Mengerian aspects of the game came from Friedman's influence.

[4] A happy Sim has an easier time staying happy, and therefore has an easier time fulfilling its needs. An unhappy Sim is likely to engage in passive aggressive behavior against the player by refusing to take actions that are in its long-term best interest, such as studying or learning skills.

[5] The game is played in an accelerated time mode. In "Normal" time, the human player experiences one second while the game character experiences one minute. There are also "High" and "Ultra" settings, in which time moves along at a few minutes per second, up to several minutes per second. Depending on the rate at which the player is playing, several hours of character time may be accomplished in several minutes, or in a few seconds, of player time.

REFERENCES

Barba, Rick. *Prima's Official Strategy Guide to The Sims: Livin' Large*. Roseville, Calif.: Prima Publishing, 2000.

Electronic Arts. *The Sims: The People Simulator from the Creator of Sim City*. Redwood City, Calif.: Electronic Arts, 2000.

Friedman, David D. *Hidden Order: The Economics of Everyday Life*. New York: HarperCollins, 1997.

Iron Thumbs. "Over 1 Million Copies of *The Sims* has Shipped." April 12, 2000. www.gamepro.com.

Iron Thumbs. "*The Sims* is Number 1." July 28, 2000. www.gamepro.com.

Laprad, David. "The Adrenaline Vault." February 10, 2000. www.avault.com/news/displaynews.asp?story=2102000-134326.

Marshall, Alfred. *Principles of Economics: An Introductory Volume*. 8th ed. London: MacMillan, 1938.

Menger, Carl. *Principles of Economics*. Translated by James Dingwall and Bert F. Hoselitz. Grove City, Penn.: Libertarian Press, 1994.

In: Expanding Teaching and Learning Horizons
Editors: F. G. Mixon, Jr. and R. J. Cebula
ISBN 978-1-60741-971-6

Chapter 14

ADAM'S APPLE: USING JOHNNY APPLESEED TO TEACH THE INVISIBLE HAND

David B. Skarbek and Joshua C. Hall

INTRODUCTION

One of Adam Smith's most important insights was that it was not from the "benevolence of the butcher, the brewer, or the baker, that we expect our dinner, but from their regard to their own interest" (Smith [1776] 1994: 15). Teaching undergrads this unintuitive result is challenging. In fact, it is often the unintuitive implications of economics that both challenge and inspire students. To this end, it is imperative to present familiar scenarios to our students but cast in a new light. Others have been successful using *The Simpsons* (Hall 2005; Considine 2006), classic films and documentaries (Leet and Houser 2003), and literary passages (Watts 1999). We extend this interdisciplinary approach to economic education with a minor alteration. While these past studies present several short examples using a particular medium, we present one story — that of Johnny Appleseed — and identify several of the ideas that can be introduced through this historical example. In addition, we provide a suggested classroom discussion guide as well as a suggested assignment.

JOHNNY APPLESEED: MYTH VERSUS REALITY

Most American students are at least casually familiar with the story of Johnny Appleseed. Children's books and cartoons present him as a lovable (if not buffoonish) odd-ball, who walks the frontier with a potato sack as a shirt, a cooking pot for a hat, and no shoes to be found. Appleseed's love of nature and humanity lead him to plant apple seeds all across the land. Stories handed down for generations remembered him fondly. One woman opined, "...the angels did commune with the good old man, whose loving heart prompted him to go about doing good!" (Price 1954: 158). A Massachusetts Fruit Growers Association's monument captures the essence of countless memorials to Appleseed in the Midwest: "He planted seeds that other might enjoy fruit" (Price 1954: 9). The message of these stories is that selfless benevolence is the reason that apples exist in America and brave, hungry settlers survived the harsh challenges of moving west.

The history of the matter is quite different however. John Chapman (Appleseed's real name) spent the majority of his life running a number of profitable nursery and seedling businesses beyond the settled frontier. Apples were particularly crucial to settlers in this time period for two reasons. First, apples were a versatile source of nutrition year-round. They were eaten, used to make sauces in winter, turned into apple butter, and perhaps most importantly, made into hard apple cider. Appleseed historian Robert Price notes that due to its nutritional value and the lack of alcoholic substitutes, "[n]o well-established home could exist long without [cider], and usually many barrels were essential" (1954: 39). Second, an apple orchard was both *de facto,* and in many cases, the *de jure* requirement for title to a piece of land. One land grant in the Northwest Territory specifically required a settler to "set out at least fifty apple or pear trees" as a necessary component of obtaining a deed (Pollan 2002: 16). Pennsylvania had similar requirements (Price 1954: 21).

Appleseed had substantial knowledge of the wilderness and was able to estimate ten or fifteen years ahead of settlers where they would want to live. He was unique in being familiar "with the land, to judge its course of settlement, to plant in strategic spots, and to know where all the cabins were going up…" (Price: 1954: 84). With his ability to predict future migration, Appleseed ventured far beyond the settled areas and planted apple orchards. He would later sell these lots to the newly arriving settlers, turning a tidy profit and facilitating their formal and informal acquisition of land.. Price finds that "[s]o far as records now make known, no one else ever [moved his planting ahead of the frontier]" like Appleseed did (Price 1954: 38-39). In his lifetime, Appleseed owned a total of 1200 acres and had an income "considerably better than those of the average settler in the Middle West" (Price 1954: 224). Appleseed was a singularly unique entrepreneur (Skarbek forthcoming).

WHY JOHNNY APPLESEED?

Teaching about the invisible hand is easy, teaching the invisible hand well is not (Wight 2007). There are two advantages to introducing the invisible hand concept through the life of Johnny Appleseed. The first reason is that many students already know the myth of Johnny Appleseed and thus have a favorable impression of him based on their mistaken mental picture of him as an eccentric, but altruistic, do-gooder. Many students view the outcomes provided by Appleseed solely as the result of his philanthropy. While he certainly was a benevolent individual (J. Appleseed Company 2008), viewing the fruit of his labor as solely the result of altruism ignores the role that human institutions had in directing his actions toward socially beneficial outcomes.

In discussing economists' treatment of Smith's invisible, Wight (2007) shows how many descriptions of the invisible hand metaphor are incomplete because they ignore how institutions and self-command guide an individual's instincts. While self-interest is important, so are the "rules of the game" and too often teachers of economics minimize the role of social and market institutions in an effort to make it clear how self-interest often leads to socially beneficial outcomes. While self-interest is important, Smith's point is that individuals are not self-interested in isolation, but rather their self-interest is channeled in both positive and negative ways by self-command and societal institutions.

Wight (2007: 353) summarizes the importance of teaching the invisible hand properly as follows:

> These are important lessons for economic students. If human instincts are allowed to operate within incentive-compatible environments, they are capable of producing not only private benefits but, in many cases, social benefits that are not intended. Hence, one does not need to start from a virtuous motive such as benevolence to produce something of value for society. In a supportive institutional structure, decentralized action can generate a spontaneous order that yields dynamic growth with liberty. No one ideal system of political economy exists to accomplish this, and Smith noted that many variations will work tolerably well. This understanding reasonably fits the facts of the modern world: Rich industrial democracies exhibit a diversity of institutions and a range of mixed market systems. Smith, a pragmatist rather than an ideologue, was optimistic that the invisible hand instincts could naturally lead to progress over time.

We agree with Wight about the importance of teaching the invisible hand. In addition to teaching about the invisible hand in principles classes, one of us also reminds students of Smith's important insight during the first week of a public sector economics class. Yet it is not enough to read and discuss Smith, because for many students the invisible hand concept is sufficiently at odds with their core belief system that they cannot conceive of situations where individual self-interest can create social benefits. In our experience, many students view self-interested behavior negatively or at best neutrally, no matter what outcomes emerge from the self-interested behavior. It is for these students, in particular, that this approach was designed. By beginning with the myth of Johnny Appleseed as planting trees solely out of a love for apples, students see the positive benefits of his actions and commit to the proposition that the planting of apple trees provided social benefits. Then when the true story of Johnny Appleseed is introduced, students are forced to examine their implicit assumption that good intentions are necessary to achieve good results.

In addition to the invisible hand, the story of Appleseed can motivate discussion of other economic concepts. First, Appleseed responded to people's needs because he paid attention to prices. His local knowledge of geographical, social, and commercial conditions incorporated and affected prices, and as a result, his business encouraged the efficient allocation of resources on the frontier. Second, Appleseed's story highlights the fact that entrepreneurs respond to the incentives created by the government. If land titling came from crops of potatoes rather than apples orchards, frontier customers might have known him as "Johnny Potato" instead. As Baumol (1990) argues, the incentives entrepreneurs face will determine whether or not and how their abilities are used. Third, investigating the public's perception of the market economy can draw in non-economics majors, who study literature, history, and anthropology. For example, would the folk stories have ignored Appleseed if people only remembered him for his business exploits? Students can discuss the relationship between markets and literature, society, and popular culture.

An obvious downside to using Johnny Appleseed is that that not everyone is familiar with the folk story surrounding him. While American-born students are more likely to be familiar with it, international students lack experience with the myth or reality of his activities. Our experience is that the use of his myth in the classroom can help all students learn about the invisible hand even without prior knowledge about Appleseed's life. The key is to let those students who believe that Appleseed was nothing more than an eccentric apple grower move the discussion forward. Once the myth of Johnny Appleseed is established in the minds of the students, the instructor need only use the content contained in this article to show the importance of self-interest and institutions in achieving the outcomes produced by his actions.

A Classroom Discussion

In our opinion, the best way to use the myth and reality of Johnny Appleseed to teach about Smith's invisible hand is through a classroom discussion. While in our experience many students know the myth of Johnny Appleseed, only a handful of students with some prior knowledge of Appleseed's story are needed to begin a fruitful classroom discussion. We suggest starting a discussion by asking students if they have heard about Johnny Appleseed and what, if anything, they know about him. Typically, students will answer with the caricature of Johnny Appleseed's life as presented in popular culture.

For the time being, it is important to leave the myth intact and instead spend some time focusing on the positive social benefits of Johnny Appleseed's activities. Ask the students to list the ways that others in society were helped by Appleseed's actions. After compiling a list that most students can agree are beneficial, it is a good time to present the reality about Appleseed and his motivations. After laying out to students his motivations as well as the institutional environment underlying his actions, ask the students if it changes their opinion of Appleseed. What about his work? What about the social benefits of his actions? If students answer in the affirmative, this provides an opportunity to ask follow-up questions about the relationship between self-interest and economic progress such as "Is it necessary for people to intend to do good in order to do good?"

After discussing the relationship between intentions and results, we suggest reading aloud to the class the famous invisible hand quote from Book IV of *Wealth of Nations* (Smith [1776] 1994: 512-513):

> As every individual, therefore, endeavors as much he can both to employ his capital in the support of domestic industry, and so to direct that industry that its produce may be of the greatest value; every individual necessarily labors to render the annual revenue of the society as great as he can. He generally, indeed, neither intends to promote the public interest, nor knows how much he is promoting it. By preferring the support of domestic to that of foreign industry, he intends only his own security; and by directing that industry in such a manner as its produce may be of the greatest value, he intends only his own gain, and he is in this, as in many other cases, led by an invisible hand to promote an end which was no part of his intention. Nor is it always the worse for the society that it was not part of it. By pursuing his own interest he frequently promotes that of the society more effectually than when he really intends to promote it.

The discussion can then focus on the invisible hand concept with reference to Johnny Appleseed. Is Johnny Appleseed an example of the invisible hand in action? What economic, political, or social institutions were necessary to channel his activities towards economic progress? What does Smith mean when he says "[b]y pursuing his own interest he frequently promotes that of the society more effectually than when he really intends to promote it?" Can we think of some examples where good intentions have made society worse off?

At this point, the discussion can go in many directions depending upon the preferences of the instructor. For example, a discussion of the importance of property rights stems from noting the importance of the underlying institutions that guided Appleseed's activities. Fruitful extensions about the role of the entrepreneur (Schumpeter 1950, Kirzner 1974) and local knowledge (Hayek 1945) are fertile topics easily at hand.

An Out of Class Assignment

While the classroom discussion described above is our preferred approach to using Johnny Appleseed in the classroom, we recognize it is not appropriate for all instructors or classrooms. Some classrooms, for example, are too large to have the type of discussions described here. Or the need to cover a large body of material may not allow for such an involved classroom discussion of the invisible hand. In these cases we have used (and would suggest) that instructors use the following out-of-class assignment to build upon whatever classroom discussion of the invisible hand the instructor was able to provide.

This brief assignment presents students with some background information on the reality of Johnny Appleseed and gives students the opportunity to apply what they have already learned about the invisible hand from class. Here is the prompt used in one of the author's classes:

> Few people know that Johnny Appleseed was a real person and not just the main character of countless folk stories. The most familiar depiction of Appleseed is as a humanitarian and environmentalist who selflessly planted apple trees across the frontier for the benefit of brave settlers moving west.
>
> The truth, however, is that he was a lover of nature but his motivation was not selfless, it was profit driven. He had a nursery and orchard business in the deepest part of the frontier. Settlers enjoyed apples for their nutritional value.
>
> Orchards were also a sign of permanency, so they played a key role in the process of claiming unowned land. Appleseed planted orchards and sold them to settlers upon their arrival. This allowed the settlers to take immediate legal ownership and begin improving their land.
>
> Appleseed died with a small fortune from his many years in business. Compare and contrast the real life Appleseed and the storybook version. Should we think less of Appleseed because his motivation was self-interested rather than altruistic? Would settlers have been better off if Appleseed had never existed? How does this relate to Adam Smith's 'invisible hand'?

This assignment has been used in three different principles classes at a small, nationally-ranked liberal arts college. A sampling of student responses indicates the effectiveness of the story to induce student thought on the invisible hand and the market process in general.

It is clear from student responses that most of them understood the basic idea behind the invisible hand metaphor. Consider one student's comment. "Market forces and self-interest led Appleseed to become rich in terms of money and settlers to become rich in terms of apples, so everybody wins." Several students exhibited a much deeper understanding and appreciation of how economic, political, and social institutions shaped and influenced Appleseed. One student, for example, noted that without him "[t]hey would be worse off because they would have had to have found another (and possibly costlier way) to claim their property and would not have the extra benefit of apples." Another student noted that "Appleseed would not have done it solely for the purpose of altruism. What he did was, he took advantage of something he knows best – planting apple trees, and 'convinced' the settlers it is in their better interest to buy them."

Most surprisingly, several students who recognized the socially beneficial results of Appleseed's actions admitted that they thought less of him after learning his true story. In the words of one student, "the myth of his life is much more honorable." What is interesting, however, is that the remainder of their answers made it clear that they understood the concept of the "invisible hand" and the benefits of Appleseed's actions. Other students exhibited mixed sentiments about Appleseed's business acumen, "Certainly the real Johnny Appleseed is not as good of a story for little kids about altruism and helping others. But in a way, I think the real Appleseed might have helped settlers more because he provided them with a permanent claim to land rather than a bunch of apple trees."

Conclusion

The magic of literature, movies, and art is that it can cast the familiar in a novel light and allow one to obtain greater appreciation for an underlying theme. Allegories, like the Wizard of Oz (Rockoff 1990; Hansen 2002; Dighe 2007), let the reader consider a position or belief without being prejudiced by one's past experience and commentary. In much the same way, conveying the story of Johnny Appleseed and connecting it back to the historical record can allow students to reconsider their view of markets without prejudice. By showing that his entrepreneurial endeavors made many settlers better off, instructors can reframe students' view of market exchange and deepen their understanding of Adam Smith's invisible hand.

References

Baumol, William J. (1990) "Entrepreneurship: Productive, Unproductive, and Destructive." *Journal of Political Economy* 98(5): 893-921.

Considine, John. (2006). "The Simpsons: Public Choice in the Tradition of Swift and Orwell." *Journal of Economic Education* 17(2): 217-228.

Dighe, Ranjit. (2007). "The Fable of the Allegory: The Wizard of Oz in Economics: Comment." *Journal of Economic Education* 38(3): 318-324.

Hall, Joshua C. (2005). "Homer Economicus: Using the Simpsons to Teach Economics." *Journal of Private Enterprise* 20(2): 165-176.

Hansen, Bradley A. (2002). "The Fable of the Allegory: The Wizard of Oz in Economics." *Journal of Economic Education* 33(3): 254-264.

Hayek, F. A. (1945). "The Use of Knowledge in Society." *American Economic Review* 35(4): 519-530.

J. Appleseed Company. 2008. "The Story of Johnny Appleseed." Online article: http://swedenborg.org/jappleseed/history.html. Accessed: 9 September 2009.

Leet, Donald and Scott Houser. (2003). "Economics Goes to Hollywood: Using Classical Films and Documentaries to Teach an Undergraduate Economics Course." *Journal of Economic Education* 34(4): 326-332.

Pollan, Michael. (2002). *The Botany of Desire: A Plant's Eye View of the World*. New York: Random House.

Price, Robert. (1954). *Johnny Appleseed: Man and Myth*. Bloomington: Indiana University Press.

Rockoff, Hugh. (1990). "The 'Wizard of Oz' as a Monetary Allegory." *Journal of Political Economy* 98(4): 739-760.

Schumpeter, Joseph A. ([1948] 1962). *Capitalism, Socialism, and Democracy*. New York: Harper Perennial.

Skarbek, David. Forthcoming. "Alertness, Local Knowledge, and Johnny Appleseed." *Review of Austrian Economics*.

Smith, Adam. ([1776] 1994). *An Inquiry into the Nature and Causes of the Wealth of Nations*. New York, NY: Random House.

Watts, Michael. (1999). "Using Literature and Drama in Undergraduate Economics Courses." In William. E. Becker and Michael Watts, eds., Teaching Economics to Undergraduates: Alternatives to Chalk and Talk. Cheltenham: Edward Elgar.

Wight, Jonathan B. (2007). "The Treatment of Smith's Invisible Hand." *Journal of Economic Education* 38(3): 341-359.

In: Expanding Teaching and Learning Horizons
Editors: F. G. Mixon, Jr. and R. J. Cebula
ISBN 978-1-60741-971-6

Chapter 15

ASYMMETRIC INFORMATION ABOUT PERFECT COMPETITION: THE TREATMENT OF PERFECT INFORMATION IN INTRODUCTORY ECONOMICS TEXTBOOKS*

Scott A. Beaulier and Wm. Stewart Mounts, Jr.

INTRODUCTION

The theory of perfect competition sets the frame of reference for all presentations of economic theory, both microeconomic and macroeconomic. As such, it serves as the efficiency benchmark when evaluating economic outcomes, both on the chalkboard and in the measurement of reality. In addition, it remains the starting point for discussions of the theory of the firm [1]

Among the faithful, the market structure of perfect competition requires five necessary assumptions:

(1) Firms sell a homogeneous product;
(2) There are a large number of small firms;
(3) Firms are price takers;
(4) There are no barriers to entry and exit in the long-run; and
(5) Firms and consumers have perfect information.

While we suggest there is general agreement in the profession that all five are necessary for the theory of perfect competition to hold, some textbooks only rely on two or three of them when telling the introductory story of perfect competition.

Yet, an assumption that textbook authors often drop or, at the very least, treat fast and loose is that of perfect information. Take Mankiw's (2004) treatment for example. He simply chooses not to mention it. This failure is problematic. For example, information economics, which most textbooks do cover within market failure, assumes imperfect information. How can students understand the importance imperfect information when the topic of perfect information has been largely omitted or treated lightly? In many cases, students are introduced to information-related problems in economics without having any clear benchmark against which to judge the problem. If the instructor wishes to speak clearly about information asymmetries, [2] lemons, and missing markets, imperfect information must be compared to the world of perfect information.

In this paper we survey 11 of the market-leading micro principles textbooks by asking two different questions. First, do they mention perfect information anywhere in the text? And, second, do those that mention perfect information include it as an assumption when discussing perfect competition? From this survey it is clear that most textbooks lack a clear treatment of perfect information. In most cases, the perfect information assumption has been omitted from the theory of perfect competition. Since the perfect information assumption plays a crucial role in discussions of imperfect markets, it is difficult then to understand why textbook authors treat the assumption of perfect information as they do.

The Heavy Lifting of Perfect Information within Perfect Competition

The theory of perfect competition and the general economic equilibrium analysis resulting from it remain the cornerstones of neoclassical welfare economics. If a perfectly competitive market structure exists, and if we make a few subsidiary assumptions about maximizing behavior and convexities, Pareto optimality can be attained, but more importantly, explained.

When we model firms as perfectly competitive enterprises, all five assumptions must hold. The producer's output must have no significant effect on the market price. The producer is producing a homogeneous product, which is in every way identical to other output being produced in the industry. If things change for the worse, the producer is free to get out of the market at any time; if things improve, other entrepreneurs will enter the industry (quickly).

How does the firm owner know how much to produce at current market prices? Clearly, profit-maximizing behavior takes him or her to the place where marginal revenue equals marginal cost. Yet, he or she does not know how much to produce unless we make some kind of assumption about the nature of the information that is available.

Consumers must have perfect information about all relevant prices. Resource owners, such as laborers and capital equipment providers, must know the current and alternative values of their resources. The individual producer is said to have perfect information about all relevant costs of production. In fact, the firm owner has perfect information about costs before production is ever undertaken. The firm owner also has perfect information about the market demand curve and the firm's marginal revenue curve. Profit-maximizing behavior becomes an easy exercise for the well-informed firm owner.

Without an assumption about information, well-informed decisions cannot be made. We cannot even begin to understand a firm's decisions without making some kind of assumption about the knowledge available in the industry. Without perfect information, the decision to enter or exit an industry is not apparent to the profit seeker: the firm owner does not even know the shape of relevant cost curves; the owner also lacks information about future costs and prices. In fact, in the absence of perfect information, producers are not even sure whether their output levels are the profit maximizing points of production. It seems clear, then, that the theory of perfect competition requires the perfect information assumption for there to be consistent logic in presentation.

In the end, the perfect information assumption does the heavy lifting when it comes to understanding individual decision-making within perfectly competitive firms. No other assumption is this far reaching as necessary to make the analysis logically consistent. As Stiglitz (1997 [1994]: 110) puts it, "When information is imperfect - or in sectors of the economy where innovation is important - markets will essentially always be imperfectly competitive."

FROM PERFECT TO IMPERFECT INFORMATION

If so much is dependent on the assumption of perfect information, then it seems reasonable to ask how economists present it in an introductory course. Principles classes are the places where potential majors are initially developed. Texts are complementary to this farming activity. More importantly, however, principles classes are the only place the overwhelming numbers college education citizens are exposed to the power of competition and competitive markets. For this purpose alone, economics text must present the argument that competition and competitive forces are all for the social good. In this context, how do texts present perfect information if they do at all?

As shown in Table 1, only four of the 11 textbooks surveyed include perfect information as an assumption of the perfectly competitive market. In fact, only six of the 11 leading textbooks even make mention of perfect information anywhere in the text.

Table 1. Mentions of perfect and imperfect information in leading textbooks

Textbook	Mention Perfect Information	Include Perfect Information in Perfect Competition Assumptions
Ayers and Collinge		
Baumol and Blinder	✓	✓
Case and Fair	✓	✓
Gwartney, Stroup, et al.		
Hall and Lieberman	✓	
Krugman and Wells		
Mankiw		
O'Sullivan and Sheffrin		
Parkin*	✓	✓
Ruffin and Gregory	✓	✓
Stiglitz and Walsh	✓	✓

*Parkin (2005: 238) does not explicitly assume perfect information. He assumes that "[s]ellers and buyers are well informed about prices."

Moreover, when we take a qualitative look at the actual discussions of perfect information, many of the textbooks gloss over perfect information rather quickly. Baumol and

Blinder (2005: 156) provide one of the best definitions of perfect information when they write:

> *Perfect Information.* Each firm and each customer is well informed about available products and prices. They know whether one supplier is selling at a lower price than another" (italics in original).

While Baumol and Blinder point out that a firm owner knows the cost curves of other firms in the industry, they do not say a word about perfect information anywhere else in their textbook. In essence, perfect information is nothing more than a footnote when, in fact, it should be playing a central role in their discussion of perfect competition.

Stiglitz and Walsh (2002: 228, 287) offer a more extensive discussion of perfect information. They list perfect information as a "key assumption" of the competitive model (2002: 228), and they provide readers with a nice intuitive explanation of an environment with perfect information when they write:

> ...buyers know what they are buying, whether it is stocks or bonds, a house, a used car, or a refrigerator. Firms know the productivity of each worker they hire, and when workers go to work for a firm, they know exactly what is expected of them in return for the promised pay (228).

Case and Fair (2004: 103) provide the best treatment of perfect information.

> ...households and firms possess all the information they need to make market choices. Specifically, we assume that households possess knowledge of the qualities and prices of everything available in the market. Firms know all that there is to know about wage rates, capital costs, and output prices.

Later on, they remind the reader of the complete information assumption when they begin their discussion of imperfect information (321). Their discussion of imperfect information explicitly compares imperfect information to perfect information. They tell the reader that

> [b]ecause the market handles many information problems efficiently, we do not need to assume perfect information to arrive at an efficient allocation of resources (323).

Baumol and Blinder (2005), Case and Fair (2004), and Stiglitz and Walsh (2002) handle the assumption of perfect information quite well. When discussing imperfect information, Hall and Lieberman (2005: 154) briefly note:

> [i]n our model, consumers are assumed to *know* exactly what goods they are buying and the prices at which they can buy them. But in the real world, we must sometimes spend time and money to get this information. (emphasis in original)

Hall and Lieberman's treatment of perfect information tells readers nothing about the information assumptions economists make on the production side, and readers will find no other references to perfect information in the Hall and Lieberman text. Some mention of perfect information is probably better than no mention, however. At least Hall and Liberman (2005) compare an environment with imperfect information to one with perfect information.

The six textbooks that completely fail to mention perfect information are more troubling when the extent of market share each holds is considered. Consider the ever popular Mankiw (2004: 480-484, 489-493). He concludes his textbook with discussions of asymmetric information and behavioral economics. After discussing the basics of asymmetric information, he concludes by saying, "[t]he study of asymmetric information gives us new reason to be wary of markets" (484). Nowhere does he note that asymmetric information is one extreme view of the world, which stands in stark contrast to perfect information—the alternate view of the world. Mankiw's discussion of behavioral economics (489-493) is also frustrating. It contrasts a behavioral/satisficing individual against *home economicus*. Yet, a clear discussion of what economists mean by 'well informed people' cannot be found.

Similar problems can be found in many of the other leading textbooks. Our purpose is not to engage in an exhaustive content analysis of all of the leading textbooks, but, rather, to show that different textbooks treat the theory of perfect competition differently. Some completely avoid the assumption of perfect information; others discuss it quite loosely; and some remain true to the original theory and its believers. In sum, there is a general lack of consistency in the way textbook authors deal with perfect information.

Given the theory of perfect competition's important place in microeconomic theory, the widely varying treatments of perfect information in the textbooks should be viewed as troubling. The loss of perfect information in the textbooks raises the question: why have textbook authors been dropping perfect information from their discussions of perfection competition and what can be done about it? Clearly, it is needed for a logically consistent presentation of the benchmark of all of economic theory.

WHY WAIT?

Nearly every topic in intermediate microeconomics—whether it be consumer choice theory, elasticity, or the theory of the firm—was introduced to students in micro principles. Even indifference curves can be found in appendices of many principles textbooks. But, as we have pointed out above, information is a topic that is sidestepped or avoided entirely at the principles level. Since information is a topic that receives a good deal of attention at the intermediate level, it is interesting to wonder why there is an implicit opinion among the textbook industry and its economists that it is ok to wait. Why? Is information so different and so difficult that it is only meant for upper level economics students?

It may be the case that a well-informed student only really needs to know certain things about competition. That is to say, there is an optimum amount of the theory of perfect competition that anyone needs to know. We agree that it is possible to tell people too much. In determining the optimal amount of coverage of perfect competition, the textbook industry has produced a competitive result that has left perfect information out of discussions of perfect competition.

Another possibility is that there is a certain amount of inertia in the textbook industry. In other words, principles textbooks have been slow to discuss information at greater length because the information revolution in microeconomics is relatively new and difficult to discuss. When faced with real page constraints, textbook authors have collectively chosen to stick with what has worked in the past rather than delve into new topics like perfect information. In such a view, new things find it difficult to compete for limited page space. Clearly, the recognition of the importance of perfect information is new to the timeline that is economic progress. It just might not be the time for a full presentation of its importance.

Perhaps, instead, its discussion is simply too complex for principles students. As any professor of principles knows, the mere mention of 'ratio' , 'tangency', and 'marginal rate of substitution' creates fear enough with the average undergraduate not destined to be an economics major. A discussion of perfect information may stir the same kind of fear.

In the end, we don't know. Our main hope in this paper is to get the interested reader to wonder for themselves about what the textbooks have done with perfect information.

Conclusion: Is There a Future for Perfect Information?

Perfect competition has withstood the test of time as a central idea in microeconomic theory. Central to perfect competition has been the assumption of perfect information. Without perfect information there can be no perfect competition. Given the fact that perfect information is crucial to understanding market processes, it is puzzling to see introductory textbooks dropping the perfect information assumption.

The loss of perfect information is problematic for a number of reasons. Notions like efficiency, market coordination, and market failure do not make sense in the absence of perfect information. As Stiglitz (2000: 1460; emphasis in original) has correctly pointed out, if we completely abandon the perfect information assumption, the following outcomes could result:

> demand could differ from supply *in equilibrium*. Labor markets could be characterized by [involuntary] unemployment; credit markets by credit rationing...

If textbook authors wanted to be consistent, discussions of competitive markets, without concomitant discussion of perfect information, should lead to discussions of market failures and the inability of markets to clear. Instead, and much to Stiglitz's discontent, we still find textbook authors talking about supply meeting demand *in equilibrium*, the market only producing voluntary unemployment.

Notes

[1] Makowski and Ostroy (2001) provide a nice contemporary survey of the main criticisms of perfect competition.

[2] In this case the pun is intended.

REFERENCES

Akerlof, G. (1970). "The Market for 'Lemons': Qualitative Uncertainty and the Market Mechanism," *Quarterly Journal of Economics* 86: 488-500.

Ayers, R., and Collinge, R. (2005). *Microeconomics: Explore and Apply*. Upper Saddle River, NJ: Pearson Prentice Hall.

Barone, E. (1908). "The Ministry of Production in the Collectivist State," in F.A. Hayek, ed. (1935) *Collectivist Economic Planning*. London: Routledge.

Baumol, W., and Blinder, A. (2005). *Microeconomics: Principles and Policy, 9th ed.* Mason, OH: Thomson South-Western.

Case, K., and Fair, C. (2004). *Principles of Microeconomics, 7th ed.* Upper Saddle River, NJ: Pearson Prentice Hall.

Gwartney, J., Stroup, R., Sobel, R., and Macpherson, D. (2006). *Microeconomics: Private and Public Choice, 11th ed.* Mason, OH: Thomson South-Western.

Hall, R., and Lieberman, M. (2005). *Microeconomics: Principles and Applications, 3rd ed.* Mason, OH: Thomson South-Western.

Hayek, F.A. (ed.). (1935). *Collectivist Economic Planning*. London: Routledge.

Krugman, P., and Wells, R. (2005). *Microeconomics*. New York: Worth Publishers.

Makowski, L., and Ostroy, J. (2001). "Perfect Competition and the Creativity of the Market," *Journal of Economic Literature* 39 (2): 479-535.

Mankiw, N.G. (2004). *Principles of Microeconomics, 3rd ed.* Mason, OH: Thomson South-Western.

O'Sullivan, A., and Sheffrin, S. (2003). *Microeconomics: Principles and Tools*. Upper Saddle River, NJ: Prentice Hall.

Pareto, W. (1971 [1906]). *Manual of Political Economy*. New York: August M. Kelley.

Parkin, M. (2005). *Microeconomics, 7th ed.* USA: Pearson Addison Wesley.

Ruffin, R., and Gregory, P. (2001). *Principles of Microeconomics, 7th ed.* USA: Addison Wesley.

Stiglitz, J. (2000). "The Contributions of the Economics of Information to Twentieth Century Economics," *Quarterly Journal of Economics* 115 (4): 1441-1478.

-------. (1997 [1994]). *Whither Socialism?* Cambridge, MA: MIT Press.

Stiglitz, J., and Walsh, C. (2002). *Principles of Microeconomics, 3rd ed.* New York: W.W. Norton.

Thaler, R. (1992). *The Winner's Curse*. Princeton, NJ: Princeton University Press.

In: Expanding Teaching and Learning Horizons
Editors: F. G. Mixon, Jr. and R. J. Cebula

ISBN 978-1-60741-971-6

Chapter 16

HITTING THE RENT-SEEKING CONCEPT OUT OF THE PARK IN ECONOMICS PRINCIPLES COURSES: THE CASE OF PROFESSIONAL BASEBALL STADIUMS

Daniel Box and Steven B. Caudill

INTRODUCTION

Economists define rent-seeking as the wasteful use of resources in pursuit of a government-sponsored privilege. For students of principles of economics or public choice, professional sports provide vivid examples of this concept [1]. For instance, in exchange for moving a professional sports franchise to a city, team owners sometimes extract huge subsidies from local and/or state governments. A city or state failing to sufficiently subsidize the construction and operation of a new stadium risks losing the franchise. Economists studying these subsidies conclude that they cannot be justified on economic grounds, yet such activities continue to this day.

In recent history for example, Black Entertainment Television founder, Bob Johnson, offered to buy 51% of the Montreal Expos so that he could relocate the team to Washington D.C. Johnson noted that in order to move the team to D.C., the city would have to build a new stadium. The low-end estimate of the cost of this new stadium was $342 million dollars. Increase in local employment is often touted as one benefit of new stadium construction, but studies estimated that funding for a new D.C. stadium would create jobs at a price of about $900,000 per job. This calculation helps us understand why economists argue that these large subsidies are not justified. This paper chronicles an even more extreme case of this rent-seeking phenomenon. We examine the effort in the 1980s of Tampa-St. Petersburg, Florida, to acquire a professional baseball team. As we show, in the Tampa-St. Petersburg spent about $200 million in a failed effort to lure a professional baseball team. In this extreme case, the large expenditure purchased *nothing* for the cities.

SPORTS FRANCHISE LOCATION AS RENT-SEEKING

The concept of rent-seeking is introduced by Tullock (1967), Krueger (1974) and Posner (1975) in the late 1960's and early 1970s [2]. Rent-seeking occurs when government restrictions that produce profits for individuals lead to wasteful lobbying efforts on the part of those same individuals. When all the various forms of rent-seeking are considered, from direct pecuniary and in-kind forms (Sobel and Garrett, 2002; Mixon, Laband and Ekelund, 1994; Mixon, 1995), to indirect rent-seeking (Sobel and Garrett, 2002), the estimated costs can be substantial (Laband and Sophocleus, 1988 and 1992; Mixon and Ressler, 1998; Laband and McClintock, 2001; Sobel and Garrett, 2002).

The rent-seeking concept is easily illustrated in professional sports. Organizations such as the NFL and NBA award franchises to selected cities. In order to acquire the franchise, city governments often subsidize stadium construction and operations. In many cases, the owners gain the rights to profits from the use of the stadium. Cities compete for these sports franchises because of the alleged economic benefits to the community. Sometimes the competition between cities causes a significant misallocation of resources, or social loss. Some of this social loss is produced because cities spend large amounts of money in their campaigns to acquire a sports franchise and there can be only one winner.

RENT-SEEKING AND PROFESSIONAL BASEBALL IN ST. PETERSBURG/TAMPA

This section of our essay examines a scenario like that described at the end of the previous section. In doing so it draws heavily from Andelman (1993), to whom we are giving an omnibus citation. Usually cities promise new stadiums to owners in order to acquire the sports franchise. However, in one particularly sad episode, a city tried a build-it-and-they-will-come strategy to acquire a professional baseball franchise. In the 1980'a AND 1990'S, Tampa Bay spent huge sums of money in a failed attempt to acquire a professional baseball franchise. A few teams promised to move to the area, but all eventually located elsewhere. The city ran an expensive campaign to get Major League Baseball to award them an expansion team, but they were turned down.

The cities of St. Petersburg and Tampa Bay are only a few miles apart. When these two cities began to think about professional baseball as an economic development tool, they competed with each other, along with other cities seeking a franchise. In 1986, St. Petersburg made the first real move by committing $83 million dollars to build a baseball stadium (the Florida Suncoast Dome). This was done before the city's leaders actually attracted a team because Major League Baseball officials told St. Petersburg that they almost certainly would be awarded a franchise if they built a stadium.

Rick Dodge, an assistant city manager in St. Petersburg, played a very important role in the city's campaign for baseball. An organization called the *Tampa Bay Baseball Group* ran the campaign for Tampa Bay. Dodge's work on this project began in 1983 when the owner of the Minnesota Twins began to look into moving his team to Tampa Bay. The owner was losing money in Minnesota, and he thought that the team would be better off financially in Florida. However, the *Tampa Bay Baseball Group* decided that Major League Baseball would probably block the move because team relocation was usually bad financially for baseball overall, so the group did not pursue a deal. The Twins owner then sold the team to relieve his financial problems.

Although the Twins never actually moved from Minnesota, this episode led officials in St. Petersburg to believe they were close to getting a team. Soon they *started* construction on the stadium, and they added $25,000 to the budget to study the feasibility of *finishing* the stadium. After construction had started, many other baseball teams that were having financial troubles began to explore a move to Tampa Bay. One of these teams was the Chicago White Sox, co-owned at the time by Jerry Reinsdorf. The White Sox had been having financial problems, partly because they were trying to compete in the same market as the Chicago Cubs and partly, as they contended, because of a worn-out stadium.

As a part of their effort to acquire a professional baseball team, St. Petersburg paid for a study to assess the value of potential television rights to a baseball team in Tampa Bay. The study suggested that the rights were worth more than $10 million. This figure, and the new stadium under construction, made Tampa very attractive to Reinsdorf and the Chicago White Sox organization. Dodge and his associates flew to Chicago many times to help speed the process along. However, the Illinois Senate and House of Representatives voted, by a narrow margin, to fund construction of a new stadium for the White Sox. Reinsdorf had promised to stay in Chicago if the city built a stadium. He kept his promise and decided not to relocate to St. Petersburg. The citizens of Tampa-St. Petersburg had been disappointed again.

Meanwhile, the two city governments continued to spend money on the stadium. The area's Tourist Development Council gave $125,000 to the effort. The *Tampa Bay Baseball Group*, still hoping it could build the stadium in the city of Tampa Bay, spent $100,000 tearing down their minor league stadium in order to create a site for a larger one. The city of St. Petersburg spent $13 million to develop a site in their downtown area, and, at a cost of $1,200, they sent four people to domed stadiums around the country to get ideas for how they should build their stadium. Both cities were wasting some of this money competing with each other until they decided to make a concerted effort to acquire a team which would play in St. Petersburg.

By 1989, the stadium was finished and the White Sox had decided to stay in Chicago. St. Petersburg officials began to focus on an upcoming expansion of Major League Baseball. A four-person board was appointed to select two U.S. cities that would receive expansion teams. The board would not make their selections until 1992, so cities that were vying for a new franchise had ample time to develop proposals. Because St. Petersburg already had a stadium, they were initially the board's first choice.

Around this time, St. Petersburg started a campaign to show how much its citizens would support baseball. Dodge and Frank Morsani, the head of the *Tampa Bay Baseball Group*, managed the drive. The drive, called *Join the Team*, called for people to reserve season tickets for the first season of play of Tampa's future franchise. The reservations would cost $50 each. Dodge, Morsani, and their committee spent time rallying corporate support for the campaign. They paid a sportscaster $2,000 to do a voice-over for a promotional video. The group placed *Join the Team* ads in almost all of the prominent locations and in newspapers in the area. A $275,000 allocation in the budget for the baseball stadium covered employee salaries, printing costs, and other expenses. Despite the limited budget, the promotion worked very well. In the four weeks that the campaign ran, 22,697 people reserved season tickets.

In addition to selecting where to place the teams, the MLB expansion committee also selected ownership groups. In most of the cities vying for a team, several groups applied to be considered for franchise ownership, and the committee had to choose. Three different groups applied for ownership in Tampa. Frank Morsani headed one of these groups. Most people in Tampa Bay preferred his group to the others, but his group's candidacy was later downgraded when it got into financial trouble. Since the inception of the *Tampa Bay Baseball Group*, Morsani had paid most of the group's expenses. Some of these expenses included $1,000 a month for the group's office space and $100,000 in architect's fees for planning the new stadium. Morsani also paid the $100,000 application fee for ownership of an expansion team. Over the years, Morsani spent more than $2 million covering the group's operating costs.

The payouts listed above drained almost all of Morsani's bank accounts, and the group that was awarded ownership of a team in Tampa Bay would ultimately have to pay $95 million to buy the team. Morsani was out of the picture, and as a result other members of his ownership group scaled back on their contributions to the cause. On December 18, 1990, the expansion committee narrowed its list of prospective host cities to six. They also picked an ownership group from Tampa Bay, and it was not Morsani's.

The group that the expansion committee selected was headed by Stephen Porter and Joel Schur. These two men had not previously been on good terms with city officials in St. Petersburg due to several arguments over the terms of the lease for the stadium. When the expansion committee visited Tampa to tour the stadium, the city had to cover all expenses, without contributions from Porter and Schur.

In the other cities in the competition, the ownership groups had paid these expenses. In an attempt to get past their problems, the city supported Porter and Schur as much as possible once they were selected.

All of this effort by the city of St. Petersburg was for naught because Porter's group began to have the same monetary problems that doomed Morsani's efforts. Important partners backed out of financial commitments. Porter found that he could not pay as much of the $95 million fee as he had promised. Although St. Petersburg had done almost everything else right, the expansion committee announced on June 10, 1991, that they would place franchises in Miami and Denver. The overriding factor in the decision was that Major League Baseball could not afford to have an ownership group that was not able to pay for its team.

Instead of giving up after this huge setback, St. Petersburg continued its campaign. They renewed the season ticket reservation drives and continued to look for existing franchises that wanted to relocate. Rick Dodge kept track of every MLB team's financial performance so that he could contact troubled franchises in an effort to get them to move to Tampa. He found an opportunity when, almost immediately after the expansion committee's decision, the Seattle Mariners began to discuss relocation. Dodge knew that the team was losing money, and he was in contact with owner Jeff Smulyan about relocating the Mariners even before Tampa lost their expansion bid.

Smulyan saw much more potential for profit in Tampa, but he was not able to relocate immediately. St. Petersburg and Seattle soon began spending money competing with each other for the Mariners. The *Join The Team* organization spent $3,600 printing 25,000 postcards used to promote the Florida Suncoast Dome at baseball meetings and to Mariners representatives.

In Seattle, one part of Smulyan's lease with the city for their stadium stated that he could not relocate the team in any year in which they reached certain attendance levels. At the end of 1991, the city decided to buy $450,000 worth of unsold tickets to meet the sales requirement and force the Mariners to stay another year.

Meanwhile, Smulyan put the team up for sale, stating that he would otherwise relocate to Tampa because he could not afford to maintain the Mariners in Seattle. He preferred to keep the team himself, but executives from Nintendo offered to buy it. Because of another clause in the lease, he was not able to refuse this offer. Nintendo took over the Mariners organization and it remained in Seattle. Officials in St. Petersburg did not take this news well as frustration mounted over the city's repeated baseball failures.

However, Dodge continued to search for teams interested in relocation. He soon found that the San Francisco Giants owner was in a bad situation. The Giants played in Candlestick Park, which many people claimed was the worst stadium in baseball. Candlestick was cold, windy, and run-down.

The Giants' owner, Bob Lurie, got the cities of San Francisco and San Jose to hold repeated referenda in an effort to get voters to support a new baseball park, but none of these referenda passed. Lurie decided to sell the team to the first group that made an acceptable offer. This time Dodge put together a group with good financial backing, and the group actually signed a contract with Lurie to buy the Giants franchise for $115 million and relocate it to St. Petersburg.

This was the closest that St. Petersburg/Tampa had come to actually getting a team. Excitement in the area grew, and the city spent $34,000 distributing seven million cards with pre-printed thank-you messages that people could send to baseball commissioners or Lurie. Once again, though, the relocation deal was blocked because of outside business interests. CBS owned the television rights to baseball at that time, and they thought that moving the Giants would eliminate an important viewership market.

The owner of the new expansion team in Miami fought vigorously against having another team in his television market. A group of investors in San Francisco made a $100 million offer for the team, and Major League Baseball voted to block the Tampa deal and accept the San Francisco offer.

This episode ended Tampa Bay's last real chance to get a baseball team anytime in the near future. The city of St. Petersburg decided to sue MLB and the San Francisco government for violating contractual agreements. In doing so they attempted to convert the $1.5 million fund from the *Join the Team* campaign into a legal defense fund. Frank Morsani and the Tampa Bay investors who had made the deal with Lurie also filed large lawsuit claims.

In the end, St. Petersburg was left with no baseball team, an unused stadium, and a huge amount of money wasted. The total cost to the city of St. Petersburg and the *Tampa Bay Baseball Group* was $100,265,800 (See Table 1).

Besides the monetary cost, many people, especially Dodge and Morsani, consumed significant amounts of time in their efforts to lure professional baseball to the west coast of South Florida.

For more than ten years, Dodge, Morsani, and many other city officials made the acquisition of a baseball a priority. They spent months traveling around the country investigating various possibilities. In addition, the repeated rejections hurt Tampa Bay citizens' pride in their city.

Table 1. Total Expenditures on Baseball for St. Petersburg/Tampa Bay, 1978-1993

Year	Transaction	Cost
1986-1989**	Building Florida Suncoast Dome	$ 83,000,000
1988**	Study of finishing costs	$ 25,000
1978	Match of fundraiser by tourism council	$ 125,000
1982**	St. Petersburg land development	$ 13,000,000
1986**	Tearing down Tampa's minor league stadium	$ 100,000
1984	Visits to domed stadiums around the United States	$ 1,200
1989	Employees and materials for Join The Team campaign	$ 275,000
1982**	Architect's planning fee	$ 100,000
1982-1989	Tampa Bay Baseball Group expenses	$ 2,000,000
1989	Sportscaster contract for promotion video	$ 2,000
1990**	Application fee for expansion team	$ 100,000
1991	Postcards distributed to Mariners organization	$ 3,600
1992	"Thank you" cards after Giants deal	$ 34,000
1992**	Legal defense fund against baseball and San Francisco	$ 1,500,000
		$100,265,800*

This figure does not include costs of plane tickets and various other minor expenses for which were not given in Andelman (1993). ** denotes an approximate time frame.

CONCLUSION

Tampa came close to getting a baseball team on several occasions, but they could never finish the deal. This led them to continue spending money in the belief that they were just a few dollars short of a successful effort. One unique part of the Tampa/St. Petersburg situation was that a stadium had been built without any certainty that a team was coming, something that most other cities would not have even considered. In these ways, rent-seeking efforts to acquire an MLB franchise had drained taxpayers' (and some private citizens') money. The competition for economic rents among baseball owners and potential baseball owners generated a huge social waste. Paying attention to the problems associated with this particular rent seeking episode in professional baseball could eventually save other cities from the same fate.

Eventually baseball found a home in the area when, in 1998, the Tampa Bay Rays began play in St. Petersburg.

NOTES

[1] Interestingly, in a study published more than a decade ago Mixon and Ressler (1998) discuss the importance of integrating the rent-seeking concept into economics principles courses.

[2] For more on the origin of the rent-seeking concept, see Tullock (2003). For a good survey on the concept, see Tollison (1982).

REFERENCES

Andelman, R. (1993) Stadium for Rent: Tampa Bay's Quest for Major League Baseball, Jefferson, NC: McFarland and Company.

Krueger, A.O. (1974) "The Political Economy of the Rent Seeking Society," *American Economic Review* 64: 291-303.

Laband, D.N. and McClintock, G.C. (2001) *The Transfer Society*, Washington, D.C.: The Cato Institute.

---------- and J.P. Sophocleus (1988) "The Social Cost of Rent Seeking: First Estimates," *Public Choice* 58: 269-275.

---------- and ---------- (1992) "An Estimate of the Resource Expenditures on Transfer Activity in the United States," *Quarterly Journal of Economics* 107: 959-983.

Mixon, F.G., Jr. (1995) "To the Capitol, Driver: Limousine Services as a Rent Seeking Device in State Capital Cities," *Rivista Internazionale di Scienze Economiche e Commerciali* 42: 663-670.

Mixon, F.G., Jr., D.N. Laband and R.B. Ekelund, Jr. (1994) "Rent Seeking and Hidden In-Kind Resource Distortion: Some Empirical Evidence," *Public Choice* 78: 171-185.

Mixon, F.G., Jr. and R.W. Ressler (1998) "Integrating the Concept of Rent-Seeking into the Economics Classroom: Evidence from Survey Data," *Journal of Education for Business* 74: 24-27.

Posner, R.A. (1975) "The Social Costs of Monopoly and Regulation," *Journal of Political Economy* 83: 807-827.

Sobel, R.S. and T.A. Garrett (2002) "On the Measurement of Rent Seeking and its Social Opportunity Cost," *Public Choice* 112: 115-136.

Tollison, R.D. (1982) "*Rent Seeking: A Survey*," Kyklos 35: 575-602.

Tullock, G. (1967) "The Welfare Costs of Tariffs, Monopolies, and Theft," *Western Economic Journal* 5: 224-232.

---------- (2003) "The Origin of the Rent-Seeking Concept," *International Journal of Economics and Business* 2: 1-8.

PART III.
THE SOCIOLOGY OF ECONOMIC EDUCATION

In: Expanding Teaching and Learning Horizons
Editors: F. G. Mixon, Jr. and R. J. Cebula
ISBN 978-1-60741-971-6

Chapter 17

A Differentiated Model of Doctoral Training in Economics

Stuart D. Allen and Kenneth A. Snowden, Jr.

Introduction

In 1991 the Commission on Graduate Economic Education (COGEE) concluded that a single approach to doctoral education dominated the training of economists in the U.S. even though the Ph.D.s went on to pursue a variety of career paths in academia, government and business (Krueger, 1991, 1053). This "traditional" model, which continues to dominate graduate programming, emphasizes theory and techniques over application and mathematical formalism over historical and institutional context. The COGEE established two generalizations that help to explain the widespread use of the traditional model: 1) faculty who taught in graduate programs and their students both believed that the focus of the traditional curriculum was appropriate and 2) the Ph.D. afforded new economists faster placement and higher starting salaries than recently trained graduates in other social sciences. The COGEE reported other evidence, however, that suggested important weaknesses in the traditional curriculum: 3) alumni of graduate economics programs reported significant gaps between what they were taught and what they needed in their careers and 4) employers found that many new Ph.D.s were inadequately prepared to conduct and communicate about applied research. In addition, evidence had begun to mount by 1990 that domestic demand for new doctoral economists had reached a long-run plateau and that interest in graduate economics training among U.S. undergraduates was declining. In light of these troubling signs the COGEE expressed surprise and concern that the doctoral curriculum in economics had not become more differentiated so that it could better serve a diverse student audience (Krueger, 1991, 1053).

This paper describes a different approach to doctoral training that addresses many of the concerns that the COGEE and others have raised regarding the traditional curriculum. The differentiated model of doctoral training described here is not a proposal; it was designed and actually implemented at The University of North Carolina Greensboro (UNCG) in 2004 and differs from the standard model in three key respects. First, it is intended to train only applied microeconomists in the fields of public, labor and health economics. Second, it is integrated with and supported by a terminal, professionally-oriented M.A. program in Applied Economics. Third, the program's core course sequence is explicitly designed to emphasize the applications of theory and econometrics that are most relevant for labor, public and health economists. Each of these innovations would be problematic or even inappropriate if embedded within a traditional Ph.D. program that offered a diverse set of specializations. Taken together, however, they represent an alternative approach to doctoral education that can be used to train applied economists in other narrowly-focused areas of specialization for careers outside research-oriented departments of economics.

Differentiated doctoral programs in economics will become attractive alternatives to the traditional model only if prospective students, academic advisors and employers accept their relative strengths and weaknesses. We discuss these strengths and weaknesses in the conclusion of the paper and their implications for the quality and viability of differentiated doctoral programming. We lead up to that assessment by first reviewing what we have learned about graduate education in economics from and since the COGEE report. We then describe how the three curricular innovations that are emphasized here—a narrow focus, a specialized core and integration with a terminal, professional masters' program—have been combined in the differentiated doctoral program in applied microeconomics at UNCG.

What We Have Learned From and Since the COGEE

In its 1991 report the COGEE documented and gave voice to concerns within the economics profession regarding the direction, content and structure of doctoral education. Since this groundwork was laid, a variety of researchers have extended, amplified and updated the COGEE's analysis on a regular basis. We briefly review that literature in this section to highlight developments in graduate education in economics over the past sixteen years that provide context and motivation for the curricular innovations that are described later. The discussion focuses on three broad themes that have resonated since the COGEE report: the strengths and weaknesses of the standard doctoral curriculum in economics; the profession's resistance to changing this traditional model; and the impact that the adherence to the curriculum has had on the number, composition and career profiles of Ph.D. economists who are being trained in the U.S. These three developments, when viewed together, indicate a continuing need for the development of differentiated doctoral programs in economics.

The Strength and Weaknesses of the Standard Model

The overwhelming majority of graduates from doctoral programs in economics follow one of five career paths:

(a) researcher/teacher in a department of economics with a graduate teaching mission.
(b) teacher/researcher in a department of economics with an undergraduate teaching mission.

(c) researcher/teacher in professional graduate school of public policy, education, health or business.
(d) researcher/policy analyst in government or in a non-academic research organization.
(e) researcher/practitioner employed by a business enterprise.

The concern of the COGEE that we focus on here is its conclusions that the standard doctoral curriculum in economics is designed primarily to prepare students for the first career path and provides less effective training, as a result, for the other four [1]. The seriousness of this problem is underscored by the fact that four out of every ten new Ph.D.s economists work outside of academia—a share that has not changed in the sixteen years since the COGEE report [2].

The COGEE based its conclusions and recommendations on several types of evidence regarding curricular focus and emphasis that were assembled and reported by Hansen (1991). First of all, he asked faculty serving in graduate programs and their students to rate the importance that was given to seven specific areas of knowledge and six different skill sets within their doctoral programs; he also asked respondents to rate the importance that each knowledge area and skill set should have been given [3]. Both groups reported that the knowledge profile of the curriculum was appropriate—theory was and should have been more important than econometrics, empirical technique or policy applications while the least emphasis was correctly placed on knowledge of institutions, history and the economics literature. The faculty and students also had a common view of the appropriate mix of skills—the greatest emphasis should have been given to analytics, critical judgment and creativity; less emphasis on the ability to apply abstract concepts to real-world issues; and the least on mathematical, computational and communication skills. Both groups agreed, however, that too much emphasis was actually placed on mathematical and computational skills and too little on critical judgment and creativity. Hansen's survey established that the faculty and students most intimately connected to graduate education shared a common view of the doctoral curriculum in economics, and one that was generally positive.

Hansen (1991, 1068-75, 1083-5) also surveyed alumni of Ph.D. programs in economics (the 1977-78 class) to elicit their views concerning the focus and effectiveness of the doctoral curriculum. The survey indicated that there had been little change in the basic focus of doctoral training in the years leading up to the COGEE report as the alumni reported that the programs they had attended a decade earlier provided virtually the same mix of knowledge and skills that were reported by current Ph.D. students. The older Ph.D.s reported, however, that the knowledge and skill sets that were important in their postgraduate careers turned out to be different from those that were emphasized in graduate school. In particular, theory, econometrics, mathematics and computational skills were considerably less important in their careers than they had been in their doctoral programs. Knowledge of policy applications, empirical techniques and communication skills, on the other hand, proved to be much more important. Ph.D.s with academic careers in both graduate and undergraduate departments of economics voiced these impressions, but the mismatch in knowledge and skills was judged to be particularly severe by Ph.D.s who worked outside of academia.

Employers of new Ph.D.s also gave mixed reviews to the knowledge and skill sets that were provided by the traditional doctoral curriculum (Hansen 1991, 1082-3). Both non-academic employers and chairs of graduate and undergraduate departments of economics rated Ph.D. knowledge of economic theory and econometrics high, their command of history and institutions low; and their understanding of policy, application and economic literature somewhere between these extremes [4]. All employer groups also rated the mathematical, analytic and computational skills of the new Ph.D.s the highest, followed closely by their critical judgment. On the other hand, nearly all employers gave the lowest ratings to the application and communication skills of the new graduates. In fact, non-academic employers and department chairs at top-tier graduate programs joined in ranking the application skills of new graduates as actually being "less than adequate". The non-academic employers revealed even broader dissatisfaction with the doctoral curriculum in face-to-face interviews. They generally acknowledged that new Ph.D.s were well-trained in theory, econometrics, mathematics and analytics, but they "urged" that doctoral programs do better jobs preparing students to conduct and communicate about empirical research and providing them with knowledge about real-world applications and data (Hansen, 1991, 1085).

Hansen's evidence established that graduate faculty, current and past graduate students, and employers of all types held similar views of the strengths and weaknesses of doctoral training in economics. These responses reinforce the generalization that Hansen drew from information he collected from descriptive brochures, course syllabi and comprehensive examinations—doctoral programs in economics were strikingly similar in structure across all departments (Hansen, 1991, 1061-3). This singular approach emphasizes technique over professional knowledge and skills because "graduate programs concentrate their efforts almost exclusively on preparing Ph.D.s for academic, research-oriented jobs" (Hansen, 1991, 1085), Colander (1998, 605) stated the case differently—in his view the traditional doctoral curriculum emphasizes the formal, deductivist tradition of theoretical economics at the expense of the general, inductivist approach that is important in applied work.

This backdrop frames two recommendations made by the COGEE that we focus on throughout this paper. First, the report encouraged departments to differentiate their doctoral programs by providing training that was appropriate for the career paths most frequently pursued by their own graduates (Krueger, 1991, 1051-3). Second, the COGEE identified the core as the logical focal point for curricular innovation and improvement. More specifically, the COGEE suggested that departments take collective responsibility for core courses, emphasize more application of theory within the core, and connect the core more effectively to field courses (Krueger, 1991, 1043-6). Both recommendations play a central role in the design of the differentiated doctoral program described below.

Continued Adherence to the Standard Model

Nearly a decade after the COGEE report, Colander (1998) characterized the profession's response as "The Sounds of Silence". He was not alone. Siegfried and Stock (1999, 133) found it "peculiar" that there was so little evidence of program differentiation eight years after the COGEE report and Krueger (1999, 156), who chaired the commission, remained "puzzled" by the lack of innovation. Coats (1992, 344), in contrast, had predicted resistance to the implementation of the COGEE's recommendations because the faculty and students most directly involved in doctoral programs were generally satisfied with the traditional curriculum, while dissatisfaction with the approach was concentrated among alumni and employers. Coats (1992, 348) also placed the resistance to change in a broader historical context by noting that Bowen (1953) had some four decades earlier raised concerns about graduate education in economics similar to those raised by the COGEE; Coats took this as evidence that a "narrowly technocratic species of professionalism" had dominated the economics profession and shaped graduate education since at least World War II. On the other hand, Siegfried and Stock (1999, 133) speculated that graduate programs were reluctant to innovate COGEE's recommendations because differentiation represented a poor competitive strategy given the uncertainty and information problems prospective graduate students faced when evaluating their postgraduate career options.

Whatever the cause for the reluctance to change, the traditional doctoral curriculum in economics continues to be widely employed well after the COGEE's report called for greater program differentiation. Colander (1998, 604) found that some departments outside the elite tier of graduate schools had refocused their doctoral programs on specific, "niche" specializations or on training undergraduate teachers, but he emphasized that many of these were responses to idiosyncratic university-based initiatives and not to the COGEE report [5]. Some five years later Colander (2005) also reported that the research conducted by doctoral students in elite programs was more empirical and relied on more diverse theory than had been the case in the late 1980s. But the change in research focus was not, in his judgment, due to curricular innovation. Instead: "the pedagogical institutional structure has not kept pace with the changing research technologies. My critique of economics now is not about economics, but about pedagogy—specifically the structure of the core in graduate education" (Colander, 2005, 197).

Hansen and Stock (2004) found additional evidence of the profession's slow response to the concerns raised by COGEE in their replication of Hansen's (1991) survey of doctoral alumni. In the later study, as in the original, the respondents were asked to compare the importance of the knowledge areas and skills that were emphasized in their Ph.D. programs to those that were required in their careers. This time, however, members of two cohorts were surveyed—those from both the 1996-1997 and 2001-2002 graduating classes. The survey revealed little change in the doctoral curriculum in the decade after the COGEE report. More than 50 percent of both cohorts reported that their programs had placed "too little" emphasis on the application of theory to the real world, and one-third reported that "too little" emphasis had been placed on using theory in empirical applications. The skill gap between doctoral training and professional requirements was also unchanged from 1991—mathematics and computation were more important in graduate school than on the jobs, while the reverse was true for application and communications. Moreover, the disparity between the knowledge and skills taught and those subsequently used was, once again, larger for respondents in non-academic professions [6]. In light of these results Stock and Hansen concluded in 2004, as the COGEE had thirteen years earlier, that greater emphasis on applications of economic theory, empirical research and communication skills had to be built into the graduate economics curriculum if it were to better serve the professional aspirations of a diverse student body.

The Effects of Adherence to Standard Curriculum

Between 1977 and 2001 around 700 new, domestically-trained Ph.D. economists entered the U.S. labor market each year; over the same period the number of these new Ph.D.s who were U.S. citizens declined from 550 to around 350 (Siegfried and Stock, 2004, 273-4) [7]. To place these trends into perspective note that the number of Ph.D.s awarded to U.S. citizens in all science fields doubled over this period, and more than doubled in other social sciences (Siegfried and Stock, 2006, 1). In stark contrast, the number of U.S. citizens who will begin careers each year as doctoral economists will soon fall to levels not seen since the Eisenhower administration (Siegfried and Stock, 2006, 1).

These trends in the number and composition of new Ph.D. economists were already established at the time of the COGEE report, and several observers predicted that they would continue unless the COGEE's recommendations were taken seriously. Hansen (1991, 1085) and Coats (1992, 348), for example, expressed concern that the demand for new Ph.D.s economists would remain flat in the U.S. so long as the gap existed between the knowledge and skill sets emphasized in doctoral programs and those required for professional careers outside of research-oriented economics departments [8]. They argued that the mismatch increases the on-the-job training costs employers face when hiring economists as applied researchers and policy analysts and, therefore, provides incentives to replace Ph.D. economists with graduates from professional schools of business, public policy and health who are better prepared for these roles.

Other observers expected a continuation in the decline in the number of U.S.-trained undergraduates who completed the Ph.D. in economics—although the forecasts were based on different views of how the trend was connected to the traditional curriculum [9]. Kaspar (1991) examined the interest in graduate education among economics majors at elite liberal arts colleges and concluded that many undergraduates who became interested in economics as a method of examining applied, real-world issues decided not to pursue graduate training in the field because it had become too abstract and technical. Colander (1998, 604), on the other hand, argued that U.S. undergraduates with strong empirical interests and talents are being disproportionately excluded from doctoral programs because admission committees favor mathematical aptitude and training. Hansen (1991, 1081-3) conjectured that the declining number of U.S. undergraduates earning Ph.D.s results from higher attrition after matriculation due to poor preparation. But Finegan, Stock and Siegfried recently found no difference in matriculation behavior, attrition or time-to degree between U.S. citizens and international students [10]. They conclude, in fact, "that the mains source of that decline [in Ph.D.s earned by U.S. citizens] must lie earlier in the recruitment process" (Finegan, Stock and Siegfried, 2006, 457).

Doctoral programs in economics in the U.S. have succeeded over the past several decades in training outstanding basic research scientists who make significant contributions to economic theory, econometrics and cutting-edge application of these tools in a variety of fields. In pursuing this mission they have attracted a pool of talent that is increasingly international in composition and who in increasing numbers seek and find postgraduate employment opportunities abroad. Over the same period the numbers of new Ph.D. economists who are absorbed into the domestic labor market each year has remained virtually flat while the production of Ph.D.s from professional schools of business, education, public policy and health has been increasing. If increasing numbers of applied social scientists are to be trained in economics departments, some modifications need to be made to the doctoral curriculum in economics.

A Differentiated Ph.D. Curriculum

Three factors shaped the focus and structure of the differentiated doctoral program in economics as it was developed and implemented at UNCG between 2002 and 2004. First, the COGEE report provided context and an underlying rationale by calling for the development of doctoral programs that better served specific professional audiences. Second, the Ph.D. was brand new and not a modification of an existing program; as a result, all features of the curriculum, and especially the doctoral core, could be designed from the ground up. Finally, a set of curricular components that was appropriate for the new doctoral program was already being offered at UNCG in its innovative, professionally-oriented masters' program in Applied Economics. Taken together these three factors created the opportunity to build an innovative, narrowly-focused and differentiated Ph.D. program and in this section we describe how it differs from the traditional Ph.D. in economics.

Narrowly Focused Training

The first, and easiest, decision concerning the new doctoral program at UNCG was the choice of specialized fields that would be offered to students. A key input into any Ph.D. program, and especially a new one, are the faculty who mentor students as they define and develop quality research agendas. The economics department at UNCG had decided in the mid-1990s to recruit and retain faculty who specialized in empirical microeconomic research in health, labor and public economics. The idea was to assemble a strong core of research faculty who could collectively produce research comparable in quantity and quality to faculty at departments of economics with Ph.D. programs [11]. The research strength of the faculty was already concentrated in empirical labor, health and public economics when the new doctoral was first proposed and so only those fields were offered in the new doctoral program.

The COGEE report provides persuasive evidence that the traditional doctoral curriculum in economics is not appropriate for a program with such a narrow focus. Many, if not most, Ph.D.s who specialize in applied microeconomics seek and find attractive career alternatives outside departments of economics—in government agencies, in professional schools of health, education or public policy, or in private research organizations. We have seen above that employers in these sectors express dissatisfaction with the knowledge and skill sets that are emphasized in the traditional economics curriculum and are particularly concerned about the quality of training it provides in applied economic research and real-world policy analysis. Taking this evidence into account, the economics faculty at UNCG determined that a program that offers specialized training in applied microeconomics needed to incorporate significant curricular features that differentiated it from the traditional doctoral curriculum.

Integration with a Professionally-Oriented M.A. Program

One source of curricular innovation for the new Ph.D. program was the professionally-oriented M.A. program in Applied Economics that had been operating at UNCG since 1997.[12]. Because the Applied M.A. program was itself shaped by the COGEE report, its complementarities with the new Ph.D. program are not coincidental. Up until the early 1990s the masters' program at UNCG was a high-quality, traditionally-structured terminal program comprised of a core, elective field course requirements and an independent thesis. By 1994 alumni from this program who did not pursue doctoral training were voicing concerns similar to those identified in the COGEE report—they left the program with excellent technical skills and knowledge but were not adequately prepared for the applied research responsibilities that were important in their postgraduate careers. In response to these observations the M.A. program was redesigned to place greater emphasis on application, professional writing, data management and computational skills—just as the COGEE had recommended for doctoral programs. The curricular mechanism was a four-course sequence in applied research methods: a course in which students learn how theory and econometrics are used in applied microeconomic analysis; a seminar in which students write a substantial, independent literature review; a course in which students learn to compile, manage and manipulate very large and complex datasets; and a seminar in which each student completes a substantial, independent research project. By the time the new doctoral program was first considered, the Applied M.A. program at UNCG was a proven success as alumni and their employers reported that the curriculum provided high-quality and marketable training in applied research [13].

Ph.D. economists who supervised graduates from the Applied M.A. program provided feedback that had a particularly important impact on the formulation of the new Ph.D. curriculum. These individuals recognized the quality of the training that was being provided in the applied research methods component of the masters' program, but they also volunteered that similar training would have been a valuable component of their own doctoral training. Based largely on these observations, the applied research methods sequence was incorporated as a curricular requirement in the new Ph.D. program. When asked to review the proposed doctoral program, non-academic employers of Ph.D. economists were particularly impressed with this curricular component: [14]

> "The strength of the proposal is the practitioner-oriented emphasis...we look for accomplished students who are well-trained in applied econometric tools and methods. Because the proposed program will emphasize these skills, it will address an important market segment."
>
> The applied-practitioner orientation of your proposed program makes a lot of sense...Mastering theory or econometric technique is vital, but does not suffice by itself. What is required is sustained exposure to the interplay between observation, broadly defined, and economic reasoning.... Your program strikes me as much more like what many of them will be called upon to do after graduation."

Students in the doctoral program at UNCG complete the twelve credit hour research methods sequence within their first three semesters. As a result, they receive training in the entire skill set that is required to perform high-quality, applied economic analysis before they enroll in field courses or undertake dissertation research. The applied research methods sequence at UNCG, although originally developed for an M.A. program, represents an innovation that specifically addresses key weaknesses that the COGEE identified in the traditional doctoral curriculum.

An Innovative and Specialized Doctoral Core

Most of the specific curricular recommendations made by the COGEE involved changes to the doctoral core. It recommended, in particular, that the core become an integrated departmental "public good" that was connected to field courses by the incorporation of more applications of economic theory and econometrics (Krueger, 1991, 1043-46). Colander (1998, 606) proposed a more radical modification—that doctoral programs offer separate core sequences to students who specialize in formal theory and those who pursue careers as applied researchers or undergraduate teachers. Regardless of the merits of these specific suggestions, these proposals make clear that the doctoral core should be a focal point for meaningful curricular innovation within graduate economics education.

Against this backdrop the economics faculty at UNCG designed a three-stage doctoral core that is specifically designed for applied microeconomists [15]. In the first stage the student satisfies a prerequisite—the completion of a masters-level core that includes courses in microeconomic theory, macroeconomic theory and applied and theoretical econometrics. "Masters-level" refers here to calculus-based treatments of theory and econometrics that emphasize application rather than formal proofs and which rely on texts such as Nicholson (microeconomics), Romer (macroeconomics) and Greene (econometrics). Students who enter the differentiated Ph.D. program with bachelor's degrees are required to take the one semester core sequence offered in the Applied M.A. program at UNCG before beginning their doctoral coursework; this requirement is waived for students who have earned comparable masters' degrees from other institutions.

The second stage of the doctoral core in the differentiated program is similar in structure, rigor and emphasis to core sequences in traditional doctoral programs. It differs from the familiar model, however, in that students take only one course each in microeconomic theory, econometric theory and mathematical economics (including mathematical statistics). Within this one semester sequence students are given a rigorous exposition of the theory of the consumer, firm and markets and the foundations of parametric and non-parametric estimation and inference. One reason that this material can be covered in one semester is that the students have already been exposed to many fundamental concepts in their M.A. core courses. A second reason, of course, is the absence of additional advanced coursework in macroeconomic theory. As a result, the second stage of the doctoral core in the differentiated program is briefer and more selective in focus than the core in a traditionally-structured doctoral program.

The third stage of the doctoral core represents the second important curricular innovation in the differentiated program. After completing the second stage, students take a sequence of four required, half-semester courses in both applied theory and applied econometrics. Each of these courses is designed to treat specific topics that are usually examined separately in both core and field courses within the traditional curriculum—such as information and intertemporal economics, game theory and public goods. The four topics covered in the applied econometrics sequence are limited dependent variables, panel data and duration models, treatment effects and sampling methods. Within the differentiated program the formal presentation of each topic is combined in the half-semester two credit hour coursess with the applications that are most relevant to health, labor and public economists. As a result, application is balanced with formalism and students enter specialized field courses with a clear understanding of how formal theory and econometrics are actually used.

THE QUALITY AND VIABILITY OF A DIFFERENTIATED PH.D. PROGRAM

The doctoral program in applied microeconomics at UNCG is differentiated from the traditional doctoral curriculum by a three-stage doctoral core that is specially designed for applied microeconomists and an innovative four-course sequence that trains students in applied research methods, data management and communication. Both innovations represent significant curricular responses to weaknesses that the COGEE and others have identified in the training that applied research economists receive within the traditional doctoral model of education. Nonetheless, questions will and should remain about the overall quality of training that students will receive in such a program and whether they will be viable.

The quality issue will ultimately be resolved, of course, by the program's track record in placing students and their postgraduate successes. But these outcomes will be determined, in part, by the impact of tradeoffs that have already been built into the differentiated curriculum. The program has been designed to offer training in applied microeconomic theory and specialized field courses that is comparable to the training students receive at the best doctoral programs and training in applied microeconometrics and research methods that is even better. To accomplish these goals students in the differentiated program students receive formal, rigorous training in a relatively narrower range of microeconomic theory and none in macroeconomic theory [16]. Some will argue that these tradeoffs cannot improve the overall quality of doctoral training even for applied microeconomists, but one of the important lessons of this paper is that explicit tradeoffs like these have to be made to build a differentiated doctoral programs such as the one described here.

Assuming that the curriculum will provide outstanding training, program viability will primarily be determined by success in attracting and retaining outstanding faculty and outstanding students. It turns out thus far that the presence of a differentiated doctoral program has, if anything, provided an advantage in faculty recruitment at UNCG. There is the obvious impact, of course, of research synergies that are created when building a narrowly-focused research core, but it turns out that outstanding applied microeconomists are also attracted to a program in which the doctoral core clearly supports their areas of specialization and in which they have an opportunity to teach applied theory and econometrics in addition to standard field courses.

A differentiated doctoral program faces much greater challenges recruiting students. Hansen (1991, 1081-1083) makes the point that prospective Ph.D. students face considerable uncertainty concerning their choice of career paths within economics and may not fully understand the different knowledge and skills that will be required in the different areas. Matriculation into a differentiated, specialized program like the one described here would seem to foreclose the flexibility that students naturally value in this situation, but it turns out that the presence of a high-quality, terminal M.A. degree program provides a set of alternative career paths that some students prefer to the career options available in a larger doctoral program. The curricular structure of the two programs at UNCG provides prospective students with three excellent options after entering the differentiated Ph.D.: 1) to complete the combined M.A./Ph.D. program, 2) to transfer into the three-semester, terminal applied M.A. program after either the first or second semester; or 3) to use the terminal master's program to prepare for a doctoral program that better suits their interests and abilities [17]. The recruiting strategy, therefore, has been to attract outstanding students—and there are many--who have yet to decide whether to pursue a Ph.D. or earn a professionally-oriented, applied masters' degree. Thus far, two-thirds of the Ph.D. students at UNCG have entered the program through this mechanism.

Besides providing advantages in student recruitment, the integration of the Applied M.A. and Ph.D. program at UNCG has helped to resolve at least some of the problems that arise in a small-scale graduate program [18]. There is a strong presumption that a department of economics cannot simultaneously maintain a high-quality masters alongside a Ph.D. program. A second important message of this paper is that this conventional wisdom can be turned on its head for the case of a professionally-oriented masters' program and a differentiated, specialized doctoral program. If they are carefully structured and well-integrated programs like these can support and strengthen each other, rather than compete.

NOTES

[1] Colander and Klamer (1987) and Coats (1992) argued forcefully that the training provided by the doctoral curriculum had become inappropriate even for the basic research path.

[2] Hansen (1991, 1060) reported that 57.5% and 54.5 % of economics Ph.D. students planned to pursue academic careers in 1977 and 1987 respectively; Stock and Siegfried (2004, 275) estimated that 58.8% of the 2001-02 cohort of Ph.D. graduates actually did so.

[3] The knowledge areas specified by Hansen (1991, 1068) were economic theory, econometrics, institutions and history, economic literature, economic application and policy issues, and empirical economics. The skill areas (see Hansen, 1991, 1070) were critical judgment, analytics, applications, mathematics, computation, communication and creativity.

[4] Because of low survey response rates from non-academic employers, Hansen (1991, 1083-4) supplemented their survey responses with face-to-face interviews with a smaller sample.

[5] Colander (1998, 604) discussed seminars on teaching, area studies programs and programs in alternative approaches to economics as examples of program innovation. Krueger (1999, 156) also acknowledged the existence of some narrowly focused "niche" programs.

[6] Stock and Hansen (2004, 269) reported that slightly more than one-third of the graduates were in non-academic professions in both survey years.

[7] The modest increase in the average annual production of Ph.D. economists in the U.S. over these same three decades was completely attributable to students who accepted employment abroad after graduation—for example, from 119 in 1977 to 244 in 2001 (Siegfried and Stock, 2004, 273).

[8] Hansen (1991, 1085) makes the point based on interviews with non-academic employers while Coats (1992, 348) focuses on differences in the focus of graduate training in economics departments and professional schools of business, public policy and health.

[9] The number of U.S. citizens receiving Ph.D.s in economics each year is predicted to fall below 300 by 2009 (Siegfried and Stock, 2006, 1). The decline (from around 550 in the early 1970s) is particularly striking given that the number of undergraduate majors in economics has increased (although sporadically) by 25% over the same period—from 16,674 in 1977 to 24,402 (1987), 17,896 (1996) and 20,377 (2001), (U.S. Department of Education, 2007, Table 43).

[10]See Finegan, Stock and Siegfried (2006) on matriculation; Stock, Finegan and Siegfried (2006) for attrition and Stock and Siegfried (2006) on time-to-degree.

[11]At the time the differentiated doctoral program was proposed the department of economics at UNCG was ranked 178th in the world in research according to Kalaitizidakis, Mamuneas and Stengos (2003) with a particularly strong record of funded research in health and labor.

[12]See Allen and Snowden (2007) for a detailed description of the M.A. Applied Economics program at UNCG and a discussion of its origins. Briefly, its lock-step curriculum combines a core of theory and econometrics in the first semester, courses that emphasize the application of research tools in the second semester, and seminars on advanced data management skills and independent research in the third semester. Overlaying this basic structure are three broader principles: that applications would be integrated into courses wherever useful and practical; that every econometric course (six in all) would have a weekly laboratory component; and that each student would be required to complete a major writing requirement and substantial independent data project.

[13]Before designing the Applied M.A. program a survey was given to alumni of the traditional M.A. program that was similar in structure to the one reported by Hansen (1991). The information gathered in this survey was important to its ultimate success.

[14]During the proposal process the design of the new program was reviewed not only by academics but also by representatives from federal government agencies, private research organizations and business.

[15]To implement a multi-stage core sequence students must be required to follow a lockstep curriculum until they enroll in specialized field courses. This innovation makes sense, therefore, only in a program that supports closely related fields of specialization.

[16]Students do take a masters' level macroeconomics course and receive doctoral-level training in intertemporal modeling in one of the applied economic theory modules.

[17]The seamless transition between the two programs also provides the faculty with precise information about the ability and temperament of a student to pursue the doctoral degree. This is used at UNCG in both recruiting into the doctoral program and advising students out of the program.

[18]These efficiencies include sharing the required research methods course sequence, using doctoral students as graduate assistants in M.A. coursework, and sharing the fixed costs of program administration.

REFERENCES

Allen, Stuart D. and Kenneth A. Snowden, Jr., 2009, "The Implementation of a Terminal Master's Program in Applied Economics." *Journal of Economics and Finance Education*, forthcoming

Bowen, Howard R. 1953. "Graduate Education in Economics." *American Economic Review* 43(4) part 2: 1-223.

Coats, A.W. 1992. "Changing Perceptions of American Graduate Education in Economics, 1953-1991." *Journal of Economic Education*, Fall 1992: 341-52.

Colander, David. 1998. "The Sounds of Silence: The Profession's Response to the COGEE Report." *American Journal of Agricultural Economics,* 80: 600-07.

Colander, David. 2005. "The Making of an Economist Redux." *Journal of Economic Perspectives.* 19 (1): 175-98.

Colander, David and A. Klamer. 1987. "The Making of an Economist." *Journal of Economic Perspectives.* 1 Fall: 95-111.

Finegan, T. Aldrich, Wendy A. Stock, and John J. Siegfried. 2006. "Matriculation in U.S. Economics Ph.D. Programs: How Many Accepted Americans Do Not Enroll?" *The American Economic Review* 96(2): 453-457.

Hansen, W. Lee. 1991. "The Education and Training of Economics Doctorates: Major Findings of the Executive Secretary of the American Economic Association's Commission on Graduate Education in Economics." *Journal of Economic Literature*, Vol. 29, No. 3: 1054-1087.

Kalaitizidakis, Pantelis, Theofanis Mamuneas, and Thanasis Stengos. 2003. "Rankings of Academic Journals and Institutions in Economics." *European Economic Review.* 1(6): 1346-1366.

Kasper, Hirschel. 1991. "The Education of Economists: From Undergraduate to Graduate Study." *Journal of Economic Literature*, Vol. 29, No. 3: 1088-1109.

Krueger, Anne. O. et al. 1991. "Report of the Commission on Graduate Education in Economics." *Journal of Economic Literature*, Vol. 29, No. 3: 1035-1053.

Krueger, Anne O. 1999. "Implications of the Labor Market for Graduate Education in Economics." *The Journal of Economic Perspectives* 13(3): 153-156.

Siegfried, John J. and Wendy Stock. 1999. "The Labor Market for New Ph.D. Economists." *The Journal of Economic Perspectives* 13(3): 115-134.

Siegfried, John J. and Wendy Stock. 2004. "The Market for New Ph.D. Economists in 2002." *American Economic Review: Papers and Proceedings*. 94(2): 272-85.

Siegfried, John J. and Wendy A. Stock. 2006. "The Undergraduate Origins of Ph.D. Economists." Working Paper 06-W11, Economics Department, Vanderbilt University.

Stock, Wendy and W. Lee Hansen. 2004. "Ph.D. Program Learning and Job Demands: How Close is the Match?" *American Economic Review: Papers and Proceedings*. 94(2):266-71.

Stock, Wendy and John Siegfried. 2004. "The Market for New Ph.D.s in Economics." *American Economic Review: Papers and Proceedings*. 94(2): 272-85.

Stock, Wendy and John Siegfried. 2006. "Time-to-Degree for the Economics Ph.D. Class of 2001-2002." *The American Economic Review* 96(2): 467-476.

Stock, Wendy A., T. Aldrich Finegan, and John J. Siegfried. 2006. "Attrition in Economics Ph.D. Programs." *The American Economic Review* 96(2): 458-466.

U.S. Department of Education, National Center for Education Statistics. 2007. *Digest of Education Statistics 2006*.

INDEX

B

C

D

E

F

J

K

L

M

Q

R

S

T

U

V

W

Y